# POLITICAL

M000164122

# ANALYSIS

Series Editors: B. Guy Peters, Jon Pierre and Gerry Stoker

Political science today is a dynamic discipline. Its substance, theory and methods have all changed radically in recent decades. It is much expanded in range and scope and in the variety of new perspectives — and new variants of old ones — that it encompasses. The sheer volume of work being published, and the increasing degree of its specialization, however, make it difficult for political scientists to maintain a clear grasp of the state of debate beyond their own particular subdisciplines.

The *Political Analysis* series is intended to provide a channel for different parts of the discipline to talk to one another and to new generations of students. Our aim is to publish books that provide introductions to, and exemplars of, the best work in various areas of the discipline. Written in an accessible style, they provide a 'launching-pad' for students and others seeking a clear grasp of the key methodological, theoretical and empirical issues, and the main areas of debate, in the complex and fragmented world of political science.

A particular priority is to facilitate intellectual exchange between academic communities in different parts of the world. Although frequently addressing the same intellectual issues, research agendas and literatures in North America, Europe and elsewhere have often tended to develop in relative isolation from one another. This series is designed to provide a framework for dialogue and debate which, rather than advocacy of one regional approach or another, is the key to progress.

The series reflects our view that the core values of political science should be coherent and logically constructed theory, matched by carefully constructed and exhaustive empirical investigation. The key challenge is to ensure quality and integrity in what is produced rather than to constrain diversity in methods and approaches. The series is intended as a showcase for the best of political science in all its variety, and demonstrate how nurturing that variety can further improve the discipline.

Political Analysis Series
Series Standing Order
ISBN 0–333–78694–7 hardback
ISBN 0–333–94506–9 paperback
(outside North America only)

You can receive future titles in this series as they are published by placing a standing order. Please contact your bookseller or, in the case of difficulty, write to us at the address below with your name and address, the title of the series and one of the ISBNs quoted above.

Customer Services Department, Macmillan Distribution Ltd
Houndmills, Basingstoke, Hampshire RG21 6XS, England

# POLITICAL

# ANALYSIS

Series Editors: B. Guy Peters, Jon Pierre and Gerry Stoker

*Published*

Peter Burnham, Karin Gilland Lutz, Wyn Grant and Zig Layton-Henry
**Research Methods in Politics (2nd edition)**

Colin Hay
**Political Analysis**

Colin Hay, Michael Lister and David Marsh (eds)
**The State: Theories and Issues**

Andrew Hindmoor
**Rational Choice**

David Marsh and Gerry Stoker (eds)
**Theory and Methods in Political Science (2nd edition)**

Jon Pierre and B. Guy Peters
**Governance, Politics and the State**

Martin J. Smith
**Power and the State**

Cees van der Eijk and Mark Franklin
**Elections and Voters**

*Forthcoming*

Keith Dowding
**The Philosophy and Methods of Political Science**

Colin Hay
**Globalization and the State**

David Marsh
**Political Behaviour**

Karen Mossberger and Mark Cassell
**The Policy Process: Ideas, Interests and Institutions**

# Power and the State

Martin J. Smith

First published 2009 by
PALGRAVE MACMILLAN

Palgrave Macmillan in the UK is an imprint of Macmillan Publishers Limited, registered in England, company number 785998, of 4 Crinan Street, London N1 9XW.

Palgrave Macmillan in the US is a division of St Martin's Press LLC, 175 Fifth Avenue, New York, NY 10010.

Palgrave Macmillan is the global academic imprint of the above companies and has companies and representatives throughout the world.

Palgrave® and Macmillan® are registered trademarks in the United States, the United Kingdom, Europe and other countries.

ISBN: 978–0–333–96462–0   hardback
ISBN: 978–0–333–96463–7   paperback

This book is printed on paper suitable for recycling and made from fully managed and sustained forest sources. Logging, pulping and manufacturing processes are expected to conform to the environmental regulations of the country of origin.

A catalogue record for this book is available from the British Library.

A catalog record for this book is available from the Library of Congress.

For Jean and Anna

# Contents

# List of Tables and Figures

## Tables

## Figures

# Acknowledgements

I have been thinking about and writing this book over a long period and in that time a number of people have helped in the process of writing. First, I would like to thank my publisher Steven Kennedy for his support and incisive comments. I know that I have taken longer than he would have liked and that I have not always followed his suggestions, but he has along the way provided some excellent insights which have had an important impact in terms of shaping the book. Gerry Stoker read the whole manuscript and again helped me see how all the parts of the book link together. An anonymous referee was also very helpful in suggesting further refinements and improvements. I would also like to thank my PhD students Alejandro Garnica, Dominic Holland, Louise Strong and Adam White whose work has in different ways informed my analysis. Special thanks go to Adam who read the whole manuscript and helped in a number of ways with parts of the text. Dave Richards, as always, provided a sounding board for bouncing ideas off and through our joint projects has been involved in developing my view of the state. A large part of the book was written whilst on sabbatical leave and so thanks to the Department of Politics at the University of Sheffield for providing that time and for some funding for research assistance, and a thank you to Matt Denton who acted as research assistant. I am very grateful to Rene Bailey who went through the final text in great detail and made a number of improvements and to Keith Povey (with Nancy Richardson) for their professionalism as copy-editors. My biggest thank you goes to Jean Grugel, who listened to many of my ideas, read drafts, talked me away from some of my wackier notions, and reminded me that there is a world beyond the West. Finally, a big thank you to Anna who has read none of the text, but she has seen some of the writing process, and she persuaded me that often it is better to have a game of football.

MARTIN J. SMITH

# List of Abbreviations

| | |
|---|---|
| ALARP | As Low as Reasonably Practicable |
| ANPR | Automatic Number Plate Recognition |
| ARDA | Advanced Research and Development Activity |
| ASB | Anti-social Behaviour |
| ASBO | Anti-social Behaviour Order |
| BCS | British Crime Survey |
| BSE | Bovine Spongiform Encephalopathy |
| CDRP | Crime and Disorder Reduction Partnership |
| CIA | Central Intelligence Agency |
| CJD | Creutzfeldt–Jakob Disease |
| CMPS | Centre for Management and Policy Studies |
| DARPA | Defense Advanced Research Projects Agency |
| DES | Department of Education and Science |
| ETA | Euskadi Ta Askatasuna (Basque Homeland and Freedom) |
| FBI | Federal Bureau of Investigation |
| FDA | Food and Drug Administration |
| FRU | Force Research Unit |
| GAL | Grupos Antiterroristas de Liberación (Antiterrorist Liberation Groups) |
| GIS | Geographical Information System |
| GMO | Genetically Modified Organism |
| GP | General Practitioner |
| GPS | Global Positioning System |
| ILGRA | Interdepartmental Liaison Group on Risk Assessment |
| IRA | Irish Republican Army |
| IRLG | Interagency Regulatory Liaison Group |
| IWW | Industrial Workers of the World |
| KNWS | Keynesian National Welfare State |
| MAFF | Ministry of Agriculture, Fisheries and Food |
| MP | Member of Parliament |
| NFU | National Farmers' Union |
| NGO | Non-governmental Organization |
| NIF | Número de Identificación Fiscal |
| NKVD | Narodny Komissariat Vnutrennikh Del (People's Commissariat for Internal Affairs) |
| NPM | New Public Management |
| NSA | National Security Agency |
| PRWORA | Personal Responsibility and Work Opportunity Reconciliation Act |
| RCT | Rational Choice Theory |
| RFID | Radio-frequency Identification |
| SAS | Special Air Service |
| SUV | Sports Utility Vehicle |
| TANF | Temporary Assistance for Needy Families |
| TIF | Total Information Awareness |
| WERG | Waste & Energy Research Group |
| WTO | World Trade Organization |

# Introduction

The last twenty years have seen considerable discussion about the role and future of the state. The intention of this book is to contribute to this debate by examining the relationship between states and power. However, the focus of the book is not limited to conceptualisations of the state and power, but rather it focuses on the mechanisms that states use in order to exercise power. The core argument is that states in the developed world have been creating new mechanism of power in order to achieve their desired outcomes. Traditionally, states have relied on authority, bureaucracy and force, but recently states have supplemented these mechanisms with the use of incentives, regulation, risk and surveillance. The development of these new mechanisms has resulted in states changing their focus from collective outcomes to individual outcomes.

Recent discussion concerning the state has been dominated by several conflicting, but related, narratives. For much of the post-war period discussion of the state was limited to a number of Marxists and elitist writers (Jessop, 1982) with the focus of 'mainstream' political science being on the behaviour of voters and interest groups, or the institutions of government, narrowly defined. In the 1980s, as a response to behaviourism, a new debate was initiated on the need to 'bring the state back in' (see Evans and Rueschemeyer and Skocpol, 1985; Nordlinger, 1981). The state literature, and arguments surrounding new institutionalism, maintains that political science could only study political actors within the context of the institutions of the state which shaped behaviour, culture and attitudes. Moreover, the statist literature suggests – in response to both pluralists and Marxists – that the state did not only reflect social forces, but that state actors frequently had institutionally determined interests and that they had the potential to act on these interests autonomously. In other words, policy was not only driven by voters and pressure groups, but also by the interest of state actors (officials and politicians). This perspective was highly influential, but was relatively rapidly marginalized by the growing debates surrounding globalization and governance, which saw a much more limited role for the state in terms of supplying public goods and social organization.

1

Within the international politics field much of the original discussion of globalization suggested that the state was being undermined by the transfer of political and economic power to the international level (Ohmae, 1996; Strange, 1996). For Susan Strange, the impact of government ministers on policy outcomes is much less than in the past. It is markets that have become the masters. In Ulrich Beck's (2005: xi) hyperbole:

> Today, we Europeans act as if Germany, France, Italy, the Netherlands, Portugal, and so forth, still existed. Yet they have long since ceased to exist, because as soon as the Euro was introduced – if not before – these isolated national state containers of power and the equally isolated, mutually excluding societies they represented entered the realm of the unreal. (For a discussion of the debate see Cohen, 2003)

Domestically, the literature on governance focussed on how the activities of the state were being increasingly carried out by non-state bodies such as the private sector, voluntary organizations and parastatal or quasi governmental bodies, leading to a 'hollowing out of the state' (Rhodes, 1997; Flinders, 2008). From this perspective the state is but one of many actors involved in the making and delivery of policy (Richards and Smith, 2002) and the role of the state is increasingly confined to steering rather than rowing; in other words, setting the direction rather than actually delivering public goods (Osborne and Gaebler, 1992).

As many commentators now recognize, there are a number of problems with the more extreme 'end of the state' thesis and the less dramatic hollowing out thesis (Sorenson, 2004). As Michael Mann (1997) reminds us, the critics of the state overestimate the strength of the state in the past and underestimate its continued importance. Much of the less sophisticated globalization literature takes an international perspective and in doing so ignores the continuing importance of the state at the domestic level. Whilst it may be the case that the international economy has become more open and that the level of international exchange of goods and currency is much greater than ever, this does not mean that states have no economic choices (Hay, 2006a). The impact of global economic change continues to be mediated by states and economic policies vary greatly from state to state. Even within the European Union, despite a common monetary policy, there are considerable variations in economic and industrial policy (Harrop, 1998).

For example, France, Germany and Britain have responded to the economic changes of the last twenty years in very different ways (Schmidt, 2002). Whilst even the French state has become less directly interventionist, the type of social and economic policies followed in each country has developed as a consequence of their histories, institutional structures and internal political forces (see Levy, Miura and Park, 2006; Hemerijck and Vail, 2006; Thompson, 2006).

Even apparently weak states, which may have little influence at the international level, can have considerable domestic control. Despite significant pressure from the United States, Iran continues to have substantial domestic (and even international autonomy). Similarly, whilst Sudan is portrayed as a failed state, it managed to resist international pressure to allow UN troops into the Darfur region of the country.

The governance literature takes a less apocalyptic view of the state than some of the literature in international politics. From a governance perspective, the state is not disappearing but becoming 'de-centred' in the policy process (see for example Bevir and Rhodes, 2006). However, the problem with much of the governance literature is that it takes an Anglo-American view of the state; seeing the sorts of public management reforms introduced into the Anglo-American world as universal (see Dunleavy, 1994; Hood, 1995). The reality is that despite the prevalence of the word governance, the actual application of managerial reforms in the developed and developing world is patchy. For example, Alistair Cole and Glyn Jones (2005) suggest that France, despite administrative reform, cannot be seen as converging with a global model of new public management. The governance literature essentially presents a pluralist picture of policy making with a relatively fluid and open institutional policy process and the government acting as one actor amongst many (Smith, 2006). The notion of governance ignores the extent to which in most political systems, the central state continues to be an institution with a disproportionate impact on policy outcomes (see Marsh, Richards and Smith, 2001). In most developed countries the state has administrative, economic and political resources that far outweigh any other institution in society.

Consequently, and predictably, there has been a considerable backlash against the demise of the state argument. An increasing body of literature argues that the state is not disappearing but that it is in many ways as important as ever (see Weiss, 1998). Peter Evans (1997) proposes that globalization will not see the eclipse of the state but rather result in a 'harsher state which is less open to progressive politics'. Paul

Pierson (1995) on the other hand demonstrates that the extent to which welfare regimes are embedded makes them extremely resistant to neo-liberal projects which seek to dismantle the state. There can be little doubt that in the developed world, at least in terms of state expenditure on welfare as well as in other areas, the state's influence is not in decline but has generally increased. There is also little indication that the state is playing less of a role in the everyday lives of citizens. Jonah Levy (2006: 3) suggests that the state has shifted from a market steering to a market supporting role. For others this changing role is part a more general change in the nature of the state. According to Bob Jessop (2002: 211), 'the erosion of one form of state should not be mistaken for its general retreat. On the contrary, as the frontiers of the KNWS (Keynesian National Welfare State) are rolled back, the boundaries of the state are rolling forward in other respects.' Samy Cohen (2003: 28--9) emphasizes the resilience of the state:

> One should remember also that the erosion of sovereignty is not a general and necessarily irreversible phenomenon. When there are heavy blows the state returns, present and active, as was shown by the reactions to the September 11 attacks. The terrorists' assault made people forget the criticisms regularly made against the state. Ronald Reagan's phrase 'government is not the solution...' has given way to interventionist watchwords and measures.

There can be little doubt that the state in the developed world is an important and pervasive institution. States maintain a degree of order, fight wars, collect taxes, regulate the economy and industry and provide public goods such as education and welfare. As the report by the National Intelligence Council suggests: 'In the wake of the 2008 global financial crisis, the state's role in the economy may be gaining more appeal throughout the world'. John Ikenberry (2003: 351) concurs:

> State capacities continue to evolve, declining in some areas, rising in others. There are no rival formations – local, regional, transnational or global – that have the full multidimensional capacities of the state. No rival political formations have come close to attracting the loyalties or normative legitimacy of the state.

Indeed, despite the decline of the state argument most states continue to spend large amounts of money (see Figure 1). Indeed, what is clear is

**Figure 1** *Government spending as a percentage of national income 1995 and 2008*

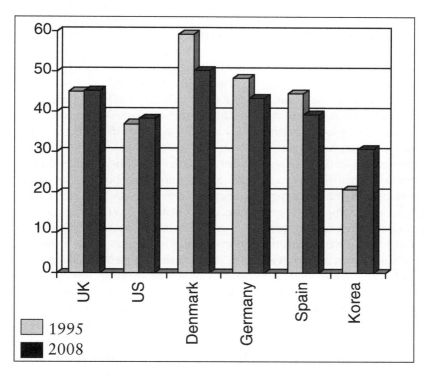

*Source*: adapted from *OECD Economic Outlook* 83 (2008).

that some have increased spending and a small number have reduced it. Even the US, the bastion of liberal economic orthodoxy, has seen a slight increase in public expenditure since 1995.

Undoubtedly the state is still a key institution in developed societies, but it is also true that states have undergone considerable change. In the late nineteenth century a number of the major states in Western Europe were Empire states attempting to develop extensive control over large territories. In the twentieth century states abandoned Empire and, faced with universal suffrage and strong labour movements, became welfare states, often with policies of considerable economic intervention. From the 1970s onwards we saw the postwar welfare settlement unravelling to varying degrees and states moving from a focus on collective provision to a focus on markets and individual behaviour. For some, this is seen as a shift from modernism to postmodernism. But the argument of this book is that whilst the state has developed new forms of power, it has done so within the framework of the existing powers of the modern state – it is, in the phrase of Rob Stones (1996), *past*modern rather than postmodern. In order to understand this change we need to make some assessment of the nature and impact of state power and how it is exercised. We also have to remember that the power of states is both fragmented and variable. States have never had a constant supply of power with which to control societies. As Joel Migdal (2001) points out, the idea of a unified state is mythical. States have always operated in a complex relationship with society and consequently the ability of states to influence behaviour varies across time, space and policy area. Sometimes states have some relative success but at others they do not. State control is always limited. States may have policies to reduce unemployment or improve literacy but there are always some people who are unemployed or illiterate. As we will see, even highly authoritarian states fail to control completely what occurs within their borders. Consequently, the notion of states losing power is a misnomer because states never have 'power'; they have a range of mechanisms of differing degrees of effectiveness with which they attempt to shape social outcomes. In order to understand state power in the twenty-first century we need to understand the concepts of state and power which hitherto have given little insight into the actual mechanisms of power available to the state.

The problem is, however, that whilst power and the state are two of the key concepts in political science, discussion of these concepts has reached an impasse, for a number of reasons. First, there is no agreement on what power is; consequently much of the literature on power is an endless debate on defining power where various authors talk past each other. Second, as a consequence of the insularity of the debate, much of the literature is impenetrable and so is ignored despite its apparent centrality. Third, whilst discussion of the state was lively in the 1970s and 1980s, little progress has been made in state theory since the state autonomy debates. To an extent discussion of the state has been subsumed into discussions of globalization and governance. Fourth, there have been few explicit attempts to link discussions of the state and power. This book aims to break this impasse by:

- Arguing for the continued importance of the role of the state, despite the suggestion from the governance/globalization debate that the state is withering, and seeing the state not as a unified and self-contained unit but as a set of fragmented and often not easily defined institutions with a variable impact on social outcomes.

- Recognizing that power is a multi-dimensional concept. Rather than looking for a single definition of power, the book will argue that the nature of power depends on where power is being exercised, who is involved in the power relations and who is the subject of power. We have to accept that the techniques of power are multiple and power operates in different ways.
- The book will illustrate the various ways that power is used by linking theoretical discussions of power to empirical examples of the exercise of power. It will examine how the modern state (meaning the developed state of 'the West') has exercised power over citizens and social and economic groups in the twentieth and twenty- first centuries. The key argument is that different conceptions of power illuminate the various and changing ways in which states control society.

States in the developed and developing world are going through processes of rapid change. The growing interconnectedness of the world economy (and of course of economic problems), changing demands of people, new types of transnational problems such as global warming and migration, and new patterns of governance, are transforming both what the state is and how we think about it. This book demonstrates that whilst the power of the state may be changing, this does not mean that the state is declining. States have varying abilities to affect outcomes and they can be strong and weak at the same time.

Notions of state power have been dominated by Marxist perspectives which see the state as the representation of a particular class interest, and Weberian approaches that characterize the state as an organization with control of violence, bureaucracy and legitimacy that provide authoritative control within national boundaries. There has been considerable debate in the late twentieth century about how the undermining of borders and the dissolution of sovereignty has left the state as a hollow vessel increasingly subject to the multiple pressures of globalization, the market, political dissolution, and growing regional and local identities. However, the argument of this book is that whilst the state may be more or less powerful than in the past – and this of course will vary from state to state – it increasingly uses new ways of exercising power. The modern state's power was built and extended through force, bureaucracy and legitimacy – what Mann (1986; 1993; see Schroeder, 2006) sees as Ideological, Military, Economic and

Political power – as its main mechanism for getting people to act in certain ways. Yet, whilst still retaining these powers, states in the late twentieth and early twenty-first century are developing new mechanisms of power or, perhaps more correctly, emphasizing different aspects of their resources in order to control or influence populations. These new powers involve: rationality, surveillance, regulation, and risk. These are all aspects of state power that have existed in the past but they have been enhanced and developed (often consciously), and they are affecting not only how states do things but what they try to do. Whereas in the past states were concerned with economies and social aggregates, nowadays they are increasingly concerned with individual behaviour; and the focus of state power is moving away from control of economies and increasingly towards the social, or even moral, behaviour of citizens. It is important not to be dogmatic about, or to exaggerate, the degree of change. As we will see in the course of the book, states have always used surveillance, regulation and rationality, and they continue to use force, bureaucracy and authority, and states have always focused on the patterns of behaviour of individuals, but what has changed is the balance. States are less interested in bureaucracy as a tool for government and more interested in how incentives, regulation, surveillance and risk management can be used to control and effect social change.

It is important to point out that when talking of the state, we are not talking of a single institution. It is a set of diverse and fragmented institutions, some of which are involved in strategic and core activities whilst others act as state authorities in more peripheral and partial ways. In addition, states are not actors. States are organizations and it is the people within them who have their own interests, who represent the interests of others, and who use the organizational resources of the state to attempt to achieve particular goals. It is also the case that states vary widely across countries and time and, as Jessop (1982) has argued, it is not possible to develop a general theory of the state. Hence the aim of this book is not to provide a framework or theory for understanding state power, but to demonstrate the different ways that are available for states (or state actors) to exercise power and how they have changed. Not all states will have these powers, or use them, but hopefully the book will offer a way of understanding the potential means that states could use for affecting outcomes.

The intention of this book is to bring together two core terms in understanding politics: the state and power. Both are terms that are highly contested, frequently used, subject to fashion and the waxing and waning of intellectual interest. Both are terms that are extremely difficult to define, although they clearly refer to different objects/concepts. Power is a concept or idea, whereas the state is in principle something that has a physical existence. However, it is clear that in many ways the state exists as much as an idea as a real physical object. Whilst some Marxist and Weberian theorists have presented the state as a unified object, or a distinct set of institutions, Migdal (2001: 15–16) has argued that this is to completely misspecify the state because:

> The state is a field of power marked by the use and threat of violence and shaped by (1) *the image of a coherent, controlling organization in a territory, which is a representation of people bounded by that territory, and (2) the actual practice of its multiple parts.* (Emphasis in original)

For Migdal, the point is that whilst the image of the state is one of unity – states are presented as sovereign, centralized and in control of a territory – the reality is that they are messy and ill-defined sets of institutions whose boundaries are fuzzy and changing. Likewise, Mann describes them as 'polymorphous' with state power inexorably linked to the social power of civil society (Schroeder, 2006: 4).

Power has always been and always will be a contested concept in political and social science. Power is intimately linked to ontological, epistemological and methodological positions. Writers such as Weber, Dahl and Foucault use the same word to describe very different social phenomena. But as Goverde *et al.* (2000: 18) state, following Wittgenstein, the uses of power

> are related, but not by any single characteristic. Rather, their relationship is formed from a criss-crossing set of commonalities that interweave into a complex tapestry of related meanings. Just as members of a family resemble each other in a diversity of ways, so, too, the usages of power overlap in a complex interweaving of meanings with no single strand running through the entirety.

Steven Lukes (2005: 69) is less circumspect, arguing that there is 'a single, comprehensive, extremely general or generic concept of power common to all cases' and that power is 'being able to make or receive any change, or resist it'. Whilst we may have a general and common sense idea of what power is, there is little philosophical agreement over the meaning of power. As Lukes highlights, power operates in different ways; there is power to and power over; power over a single issue or a range of issues; the ability to affect individual events or to change the whole context; and the issue of whether power involves intentionality. For some social scientists power is a specific observable event, whilst for others it is imbricated in every social relationship and so not easily identifiable either in terms of the exerciser or a specific event. If we look at a racist act against the idea of institutional racism it illustrates this distinction. In a racist act a bigger and more violent person may stop someone doing something because they are black. We could see that person as exercising power. In institutional racism discrimination is exercised over people not necessarily through a single observable act but through widely accepted norms, rules and forms of organization which mean white people have power over black people.

One of the aims of this book is to deal with the complexities concerning the nature of power by demonstrating that any attempt to understand power is undertaken not through further theoretical or conceptual discussion but by locating debates of power in an empirical context and examining how states use power. States are concerned with shaping behaviour but how they do that varies: it can be through force, it can be with authority, persuasion, offering incentives, watching and regulating what people do, socializing behaviour or legitimizing a series of norms. State officials are neither interested in the metaphysics of power nor logical consistency, and therefore definitions of power have little importance to everyday acts of power. States use multiple, and philosophically inconsistent, forms of power. Moreover, the ways in which states exercise power have changed, with an emphasis on different forms of power. Mann (1986) demonstrates how states have shifted from a pre-modern era of despotic power to the modern era of infrastructural (or bureaucratic) power. What we see today is infra-structural power being developed in new and different ways, with the development and emphasis on different techniques of power.

What this book argues is that states use power in a variety of ways and in manners that conform to different definitions of power. State actors do not have to be philosophically consistent and can use differ-ent types of power (sometimes at the same time). Power as it is prac-tised is multi-dimensional and states do not use power that conforms to particular philosophical traditions. States can at the same time see citi-zens as rational actors and therefore create new incentive structures in order to change behaviour, and also see them as social beings whose behaviour is governed by norms. For instance, public servants can be defined as rational actors and altruistic at the same time. Consequently, in order to understand how states exercise power, we do not have to resolve the philosophical conundrums that have occupied great minds (is power intentional; is it structural; is it possible to manipulate desires; is it possible to escape the circuits of power?), but if we identify different forms of power we can use these approaches to understand how states inconsistently and partially use a range of types of power. States can use traditional forms of power: force, authority, bureaucracy; and new (or newer forms): rationality, surveillance and risk at the same times and in different degrees according to the state, the time and the policy area. Hence the aim of the book is to demonstrate that despite the threats to the internal and external sovereignty of the state, state actors still have a range of techniques to attempt to shape the behaviour (with varying degrees of success) of their citizens.

Currently we have two separate bodies of literature, one set focused on the state and how it collectively controls societies and another based on the philosophical nature of power. Neither focuses on the actual mechanisms through which states attempt to influence social outcomes. The aim of this book is not to attempt to resolve the debate about power, but to use the different approaches to power to sensitize us to the many ways states and state actors exercise power, and to see that power can be both an intentional, observable act and a more complex process of social power where the causal chains of power are not necessarily clear. The point is that if power is a relative and multi-faceted phenomenon then the question of whether state power is increasing or declining becomes irrelevant. What we can see is a social institution with ever-changing boundaries, and complex interpenetration with civil society, exercising power in a variety of ways in different situations. At times these approaches may be successful and at other times less so. What is clear is that the reach and aims of the state are very different in the early twenty-first century than they were at the beginning of the twentieth century. In the early twentieth century Britain, France, Germany and even Russia were Empire states with extensive power over large areas, but often with little direct control over what people did. In the mid-twentieth century many states built extensive welfare states and processes of economic planning with varying degrees of success (for example, Germany built itself up to be Europe's leading power and Britain coped with political and economic decline). In the twenty-first century we see states moving away from economic intervention to more individualized interventions based on risk, surveillance and modifying behaviour and using different types of power (again with varying degrees of success). The book therefore looks at how we understand power, the changing nature of the state, and then how the traditional forms of state power – force, legitimacy and bureaucracy – have been overlain with new forms of rationality, regulation, risk and surveillance, and looks at how these different approaches are illuminated by different theories of power.

The book begins with an exploration of the nature of power and the state. Chapter 1 analyzes the traditional ways of understanding power in the literature of behavioural and rational choice approaches and Chapter 2 examines how these have been developed in what may be called radical approaches starting with the work of elitists and going on to poststructuralists. Chapter 3 looks at the ways power has been understood in terms of theories of the state. Chapter 4 brings together the various theories of power to develop a framework for understanding power and the state. Chapter 5 looks at the development of the modern state and the particular forms it takes in terms of trying to control societies. The following chapters then look at how the state has used different notions of power. What becomes apparent is that whilst state actors have little sense of ontology, they do make different assumptions about how people behave; also that different techniques of power involve different understandings about the nature of human beings and how they are likely to react to attempts to change behaviour. What is clear is that states often hold contradictory ideas about what will affect the behaviour of people, and can use numerous different types of power. Chapter 6 highlights how the key elements of the modern state have been authority and bureaucracy. Chapter 7 examines force and terror and how these techniques are present in authoritarian and democratic regimes. From Chapter 8 the book examines new forms of power starting with rationality and regulation, with Chapter 9 examining surveillance and Chapter 10 looking at risk. Chapter 11 then examines how the new forms of power have been combined to develop a new form of moral politics where states attempt to apply increasingly interventionist measures in relation to individual behaviour. Finally, as a counterbalance, Chapter 12 examines the limits to state power.

# Chapter 1

# Understanding Power: Traditional Approaches

Theories of power are not good at understanding how the state exercises power. In many ways they are more concerned with understanding how power is defined rather than how it is exercised. Power is treated as an abstract philosophical issue rather than as a mechanism used by states. Whilst political theorists and philosophers search for consistency, politicians and policy makers are concerned with achieving their goals and do not have a necessarily coherent theory of power. In the real world power exists in numerous forms. Nevertheless, existing theories do provide frameworks for understanding power which help us to analyse what states do and how they affect outcomes. The aim of this and the following chapter is to outline the key debates on power in order to illustrate the main approaches to power, but also to demonstrate that if we are to understand how the state exercises power we need to have a multi-dimensional approach that allows us to understand the complex ways in which power can be exercised. In other words, the aim is to illustrate that theories of power offer limited analytical purchase in terms of understanding the nature of state power as actually practised.

This chapter begins by outlining the traditional approaches to power which are based on 'observable' understandings of power. The point is to demonstrate that sometimes power is exercised in observable ways but that purely focussing on these forms of power would limit our understanding of how the state operates.

## The power debate

The debate about power has to some extent reached an impasse, for a number of reasons. First, discussions of power often lack any empirical reference and consequently tend to revolve around abstract questions rather than real issues. Second, many of the protagonists of power debates talk past each other. They have conflicting epistemological and ontological understandings of power and, consequently, there is no debate but a stating of positions. They even disagree about where we should look for power; some look at individuals, others look at organizations, and some look at whole societies. Such is the impasse that often one set of approaches develops theories of power without reference to others. For instance, Stefan Napel and Mika Widgrén (2005: 517–18) say: 'Scientists who study power in political and economic institutions seem divided into two disjoint (sic) methodological camps. The first one uses non-cooperative game theory ... The second one stands in the tradition of cooperative game theory. ...' What they mean is that within the particular subfield they work in there is a division over methodology. In fact they are ignoring the rest of the social sciences and the many ways power is understood. There are debates about power within rational choice theory, historical sociology, political theory and philosophy, international relations and international political economy. Nearly all of these debates are conducted within sub-disciplines; they cite and criticize each other but rarely look beyond the boundaries of their own epistemological and methodological positions. This, of course, means that there are parallel discussions of power going on which often fail to make any real progress and so they reinvent the wheel.

Third, there is an assumption, as Napel and Widgrén illustrate, that there is or can be a single definition of power. What I intend to demonstrate is that when looking at the state we need to understand power as a complex, multi-faceted concept that cannot be reduced to a single definition and, consequently, that states adopt and use different forms of power. Political actors are concerned with outcomes and not the nature of power and therefore do not develop a consistent approach to power.

The discussion of power has been in a process of continual debate in political science for over fifty years. Power is, as the oft-quoted Walter Gallie (1956) says, an essentially contested concept. In other words, there can never be any agreement because different thinkers fundamentally disagree over what power is and there is no mechanism for verifying one particular definition. For some, power is exercised by individual agents, whereas for others it is exercised by structure. For some theorists power is something that has to be observed but for others it exists within ideologies and institutions. What is clear is that there are different ways of understanding power and each definition and way of conceptualizing power provides a different insight into political phenomena.

Table 1    *Approaches to power*

| Theory of power | Ontology | Epistemology | Methodology |
|---|---|---|---|
| Pluralist | Group identities are the focus of analysis | Positivist; there is an objective reality | Case studies of decision making |
| Rational choice | Agents exercise choice – they are self-interested actors | Positivist | Modelling and quantitative |
| Institutionalist | Actors exist within an institutional context that may define interests. Structures can have properties of power | Realist | Range of methods but with the assumption that the theoretical frameork needs to reveal underlying structures |
| Post-modernist | Agents' preferences are contingent | Relativist | Histography; discourse analysis |

## Pluralism

The simplest definition of power is that provided by Robert Dahl (1957) who said that power exists when A gets B to do something that B would not otherwise have done. In this definition power is based on intention and manifests itself in actions and outcomes that can be observed. If A wants B to pay tax but B does not want to, A tells B: if you don't pay tax you will go to prison. B pays tax. In this case we can see A has exercised power over B. Likewise, Dennis Wrong (1988: 2) defines power as 'the capacity of some persons to produce intended and foreseen effects on others'. There are two important points to consider. The first is that power is seen as something we can observe – we can see and measure the effect. The second is that power is intentional. A person intends to have an effect in a particular way on another person. This could be a parent intending to make his daughter eat carrots or a prime minister intending to ensure that particular groups of youths do not undertake street robberies. However, it seems strange to eliminate from a notion of power a range of situations where the position of people is affected without any direct intention on the part of others. Frequently our lives are affected by decisions that government and businesses take without them having any intention to directly change our behaviour. Yet, to say they did not intend to affect us does not eliminate the power they have over our lives. The state has power over its citizens and can affect their lives in remarkable ways without any direct intention. As Wrong (1988: x) admits in the second edition of his book, there is a 'distinction between power as a generalized capacity to act on the world and as a specific kind of social relation'. In other words, there is a considerable difference between the type of power that a parent exercises in relation to a child and that the state exercises in relation to a citizen. There is a distinction between power to do something and power over a society or a group of people. States move between using power to achieve particular goals and power over people as a generalized capacity to ensure social order.

Consequently, if we tie the discussion of power to a simple notion of intentional actors achieving specific and specified goals, we are reducing the concept of power to one for a limited range of particular circumstances. Perhaps more importantly we are limiting the power of the 'sociological imagination' (Mills, 1970). It is not a coincidence that Dahl, who defines power in this simple way, was one of the founders of modern American pluralism. What he wanted to demonstrate was that power in the United States was limited to particular spheres, that it could be controlled, that often decisions were a consequence of agreement rather than conflict, and that the lack of opposition to a decision was an indication of contentment. Definitions of power are normative. They are linked to moral and political preferences – highlighting again why agreements on definitions of power are so difficult to achieve. On the more simple definition above, power is about winners and losers. It is something we can easily see and measure, and in a sense power is a benign concept; it is open to control. If someone has too much power we can limit it. We can see who exercises power and how they exercise it and thus we can easily create mechanisms of democratic account- ability. However, if we develop a more complex definition of power, we can start to understand the operation of power in everyday life, and not see the absence of power in the observable sense as an indication of the existence of consensus. As we will see in the next chapter, the lack of observable power does not mean that power does not exist.

For instance, in most Western developed societies the predominant form of transport is the motor car. Billions of pounds have been spent on providing roads through most major nation states. Most residential streets and city centres have been given over to the car. On one reading, the predominance of the car is not an exercise of power. Consumers have chosen to buy cars and once they buy cars they want to get from A to B as quickly as possible and they want to be able to park easily and cheaply in both A and B. Governments have taken this into account by providing the funds for road building but because the state is pluralist and open, the government does ensure that pedestrians are accommo- dated with crossings, pavements and safety regulations. A consensus is established about the role of cars in society.

Yet we can look at the issue in a more fundamental way if we ask: why do cars predominate over cycles and pedestrians, despite the economic and health costs, and why does the preference for cars exist? Why do people seemingly want bigger and more powerful cars despite the fact that they have a more dramatic impact on the environment and have little or no benefit in terms of reducing the time it takes to go from A to B? There is no essential reason for the predominance of cars to exist; when cars were first introduced into Britain they had to have a person with a warning light walk in front of the car, but of course that made the car pointless as a means of transport. It was once the case that streets were places of social interaction and not a route for loud metal- lic killing machines. It could still be the case that cars were greatly restricted in residential areas and that cars had to watch out for pedes- trians and not pedestrians for cars. The reason for cars being predomi- nant is a consequence of a particular conception of development, of individualism, of certain ideas of freedom, of advertising, big business and government. A set of power relationships has existed which has privileged the car over the pedestrian and which leads to what Herbert Marcuse (1964: 21) described as false needs. To suggest that cars be banned from residential areas is seen as lunacy, and to suggest that cars be technically limited so that they cannot go over the speed limit is an issue that is not discussed. A whole set of economic, social, political and ideological factors have combined to ensure the car predominates, but according to the definitions of Dahl and Wrong this is not power. The pluralist (and rational choice) position assumes that the choice of car drivers, their preference for cars, for money to go into roads rather than trains, and the preference for gardens to be turned into parking lots is all a free choice or a consequence of numerous contingent decisions, not a reflection of power relations. However, it is possible to see these preferences as social constructions that reflect the effects of power. Why is freedom the ability to drive a car fast and not the freedom to cross a road without the ever-present danger of a car potentially knocking a person over?

Pluralism was the dominant mode of understanding power in the 1950s and 1960s (and continues to have its advocates). However, the pluralist approach to power was undermined by a whole set of empirical and theoretical challenges. While the ink was still drying on Dahl's claim (1963: 24) that 'the theory and practice of American pluralism tends to assume the existence of multiple centres of power, none of which is wholly sovereign', blacks in the South were being killed for demanding civil and political rights. The pluralist view of power was undermined by an empirical reality of the civil rights movement, the anti-Vietnam war movement and Nixon's White House. Robert Putnam's response to the assassination of Martin Luther King, and the riots that followed illustrates the pluralist impasse: 'What the glow in the sky on that evening of the Martin Luther King assassination conveyed was a sense that there was something happening in American politics that was not encompassed by the conceptual framework we were all working with' (Merelman, 2003: 211–12).

Pluralism fails to deal adequately with the issue of state power. For pluralists, groups and democratic procedures are mechanisms for limiting the state but pluralists fail to define or analyse the nature of its power (Smith, 2006). Whilst, as Andrew McFarland (2004: 46) points out, many pluralists see institutions of government as acting independently and having a degree of autonomy, this is not presented as a mechanism of state power but as an indication that the state is not a unified institution. In other words, within government there are sets of institutions that have relations with different interests and which act as constraints on government. While the various institutions of government may be able to exercise power, it can be empirically demonstrated that that power is not exercised in the interest of a particular group and is constrained by other governmental and democratic processes. McFarland (2004: 48–9) attempts to rescue naïve pluralism by arguing that the process of countervailing powers is not simply a case where a producer group is automatically checked by a consumer group, for example, but rather that in a policy area there are likely to be a range of groups with conflicting interests and the groups allow 'relatively autonomous actions by governmental agencies'. For McFarland (2004: 49):

> Countervailing powers occurs with some frequency because it is not limited to situations in which producer groups are all on one side of an issue and well-organized citizens groups, such as environmentalists, are on the other side. Certain business groups may join public interest groups, professional associations, local property holders, and so on to form countervailing power coalitions to producer interests on specific policy issues.

For instance, the development of food policy in Europe revolves around an ever changing set of coalitions between consumer groups, environmental groups, supermarkets and farmers. It is not simply the case that producers are continually ranged against consumers and environmentalists. In the case of genetically modified food, supermarkets, consumers and environmentalists (and to an extent the media) have been in alliance against food producers and farmers.

Neopluralists develop the naïve pluralism of Dahl and acknowledge that power could be structural power (in the sense of the state privileging particular interests) and they question the notion that the political consensus is an indication of contentment rather than power (see Lindblom, 1977; 1982). Nevertheless, both forms of pluralism fail to deal with the issue of the state and do not give sufficient attention to how the state exercises power (although McFarland denies this). They emphasize much more the role of groups and say little about the way that the state operates. Pluralist studies tend to focus, as Dahl did in *Who Governs?*, on particular decisions and read power from outcomes (see, for example, Hewitt, 1974). As Dowding *et al.* (1995: 266) point out, because pluralists read interests from outcomes, they cannot really know if people get what they want. Pluralist approaches do not examine the mechanisms of power; they see power more in terms of groups shaping what states do rather than states shaping what people do. There is an underestimation of the state and the ways in which it structures many of the political conflicts within society. The state is assumed to react to groups rather than imposing policies. Pluralists fail to confront the issue of state power, seeing the state as a conduit for group interactions.

There are elements of pluralism that are useful in analysing power.

There are instances where power is observable and it does take the form of A making B do something that he would not otherwise do (see Lukes, 2005). Where a pressure group wins a concession from government or Congress votes down the President's budget, a powerful group can be observed (although there are still problems of correlation and causation). However, this is a narrow outcome power rather than a broader social power. The interesting question may not be why A wants $y$ or $z$ but why $y$ or $z$ are the options. Nevertheless, it is important in political systems to understand why $y$ is chosen over $z$. Pluralism, whilst highly influential, was undermined both theoretically and empirically. Ironically, one of the critiques of pluralism was rational choice theory, even though it shares a similar, behavioural conception of power.

## Rational choice theory

The behavioural alternative to pluralism is rational choice theory (RCT). Whilst pluralism's normative position legitimizes liberal democracy (see Merelman, 2003), rational choice developed as a critique of the liberal democratic state, highlighting how, rather than acting in the public interest, as pluralists assumed, politicians and bureaucrats (Downs, 1957) often act in their own interest. Rational choice theorists do not see the state simply as implementing the desires of groups. Moreover, Mancur Olson (1965) emphasized the constraints on group formation and collective action when the potential membership is large. Despite their differences, pluralism and rational choice theory are united by their methodological individualism (although for pluralists group identity can often be more important than individuals) and so power is the consequence of the choices of individual actions. This initial premise leads to a positivist epistemology and the belief that power is observable. For many pluralists methodology was based on case studies where they observed the operation of power, and they developed some extremely rich and detailed empirical studies such as Dahl's (1961) *Who Governs?* and Nelson Polsby's (1963) *Community Power and Political Theory*. However, the focus on particular communities made it difficult to generalize the findings (and resulted in a long debate where different case studies were pitted against each other, so that whilst Dahl and Polsby could demonstrate pluralism in New Haven, Matthew Crenson (1971) and John Gaventa (1980) could demonstrate elite rule in Gary and the

Appalachia). RCT built on the positivist approach and attempted to develop universal theories that could be tested in a rigorous scientific way. However, such a methodology leads to a narrow focus because modelling observable power limits the types of power that can be analyzed. RCT focuses on formal institutions and situations in which game theoretical approaches can be applied; power becomes focussed on the formal arena of politics.

Pluralist and rational choice theory have important differences. For pluralists power is complex (McFarland, 2004: 22). Who has power and how it affects outcomes cannot be modelled in a simple way. Rational choice theory is intent on developing parsimonious models of power that can be expressed in mathematical formulae. Moreover, for pluralists interests are dependent on identity. If I am an industrial farmer I have a different set of interests to those that I would have as an ecological biologist. Our interests relate to the groups of which we are members. For rational choice theory interests are fixed and not changed by processes and therefore the assumption of self-interest utility maximization can be used to model behaviour and to understand power. With fixed preferences it is possible to predict how actors will respond to particular sets of incentives.

The basis of rational choice theory is that:

- Individuals are utility maximizers. In other words they will do what is in the direct interest of themselves and their immediate families.
- People have clear preferences.
- Preferences are transitive. In other words, if people prefer apples to pears and pears to bananas, they will choose apples over bananas if there are no pears.
- People have the information to make informed choices.

The consequence of rational self-interest is that cooperation for the common good is difficult. The desire to achieve our own self-interest means that we will not achieve what is good for society as a whole. We may desire a world without pollution and think it would be better if cars were used less. However, we want to use our own cars and a consequence of everyone making that decision is pollution and congested roads. Building on assumptions of rational action, rational choice theorists attempt to develop predictive models concerning the behaviour of actors and have used game theory as an analytical tool for understanding collective action problems. From these assumptions they are able to model behaviour and to develop games which can be used to develop predictions about how people will behave in particular situations. RCT assumptions have led to two related approaches: game theory and the notion of power indices. Both are attempts to develop mathematical models of power.

## Game theory

Keith Dowding (1996: 8) points out that game theory 'models inter-dependent action':

> The choices of these actors are shaped by the social environment in which they find themselves, which includes the nature of the inter-relationship of players of the game. In fact, the type of game that the players are engaged upon may be said to constitute their incentive structure. Game theory provides a way of formalising social structures and examining the effects of those structures upon individuals' decisions. It therefore provides an ideal way of examining the structure of power in society.

From this definition it does not appear that the use of games provides for an analysis of power because game theory analyses choices in a structured relationship and not who has power in a relationship. Peter Bennett (1995: 22) points out that to analyse a game it is necessary to have two or more players, strategies for each of the players, 'a set of possible outcomes' and 'a set of *preference functions* specifying how good or bad each outcome is for each player' (emphasis in original).

However, games are often presented through two by two matrices. In the prisoner's dilemma two people are arrested with the equipment to commit a burglary. The police suspect that they intended to burgle a house, but have no evidence. They therefore put the two, Janet and John, in separate cells. If they can get each to give evidence against the other they can get convictions for burglary and each will get ten years in prison. If, however, both stay silent, the police only have evidence of intent to commit a crime and therefore they will get a year each. However, the police can offer a deal and say to one: you can go free if you give evidence against your colleague who will then get ten years. If one speaks and the other stays silent then one will go to prison and the other will not. This produces the matrix shown in Figure 2.

Figure 2 *The Prisoner's Dilemma*

|  | Remain silent | Inform |
|---|---|---|
| Remain silent | 1,1 | 0,10 |
| Inform | 10,0 | 10,10 |

If they cooperate and remain silent they will go to prison for a short period because of the lack of information. But the question is, can they trust the other when the police are trying to get Janet to give evidence against John and Janet has the incentive of a low sentence? As they are both rational actors they will not trust their co-thief and each will inform on the other. As a consequence of them both informing on the other, they end up with the worst outcome. The police have the evidence to send them both to jail. Presumably, it is the police and the courts who have power because they prevent Janet and John talking and set the prison tariffs, but that is not illustrated in the game, which is concerned with the choices of Janet and John and not with the actions of the police. A pure one shot 'prisoner's dilemma' is demonstrated in a game show on British television , *Golden Balls*. Contestants cooperate to win a pot of money. They then have to decide individually whether to share or steal the money. If they share they get half the money each. If one says steal and the other share, all the money goes to the one who says steal. If they both say steal they get nothing. Ideally, they should share but there is little incentive to share because the contestants cannot trust each other. By stealing there is a possibility of winning everything, and if you say share there is a chance you will lose it all; the game makes cooperation very difficult. Yet what is interesting is that whilst it is rational to steal, many people choose to share. Nevertheless, the problems of coordination posed by the prisoner's dilemma account for the existence of states; states can impose cooperation.

Another game, the chicken game, may be better at illustrating winners and losers. The chicken game is based on the idea of who will back down in a situation of conflict. Two farmers share a drainage ditch which is blocked. If they act quickly they can share the costs of mending the ditch and not have any further damage. However, being rational actors each waits for the other to act. As a consequence the blockage causes flooding which costs the farmers much more. The matrix therefore is as shown in Figure 3.

Figure 3    *The Chicken Game*

|            | Mend ditch | Leave ditch |
|------------|-----------|-------------|
| Mend ditch | 50,50     | 0,100       |
| Leave ditch| 100,0     | 200,200     |

RCT predicts the worst outcome because it is rational to wait for someone else to act over a shared problem. The chicken game has been used to analyse the Cuban missile affair. Here the relationship between the US and the USSR was a game with both waiting for the other to back down. In the end the USSR backed down and the US 'won', suggesting that the United States had power in achieving the outcome it desired. It can also be used to explain the tardiness of states in relation to taking action on global warming.

There are many criticisms of game theory, which are discussed below, and there have been attempts to make game theory more 'realistic' by assuming that players may have perceptions or misperceptions about how others will act. For instance, in the prisoner's dilemma Janet and John must know each other and how they behave will depend on whether they trust each other or whether they are lovers, relations, friends or have been forced to work together. Game theory can also factor in incomplete information and non-transitive preferences. The games can also be iterative, in other words they can be played over again, which allows trust and a reputation to be developed (which explains some of the interest in social capital as a trust-building mechanism). Of course, whilst games that are complex may introduce more variables and interest, it may be that in introducing greater complexity they lose what is their most powerful element – parsimonious explanation – and they become little more than descriptions of the choice agents may face in particular circumstances. One important development in game theory in relation to power is the notion of power indices which are used to develop models in relation to the distribution of power within parliaments and committees.

## Power indices

The development of power indices has become a complex and largely mathematical development of game theory in a variety of voting arenas ranging from elections to legislatures to committees. Power indices are based on the assumption that a single voter or coalition of voters is in a position to change an outcome. According to Jan-Erik Lane and Reinert Maeland (2006: 189) 'A power index measures the individual voting power of a player in decision making'. So for example, in a committee of seven people where there are two groups of three who always vote in coalition, then the single voter is a pivotal voter who can make a difference by voting with either coalition. As Dowding (1996: 46–7) points out:

> The full outcome power of each voter is then given by how often each is, or could be, the pivotal voter. The pivotal voter can then be defined: $Pi = m(i)/n$, where P is the power of the voter I in a set of voters $\{1,2,...,n\}$ and m (i) is the number of times that I is pivotal in securing that outcome ... Under this definition, a voter's power is determined by the number of times she is pivotal in relation to the number of possible ordered sequences.

The two most well-known power indices (Shapley-Shubik and Penrose-Banzhaf) work out the probability that each voter will affect the outcome of a vote (Lane and Maeland, 2006: 189). Lane and Maeland (2006: 193–5) are able to ascribe voting weights to states in international organizations such as the World Trade Organization (WTO) and the European Union (EU) and to demonstrate that, for example, the probability of decisiveness in the WTO is relatively low compared to the EU; and of course that the larger countries such as Germany, France and Britain have a greater probability of affecting EU decisions than smaller countries with less voting weight. The conclusion that Lane and Maeland demonstrate is that in international organizations with unanimity the probability of decisiveness is 1, whereas with majority voting it is reduced considerably, making decision making easier. They are able to illustrate how different voting systems affect the ability of states to block decisions.

Nevertheless, the notion of a power index offers a limited understanding of power. Often those who have used the power index approach are not interested in the preference of actors (Braham and Holler, 2005) and therefore power is not about what actors want and whether they achieve it, but only their voting power. It may be possible that the ability to achieve something is separate from what a person wants to achieve, but can what a person wants be separated from how they try to achieve it? For Braham and Holler power resides in the game and not in the way it is played. This leads to the accusation from Napel and Widgrén (2005) that they are being deterministic (to which of course the reply is no, since it is Napel and Widgrén who are being deterministic). As Geoffrey Garret and George Tsebelis (1999: 292) have pointed out, ignoring preferences leads to predictions about outcomes in the EU, for instance, that are empirically incorrect. In this approach power is reduced to a mathematical artefact. There is considerable doubt that it has any real empirical relevance because votes may be a reflection of decisions taken outside the formal arena. For example, in most national legislatures decisions are normally a consequence of the position of the government, not the power of pivotal voters. Indeed, this approach fails to take account of how institutional rules affect outcomes (Garret and Tsebelis, 1999: 292). For instance, the WTO has 146 members and according to Lane and Maeland the Banzhaf index of each nation is 0.000015 and the probability of decisiveness is 0.000021. However, can it seriously be suggested that the United States and Thailand have the same ability to shape outcome in international trade policy? They may have the same number of votes in the WTO but this fact tells us very little about the nature of international trade policy and whose interest it serves. The power index seems to ignore power beyond the ability to vote. It constructs an understanding of power in world trade without reference to a whole host of highly respected political scientists from a range of different traditions who point out that international trade policy has to be understood within the context of US economic hegemony and domestic US politics (Cox, 2005; Keohane, 2002; Cohen, 1988; Bauer, De Sola Pool and Dexter, 1972). As Dowding (1996) drawing on Brian Barry (1989) explains, what we may be seeing here is luck rather than power (see the discussion below).

The power indices approach highlights two criticisms of rational choice theory. First, it is an agent-based approach that actually removes choice from actors (Dunleavy, 1991: 6). Second, the assumption of utility maximization is not a universal motivation for action. C.B. Macpherson (1962) demonstrated that such a model of capitalism is historically specific and of course it does not have universal application. Many authors have pointed out that even Adam Smith's notion of markets was not based on a conception of human agents who were solely utility maximizers but rather who had a concern for general social well-being (Fleischacker, 2005). Many economists and psychologists have long demonstrated that in many circumstances people act from a range of motivations ranging from hate to love to anger to altruism (Reuben and Van Winden, 2005; Ward, 2002; Abelson, 1996). The criticism that the assumptions of rational choice theory are too narrow and that empirical evidence demonstrates that people will cooperate in prisoner dilemma situations goes back to the 1960s and 1970s (see Sen, 1977; Lave, 1962). It is increasingly accepted that there is little empirical support for utility maximization and that people have complex and mixed motives (Frederick, Loewenstein and O'Donoghue, 2002). Prospect theory highlights the way in which preferences change according to context (Kahneman and Tversky, 1990), and as Robert Abelson (1996: 26) bluntly states:

> To a psychologist, it is frankly no surprise that rational choice models receive such poor empirical support. As applied to ordinary citizens such models are at best manifestly incomplete; at worst they are seriously misleading. There is a double problem: the axiomatic requirements of rational choice are too demanding; but even were this not so, the presupposition that behaviour is necessarily instrumental to goal attainment is too restrictive.

Utility maximization has remained central to modellers, not because it is empirically correct, but because the assumption allows model building. The danger is that, as with economics, increasingly complex models are developed with little or no relation to reality. As Ian Shapiro (2005: 182) confirms, the problems addressed become artefacts of the model that is specified. As one of the leading figures in developing rational choice in political science, William Niskanen, has admitted: 'much of the [public choice] literature is a collection of intellectual games' (quoted in Friedman, 1996: 13).

Edward Hagen and Peter Hammerstein (2006: 2) maintain that 'This model of decision making was motivated as much by its analytic tractability and intuitive appeal as it was by empirical facts' (Tversky and Kahneman, 1981). Mary Zey (1998: 43) goes further: 'Support and retention of the model are more important to RCT than whether the model mirrors the data'. If we accept Weber's (1978: 24) view that social action 'may be orientated in four ways', then building mathematical and predictive models becomes extremely difficult. He identifies four types of rationality (and it is worth noting the use of the term rationality): a) instrumental rationality (which conforms to utility maximization); b) value rationality, i.e. that people may act in a specific way because of the values they hold, be they ethical, aesthetic or religious; c) affectual rationality – that we may have feelings about something; or d) traditional rationality – acting through habit (Weber, 1978: 24–5). An important question is how actions are motivated by each of these rationalities and how often it is utility maximization that is the main motivation. Even the novels of Jane Austen can be seen as a demonstration of how marriage shifted away from an institution based on instrumental rationality when people married for economic reasons to the world Austen was imagining and creating where romantic love became the driver for marriage.

For Max Weber social science is concerned with interpretive understandings. The role of the social observer is to interpret meaning and not to assume utility maximization (Weber, 1978: 4-5). Mark Blyth (2008) forcefully concludes that if we are to take ideas seriously in human motivations then predictive models of human behaviour will have little relation to social reality. If people are able to think and undertake practical reasoning when faced with a particular incentive structure it is unlikely that we can ever predict (or model) their behaviour.

Rational choice has a narrow conception of power both in terms of what it is and where it can be observed. It is arguable that rational choice theory does not take the concept of power seriously (Zey, 1998: 44; Moe, 2005). RCT examines choices within the context of a particular set of incentives and in that sense it is not interested in power, although Dowding (1996: 5) does see power as existing in the ability to change incentive structures. However, game theory does not concentrate on the setting of incentives – they are usually given – but on the choices made within the incentive structure. In this sense it looks at particular outcomes and whether or not they are in an actor's interest. In the prisoner's dilemma decisions are made independently of each other. Power would exist if they both stayed silent because they were members of the Mafia and therefore there is a powerful incentive not to inform. Moreover, understanding the incentive structure involves an historical analysis and not the sort of modelling that game theorists advocate: the explanation is not in the game but in the structure set by the leadership of the Mafia.

Game theory has been used successfully to understand sex ratios in animal species, signaling between members of groups, competition between individuals and for understanding conflicts at all levels of biological organization (between genes, between cells – this is important,  for example, in understanding cancer – and obviously between individuals and groups [Axelrod, 2008]), but biologists are not interested in power, and they are not dealing with reflexive actors. Game theory works in biology because it models causal patterns; this is not the case in social life. Rational choice theory models the choices people make (or the actions they would take if they were rational) whereas social scientists interested in power are more concerned with why people often find themselves with a particular set of options and the extent to which they have the ability to reflect and the power to act differently.

In the index approach, rational choice theorists do ascribe power to an agent – for instance the pivotal actor. Consequently, power is an object, not a relationship; something that is fixed to that particular position, although, of course, game theory sets up situations of power as a relationship. Nevertheless, game theory still ascribes fixed values to particular choices and only sees games as the whole situation of winners and losers. Rational choice theory predicts non-cooperation, whereas much current research suggests that people are more likely to reciprocate than not cooperate (Hagen and Hammerstein, 2006). Hagen and Hammerstein use the 'ultimate game' to demonstrate what many critiques of rational choice have long argued. In the ultimate game player A is given a certain amount of money, say $100, and A has to offer player B a share from $0 to $100. If B accepts the offer then B gets the amount offered and A keeps the rest. If player B rejects the offer, both get nothing. In many cases A offers more than $0 and B often rejects offers even when the amount is quite high. Both actions defy utility maximization. Hagen and Hammerstein point out that:

> Economics has long assumed that (1) individuals are rational deci-sion-makers who seek to maximise their utility where (2) utility is defined in terms of individual benefit ... Because players in the ulti-mate game often do not maximise their individual monetary profit, one or both of the above assumptions must be incorrect.

Hagen and Hammerstein conclude that utility maximization is often circumscribed by a) the opportunity to build a good reputation; b) subtle clues or relationships between participants; c) culture – as Weber might have suggested, how games are played reflects 'local, social and economic institutions'; and d) emotions. e) Many individual strategies often do not conform to utility maximization. f) They also emphasize the point developed by Amos Tversky and Daniel Kahneman (1981) that decisions are often 'framed'. In other words, the decisions people make depend on the context: 'Contributions to public goods game were higher when the game was framed as a community social event' (Hagen and Hammerstein, 2006: 7).

Moreover, game theory oversimplifies choices in a strategic situation, and it is irrefutable. As Michael Mandel (2005) argues, game theory is a dead end:

[I]t flunks the main test of any scientific theory: the ability to make empirically testable predictions. In most real-life situations, many different outcomes – from full cooperation to near-disastrous conflict – are consistent with the game-theory version of rationality... If the world had been blown up during the Cuban Missile Crisis of 1962, game theorists could have explained that as an unfortunate outcome – but one that was just as rational as what actually happened.

What is more, whilst writers such as Dowding link power to intentionality, rational choice theory in fact denies actors choice. As Colin Hay (2004a: 52) points out:

For, within any rational choice model, we know one thing above all: that the actor will behave rationally, maximizing his or her personal utility. Consequently, *any rational actor in a given context will choose precisely the same (optimal) course of action.* Actors are interchangeable (Tsebelis, 1990: 43). Moreover, where there is more than one optimal course of action (where, in short, there are multiple equilibria), we can expect actors' behaviour to be distributed predictably between – and only between – such optima. (Emphasis in original)

Indeed, Matthew Braham and Manfred Holler (2005) argue that preferences of actors are irrelevant to game theory.

Rational choice theory has been defended on the grounds that there are many empirical confirmations and there is no better alternative theory. On the first point it is possible to see cases where (some) people act as utility maximizers but many where they do not (voting, dipping headlights, getting married, buying a house, joining pressure groups, sending money to NGOs, having their aged mother around for Sunday lunch). Nevertheless, there seems to be considerable evidence that people respond to incentives (Levitt and Jacob, 2003: 843). The rational choice ontology has been widely accepted by governments in designing policies (see Chapter 8). Andrew Hindmoor (2006: 94) makes the point that 'whilst self-interested behaviour may once have been a very inaccurate assumption to make about the behaviour of most people, the academic success of public choice theory may have contributed to making it more truthful'. We do need to understand rational choice theory in order to analyse aspects of state power. It may also be the case, building on Hindmoor's point, that rational choice theory is confirmation of the arguments of Foucault and Bourdieu that are discussed below. From their perspective, the form of knowledge and ontology recognised by rational choice theorists is confirmation that late capitalism has developed a form of being and notion of power that conform to the interests of capitalists. We are self-interested utility maximizers because that best serves the interests of global capitalism! Therefore, as MacIntyre (1962) points out, utility maximizing is not a universal assumption we can make about human behaviour but it may be one that applies in particular situations where people have been defined as rational self-interested actors. Of course, because we can engage in ideas in the way Blyth (2008) suggests we can also choose to act on the basis of different rationalities.

## Conclusion

Traditional conceptions of power have been based on power as an observable and limited phenomenon. They have a clear and intuitively attractive understanding of power. It is one person shaping the behaviour of another and thereby affecting outcomes. Pluralists and rational choice theorists are concerned with outcomes and not broader forms of social power. Consequently, they have focussed on explicit, observable events where who has power can be determined or, in the case of rational choice theory, modelled. However, this provides us with a limited conception of power which is both agent-centred and ignores the way that institutions and structures may shape outcomes and affect who succeeds in achieving their interests. It probably misses more than it captures because as individuals we are rarely explicitly directed by the state or state actors, but state rules and norms affect nearly every aspect of our lives. We will see later in the book how states do explicitly attempt to direct citizens, but often state control is indirect and hidden. What is also curious about both pluralists and rational choice theorists is that they say very little about the mechanisms of power. For pluralists power is often not about conflict but consensus – it is about establishing processes for agreement. For rational choice theorists power almost doesn't exist – agents do not have choice but react to their incentive structures. Power exists in the ability to frame incentives but

RCT fails to develop any explanation of how the incentives structures come into being. Perhaps more importantly from the perspective of this book, pluralism and rational choice theory at one level have a clear definition of power philosophically – it is the ability to make an actor act in ways that she did not intend. However, both rational choice theorists and pluralists fail to take state power seriously empirically. State power is effectively ignored and not seen as a problem – despite some of their negative normative assumptions about states. Pluralists, as we will see later, see states as an arena of power and rational choice theorists actually elide the question of power by focussing on the 'choices' of actors. They ignore the core question of power, such as how a particular set of options or an incentive structure come into being, partly because these approaches are ahistorical and partly because the methods do not allow investigation of such questions.

These problems with rational choice, behavioural and pluralist conceptions have led theorists to attempt to conceptualize power in more complex ways, addressing issues such as the role of institutions and structures, the role of ideas and the notion of intentionality. The real issue is not so much what power is – it is in most definitions the ability to make a difference (Poggi, 2000: 3) – but what the processes are by which that making the difference occurs in social situations. In understanding the processes we have to understand two things: the first is abstract – defining alternative ways that power may work; the second is more concrete – examining the actual mechanisms through which preferences and actions change; in other words, the way the mechanisms that states have for achieving their desired outcomes are conceptualized. Pluralism and rational choice theory reflect ways in which politicians think about power, and both approaches have played a role in legitimizing forms of power. However as explanations of the ways in which states exercise power they are limited. In the next chapter, the book examines non-behavioural conceptualisations of power and examines the ways in which they provide for a more complex understanding of power.

# Chapter 2

# Understanding Power: Radical Approaches

The power debate, as we saw in the last chapter, is polarised around different methodologies, epistemologies and ontologies. Despite the apparent philosophical complexities of the power debate, much of the argument can be reduced to a definitional issue. Behavioural and rational choice approaches see power as a relatively defined event. It is power to achieve a specific outcome (see Morris, 2002; 2006). However, if power was simply the capability of A to get B to do something B would not otherwise do, we would not have a power debate and we would not have a problem. The nature of power would be apparent and something that could be measured. However, the field of political studies would be extremely narrow (as it is for many who adopt positivist approaches) and issues such as why some people become suicide bombers, or why some people lack any influence on the political process, or why some people drive cars, would not be issues of power but issues of choice or luck (see below).

Non-positivist definitions of power are concerned with power over – the sense of power as a social relationship and something that is implicated in complex ways into all aspects of social relations. From this perspective, power is not easily observed, partly because there is no single initiator of a decision, and also because power operates through social structures, ideas, values and norms. Power is not an individual attribute but a sociological relationship. For example, if we were to ask why there has been an increase in anorexia among young girls we could point to the power of the media, the power of the food industry, the power of parents or the nature of relations between men and women. None of these institutions had any intention of creating anorexia and there is no single cause that explains why a particular person has anorexia, but a complex set of social forces have produced this outcome and these forces are a set of power relations. Keith Dowding (1996: 16) dismisses such an approach as the 'blame fallacy', arguing that we look for a power to blame for unfortunate outcomes and he argues that without intentionality we are seeing luck rather than

33

power. However, such an approach undermines the social science enterprise by ignoring the way in which social organizations favour particular interests and limit the choices of those in less powerful positions; social explanation is replaced by fortune. A systematic failure or success at achieving outcomes is a fundamental aspect of the nature of power which needs to be explained, not reduced to fate.

This chapter is concerned with evaluating the definitions and understandings of power that challenge the simplicities of the positivist approaches. In this chapter, we will look at the so-called second and third dimensions of power, and then examine how they have been developed by structuralists and poststructuralists. The aim is to demonstrate how these approaches, whilst often incompatible epistemologically and methodologically, can sensitize the analyst to the complexity of power in the real world. It also highlights that states may not exercise power through simple mechanism of direct control but through complex processes that involve ideas, institutions and relationships.

## The other dimensions of power

Many political scientists and philosophers have demonstrated that power often occurs in ways that are not always observable, and that the exercise of power does not always depend on the direct intentions of actors or a particular set of decisions. First, Peter Bachrach and Morton Baratz (1962) pointed out that decisions could often be made through non-decision-making:

> Power is also exercised when A devotes his energies to creating or reinforcing social and political values and institutional practices that limit the scope of the political process to public consideration of only those issues which are comparatively innocuous to A. (Quoted in Lukes, 2005: 20)

In other words, what is important is not what the powerful do but often what they do not do or do not allow to happen – the ways in which issues are kept off the agenda – or are non-decisions. For example, nearly every country in the world has a maximum speed limit for cars. For every 5 kph a car goes over the speed limit, the chance of a fatal accident doubles and there is a strong relationship between increased speed and fatalities (Paine, 2004). Although the technology exists to limit the speed of cars to the national speed limit, and of course it is illegal to go above the speed limit, no country places a speed limiter on cars. Indeed, the issue of limiting the speed of cars is never discussed in a serious way. It is a non-decision. The whole idea of speed control is excluded from the agenda even though there is considerable evidence that such a mechanism would save lives. From the point of view of the second face of power, this occurs because powerful groups like the motor industry conspire to keep the issue off the agenda.

Steven Lukes (1974, 2005) was critical of the so-called second dimension of power, arguing that it continued to see power in behavioural terms. Rather than individuals deciding to do things, they decide not to do them. Lukes' 'third face of power' opens up the possibility of power being much more than a process of individuals making or not making decisions. For Lukes, power is also about the manipulation of wants; how people get to believe the things they believe and want the things they want (Lukes, 2005). In other words, Lukes is focussing on the question of how preferences and incentive structures are set. Why I want $X$ rather than $Y$ is the outcome of power, not the starting point of analysis. It is a question that is fundamental to sociological analysis from its early development in the nineteenth century: how do those without power or money sustain in positions of dominance the rich and the powerful (see Mann, 1970, 1973)? In the latest manifestation of this view Thomas Frank (2004) asks why it is that in the poorest county in the United States, 80 per cent voted for Bush in the 2000 election despite a policy platform that clearly favoured the wealthy. He sees the answer in the way the Republican party has been able to aggregate people's fears of the modern world and use an appeal to nationalism and religion as a mechanism to persuade people to vote against their apparent material interests.

This third dimension of power involves, according to John Gaventa (1980: 15):

Specifying the means through which power influences, shapes or determines conceptions of the necessities, possibilities, and strategies of challenge in situations of latent conflict. This may include the study of social myths, language, and symbols, and how they are shaped and manipulated in power processes. It may involve a focus upon the means by which social legitimations are developed around the dominant, and instilled as beliefs or roles in the dominated. It may involve, in short, locating the power processes behind the social construction of meanings.

In other words, it means examining taken-for-granted social reality and determining whose interests these constructions serve.

The third face of power can be illustrated if we return to the example of speed controls on cars. It is possible to argue that the reason that there are not speed limiters on cars is not because manufacturers oppose them but because consumers do. A government might lose votes if it proposed physically restricting the speed of cars. Most people in the West aspire to big, fast cars. Car companies sell cars on the basis of their speed. It is almost inconceivable that cars should not dominate our roads and that an expensive car is not a desirable good for the majority of people. In the United States the car is held in particular reverence. However, as Paul Harris (2006) explains, this is not a random or contingent (or luck) event but rather the consequence of conscious decisions:

> Many of those electric tram lines ended up being bought by car firms, notably General Motors. Between 1936 and 1950 a holding company backed by GM, Firestone and Standard Oil bought 100 tram firms in 45 American cities. They were dismantled and replaced by GM buses: more inefficient, more likely to lead to congestion and, in the end, more profitable to GM. Many bus lines then failed, leaving consumers with no choice but to buy cars.

Harris suggests that the dominance of cars was also helped by the urban planners who 'seemed possessed with a manic zeal to push the car at the expense of public transit'. In his view planners such as Robert Moses created cities for traffic and left open little alternative in terms of transport (see Ward, 1987). A combination of business and political power combined with an ideology of freedom and capitalism to create a situation where the dominance of the car became a part of taken-for-granted reality. There are two important points here: first, that the decision of an individual to buy a car is not the result of an intentional act of power by someone in General Motors. Second, the exercise of this power is not directly observable but is in the way that preferences are shaped through ideas, advertising, tax incentives, the structure of public transport and road building policy. A range of institutions combine to develop an unquestioning acceptance that cars are the dominant form of transport despite the number of people who are killed by cars. In the United States about 42,000 people a year are killed on the roads and in the UK the figure is about 3,600 (of whom 166 were children in 2004). These numbers are just taken as given compared to, say, the number of children murdered or US troops killed in Iraq; even though it is possible to prevent road deaths.

The growth in popularity of Sports Utility Vehicles (SUVs) provides an apparent example of how wants are manipulated. On nearly all criteria the purchase of an SUV is irrational. They are more expensive than the average car, they are intended for a particular purpose (driving off-road), but more than fifty per cent are bought by women and most drivers never use them off-road. The desire for SUVs is certainly not innate and is arguably against the collective good; they are bad for road safety, the environment and road congestion. It would seem that it is a want that has been created both by the car manufacturing industry – which incidentally makes very large profits out of SUVs – and changing perceptions.

Governments, or other institutions, can have power over others through the ability to shape the political agenda and to delineate what is or what is not acceptable behaviour. Lukes, in his third dimension, is identifying the nature of a social scientist – he is saying that the taken-for-granted is not neutral, it is not an act of God – it is socially created and in that social creation certain interests are privileged over others. This has led to considerable criticism that Lukes is taking the position of the philosopher king. The poor and powerless do not know their own interests (in Marxist terms they have false consciousness) but Lukes the social observer can determine what would really be for their good (see Hay, 1997: 48–9, cited in Lukes, 2005: 149). Lukes defends himself against this charge by pointing out that what he is talking about is the 'power to mislead' which can take many forms:

> [F]rom straightforward censorship and disinformation to the various institutionalized and personalized ways there are of infantilizing judgment, and the promotion and sustenance of all kinds of failures of rationality and illusory thinking, among them the 'naturalization' of what could be otherwise and the misrecognition of the sources and desire of belief.

It is not hard, for instance, to see that many people supported the US invasion of Iraq in 2003 because they were led to believe that Saddam Hussein had access to weapons of mass destruction, which in fact did not exist. In Britain the war was legitimized on the basis of an untrue, and unsubstantiated, claim that Iraq could prepare and use chemical weapons within 45 minutes. As Ian Shapiro (2006: 149) reminds us, we cannot make *ex ante* claims about real interests – as Marxism does

– because determining real interests is an empirical task. If people had known that weapons of mass destruction did not exist in Iraq their view on the invasion may have been different.

The other issue that is raised in Lukes' work is the role of intention. If we see power as a complex phenomenon that operates through 'shaping preferences, beliefs and desires' (Lukes, 2005: 130), which exists in all relationships and through the social fabric of society, does it mean that there has to be an identifiable agent who exercises power? For example, if President Bush says that he wants to remove Saddam Hussein from power, we can see he has intention and effect and so power. If, however, on the way to removing Saddam Hussein many Iraqi civilians are killed, whom President Bush did not intend to kill and whom he may never even have thought about, are we to say that Bush had no power over the Iraqi civilians? What Lukes is highlighting is the notion that power can be 'the ability to have another or others in your power, by constraining their choices, thereby securing their compliance' (Lukes, 2005: 74). If we see power in this way, then the narrow notion of intentionality specified by Dennis Wrong and others is not very useful. As Lukes (2005: 76) suggests: 'What actors intentionally do always generates chains of unintended consequences and it is implausible to deny that some of these manifest their power.' Often power is exercised through 'routine and unconsidered ways', without intention (Lukes and Haglund, 2005: 50). This is a key way that states do exercise power by constraining options and often having unintended impacts on the lives of citizens.

## Power: luck or structure?

Keith Dowding (1991, 1996) and Brian Barry (1991) argue that if A gets what she wants without acting then what we are witnessing is luck rather than power (and presumably the dead Iraqis are unlucky rather than powerless). Dowding goes further, arguing that when beneficial outcomes are sustained over a period of time then A is systematically lucky. He points to the example of farmers doing extremely well in the post-war years without having to do anything and therefore he sees them as also 'systematically lucky' (Dowding, 2002). However, this definition can only work because of an extreme individualist understanding of the social world (and as Lukes and Haglund [2005: 54] suggest, this is stretching the term 'luck' to breaking point). Dowding's explanation effectively ignores the social world and focuses solely on the choices of actors and, where intentional choices are not involved, their 'luck'. The farmers did well not out of luck (which surely must be random and therefore would have favoured consumers as much as farmers) but because of a whole set of historical and institutional events that favoured agricultural production.

In her book, *Hard Work*, Polly Toynbee (2003: 207) asks a chief executive of a care home company, earning at least £250,000 a year, how he justified the low wages he paid to his care staff. His answer provides a perfect example of an agency-based explanation of inequality:

> I believe this is a free country. I believe that in this modern age that everyone has their opportunity. Everyone who really wants to reach their goal is free to do it. If making money is your thing, you can go for it and make it. If it's education you want, you can get education.

Toynbee (2003: 204) sees the situation very differently:

> At the heart of the low-pay problem lies the continuation of the low valuation of what are regarded as women's skills – caring, cleaning, cooking, teaching and nursing. Things your mother did for you she did freely out of love, and there is an unspoken expectation that all women at work should be society's mothers, virtually for free. The low value put on their labour springs from a deeply ingrained belief that they do these jobs because they love them.

Toynbee is developing a social explanation (that involves power) and does not fall back on an explanation of luck. Power is about the way the position of women is constructed in relation to issues of work.

If we look at the situation the other way round then we can see the absurdity of the argument around luck. It assumes that those who don't get what they want are unlucky. By that token the fact that the murder of Stephen Lawrence was not properly investigated is an illustration not of racism, but of bad luck. Indeed, Barry (2002) seems to have recanted on his view that success may be the result of luck. He acknowledges when examining the power of capitalists that their power may indeed be unobservable, and the reason for the continued success of business is not a function of luck but of 'anticipated reactions'. He emphasizes the point made by Charles Lindblom (1977) that business has a privileged position because officials cannot afford to ignore the success of business. Indeed, the work of David Sanders (1996) demonstrates that economic competence is vital for electoral success. Government has little choice but to accommodate the interests of business. For example, it may choose to reduce the level of corporation tax in order to improve economic activity without business lobbying for such a change. Whilst this is definitely good fortune for business it is difficult to see it as luck. As Barry (2002: 177) points out, Dowding sees capitalists as lucky because they are lucky to be capitalists in a capitalist system with competitive electoral politics. Robert Dover (2007) reports for instance that the success of a British ambassador's tenure is measured by the extent to which he or she has been successful in increasing export trade for British companies. For Dowding, these companies are just lucky to have an embassy working away for their interests. However, none of these things are a consequence of luck – people do not become capitalists on a random basis, but there are a whole set of social structures that ensure there are more middle class, white, male capitalists (see Marsh, 2002). Likewise, the system is not capitalist or electorally competitive because of luck but because of a long history of political struggle which has seen some preferences succeed above others. As Barry (2002: 177) points out, the power of capitalists does not derive from their luck but 'capitalists have power over governments merely by acting as individual profit-maximising individuals'. The fact that the arms trade plays such an important role in many national economies means there is a lot of pressure on governments to act in their interests without the arms industry having to do anything. This is an illustration of their economic resources and their capacities for power rather than their luck. In other words, a whole set of individual decisions by business results in a framework which limits the options available to governments and so collectively capitalists have power over business. As Barry (2002: 182) writes:

> To say that capitalists as a class are systematically lucky is to imply that they could get outcomes they want without having to do anything. But the point is that, although no one capitalist's action is (let us again assume) essential, enough of them do have to be believed to be able to do something to exercise the means of power by making the voters worse off, and through them make the government worse off at the next election.

Likewise Steven Lukes and LaDawn Haglund (2005: 49) remind us:

A situation where one's interests systematically correspond with outcomes, even if they are interests shared with others, cannot plausibly be attributed solely to chance. It is the continuing reproduction of unequal power that allows such correspondence to continue.

The question that then arises is: do capitalists because of their privileged position have structural power?

## Power and structure

The issue of luck and systematic luck raises the question of whether power can be structural, that is, exercised through the organization of society in order to favour particular interests. Many theorists reject the notion of structural power because, as we have seen, power must involve intention. However, Marxist theories in particular see power as a structural phenomenon, particularly when talking about state power. For Nicos Poulantzas (1978), the state in capitalist society is imbued with structures that privilege the interests of the dominant class (without the state being directly controlled by that class). Poulantzas attempts to avoid determinism by suggesting that the state is not a simple instrument of the bourgeoisie but is 'the condensation of class forces'. In other words the state reflects the power struggles that exist within society – it is a set of institutions that reproduce power relations between classes. The state has a role in maintaining the dominance of the capitalist class, but this system is not closed and the dominance of the bourgeoisie is not inevitable because: 'Struggles always have primacy over, and constantly go beyond, the apparatuses or institutions' (Poulantzas, 1978: 45). As Bob Jessop (1990: 256) highlights, Poulantzas sees the state as a 'condensation of class forces', meaning that it reflects the balance of class forces within a society and, perhaps more importantly, that the structures of the state are biased to a particular interest. The state has a strategic selectivity which means it is more likely to adopt policies that favour the dominant class (not so far from Lindblom's notion of the privileged position of business, see McLennan, 1989; Manley, 1983). However, it is important to acknowledge, as Colin Hay (2002) does, that Poulantzas' later work softens the degree of structuralism by emphasizing the indeterminate nature of the state and the importance of strategy.

Theda Skocpol develops a non-Marxist structuralism when she argues that social revolutions 'should be analysed from a structural perspective, with special attention devoted to international contexts and to developments at home and abroad that affect the breakdown of state organizations of old regimes and the build up of new, revolutionary state organizations' (Skocpol, 1979: 5). Skocpol explicitly and boldly rejects the notion that revolutions are purposive and maintains that 'no successful social revolution has ever been "made" by a mass mobilizing, avowedly revolutionary movement' (Skocpol, 1979: 17). For Skocpol groups are inevitably part of revolutions but the development of revolutionary movements, and more importantly their success, depends not on groups but on 'existing socio-economic conditions and international conditions'. It could be argued that Skocpol's approach is in fact a theory of 'anti-power' rather than power, although in this and subsequent work she attributes considerable 'potential' power to the state. For Skocpol maintains that the state has the potential to act autonomously from society and has its own set of interests (Skocpol, 1979: 30 and Skocpol, 1985).

Structuralism does create a number of problems in terms of power because if events are determined by structure, where is the power? For structuralists, outcomes are not the result of decisions or actions but forces beyond the control of individuals, and whilst structural forces may be useful for explaining particular social outcomes at a general level, they do not focus on where power ultimately lies. Structuralists are effectively concerned with explaining how history unfolds from the perspective of social forces and so pay little attention to individuals. Structuralism suggests that there is no alternative and no individual choice is exercised. What we need to do if we are to understand power is develop an approach that does not simply focus on agents but at the same time does not deny that power involves choice. The next section examines what some call the poststructuralist approach to power. In the subsequent section the chapter analyzes approaches that attempt to take account of both structure and agency.

## Poststructuralism and the 'de-facing of power'

Clarissa Hayward (2000) is concerned that the traditional conceptions of power are based on a narrow definition. Power is seen as something that exists in particular actions and contexts and as a consequence there are realms where power does not exist. So if power is not being exercised on us we are in the realm of freedom. However, where there is power, there is an assumption that someone is acting upon someone else. At some point A, however far he or she is removed from B, is in some way forcing B to do something (whether directly or indirectly, intentionally or unintentionally). Hayward rejects this view and makes two points. The first is that the realm of freedom is also shaped by a whole series of social forces and practices – we cannot escape fields of power (Hayward, 2000: 37–9). The second is that a person's 'field of action is likewise delimited by actors with whom he has no interaction or communication, by actions distant in time and space, by actions of which he is, in no explicit sense the target' (Hayward, 2000: 37). A working class black boy in an inner city school finds his 'field of action' shaped by definitions, expectations and perceptions of black and working class, the structure and operation of inner city schools and the expectations and practices of teachers. For Hayward, it is not only the working class black boy who is subject to power and the teacher who exercises it, but teachers also operate within certain practices and expectations that shape, enable and constrain the way they operate as teachers and as agents. For Hayward (2000: 38) there is a need to

> focus attention on political mechanisms that comprise relevant practices. By practice I mean a complex of social boundaries to action that, together define an end or set of ends; standards such as standards of ability, character, or achievement; and a community, group, or other collectivity or individuals who pursue these ends and who accept, adhere to, and/or are measured against these standards.

Power then is the limit of human actions 'that facilitate and limit action for all actors in all social contexts'. Hayward is saying that we operate within fields of power. How our identities and roles are defined, and the institution we operate in, limit and define our action. To be a student defines us in a particular institutional relationship with a university and our parents and our teachers. It defines our rights, our scope of action and resources. Equally, the professor's scope of action is defined in different ways through similar sets of relationships. In this way the state becomes part of the field of action which is involved in delimiting the actions of citizens.

Hayward's account of power derives in large part from the work of Michel Foucault. It is necessary to pay some attention to Foucault's work because for his advocates he offers an innovative approach to the issue of power. Foucault's work has been used to develop a distinctive understanding of how the state operates in terms of power. Foucault, unlike many of the theorists discussed above, adopts a wide definition of power. Perhaps most importantly he rejects the assumption in the third face of power that there is a distinction between truth and power. Truth is constituted by power; there is no absolute and knowable truth that is separate from power relations. Truth in turn legitimizes power. In the British political system it is presented as a truth that sovereignty lies in Parliament and therefore Parliament is the core site of power; this is true because Parliament is sovereign. However, there is no absolute necessity for sovereignty to reside in Parliament – sovereignty is not a real thing and at other times and places it has been deemed to reside elsewhere: God, king, people. For Foucault, what is true is always shaped by power. Moreover, power exists in all relationships. Foucault does not see power as located in institutions but it is 'rooted in the whole network of the social' (Foucault, 2002a: 346–7). Power exists through the definition of relationship and through the definition of categories. Power is not just about government but it is also about 'a set of forces which establish positions and ways of behaving that influence people in their everyday lives' (Danaher, Schirato and Webb, 2000: 49). Foucault believed that power is about more than how we act – it is about how our identities as children, students, workers, professors, are shaped and what this implies for our behaviour.

A useful insight into the work of Foucault is provided through contrasting it with that of another famous French intellectual, Jean-Paul Sartre. For Foucault, if someone is a waiter, for example, this inculcates sets of rules and power relationships that define what a waiter is and does. For Sartre (1966), a waiter is playing a role and in playing that role, whether it is one of surly waiter or of subjugation to the customer, it is 'bad faith' because he does not realise that it is a role and that he could act differently or not be a waiter. For Sartre the possibility of liberation and fulfilment exists through recognizing the position of waiter as a role and stepping outside it and acting in what he sees as good faith. For Foucault there is no 'good faith' or truth. We are always subjects that are constructed by a whole set of power relations that we cannot control. There is nothing outside our episteme – our particular framework of knowledge. Power and the subject are indivisible. But at the same time Foucault and Sartre are saying something similar. That the roles we play are not innate but are constructed and in the construction they define how we act and what we say. When we act we reproduce power. For Foucault there is no hope of liberation, just a different role; but for Sartre there is through realising good faith.

This distinction is important because it highlights Foucault's criticism of the third dimension, and Marxist notions, of power. The third dimension assumes that there is a truth, that if actors had complete information they would act freely and know their own wants. For Foucault wants and interests can never exist independently of the way the subject is created. What Foucault (1979: 136) sees developing from the eighteenth century is increasing control over the body:

> The classical age discovered the body as object and target of power. It is easy enough to find signs of the attention then paid to the body – to the body that is then manipulated, shaped, trained, which obeys, responds, becomes skilful and increases its forces.

These are for Foucault 'projects of docility' based on more effective methods of control that were seeping outside total institutions such as prisons and monasteries into everyday life. For example, we can see from this perspective how much of the nineteenth century was about imposing a moral project on citizens in areas such as sexual morality, drinking and even cleanliness (see Chapter 12). The Victorian age is known for its attempt to impose a moral discipline on 'the body'. For Foucault, this is what he calls the 'micro-physics of power' where a whole range of forces sometimes inspired by economic necessity, epidemics or war combine to discipline the body (Foucault, 1979: 138–9).

Foucault was interested in the way the state shapes power (although as I suggest below this creates a problem in his definition of power). Foucault was concerned to analyse the mentalities of government; the ways in which governments through a wide range of agencies attempt to control and order society. According to Mitchell Dean (1999: 11):

> An analysis of government, then, is concerned with the means of calculation, both qualitative and quantitative, the type of governing authority or agency, the forms of knowledge, techniques and other means employed, the entity to be governed, and how it is conceived, the ends sought and the outcomes and consequences.

To this end Foucault is concerned with examining the different technologies of power that states used in the Middle Ages compared to those that developed after the Enlightenment. Similarly to James Scott, he suggests that for the medieval king power was based on inquiry. Foucault (2002a: 45) uses the example of how, following the Norman conquest, to 'establish order': 'William the Conqueror carried out an enormous inquiry concerning the status of properties, the status of taxes, the system of ground rent, and so on'. Foucault (2002a: 48) sees the inquiry as a particular form of 'exercising power'. He creates the state within an understanding of power but he does not really see the state as a particular organization. Rather, it is part of the overall process of power relations; as much caught up in power as any other organization or individual.

The post-Enlightenment form of governmentality (to use Foucault's term) is based on disciplinary society and this is a society of surveillance that derives for Foucault in Jeremy Bentham's panopticism. Foucault argues that in modern society panopticism has three elements, 'supervision, control and correction', which are 'a fundamental and characteristic dimension of power relations that exist in our society' (Foucault, 2002a: 70). This is a form of power

> that rests not on the inquiry but on something completely different, which I will call the 'examination' ...With panopticism, something altogether different would come into being; there would no longer be an inquiry but supervision [*surveillance*] and examination ... A constant supervision of individuals by someone who exercised power over them – schoolteacher, foreman, physician, psychiatrist, prison warden – and who, so long as he exercised power, had the possibility of both supervising and constituting a knowledge concerning those he supervised. A knowledge that now was no longer about determining whether something occurred; rather, it was about whether an individual was behaving as he should. (Foucault, 2002a: 58–9)

In the Middle Ages, the king's distance from the people meant he had no mechanism for controlling day-to-day behaviour (although it could be argued that the church embodied this role) and so wrong-doing was tackled *post hoc* and an inquiry was necessary to reconstruct the events and establish 'truth'. In a disciplinary society, the state orders and surveys its population but also creates and defines its behaviour; what is good, what is deviant; what is mad, what is normal. Thus Barry Hindess (2006: 119) sees governmentality as developing as a particular process in contemporary government:

> [A]s a specific rationality of government, a way of thinking about the problems involved in governing a state and its population and about the resources that could be employed for this purpose. They

describe it as favouring the use of the market and audit regimes, and the more general promotion of individual choice and empowerment in the government of domains which earlier forms of liberalism had subjected to more direct forms of regulation.

This conception of power has resonance with Michael Mann's (1984) infrastructural power. Under absolute monarchies the power of the state reached as far as its force; in modern states it works through the inculcation and incorporation of bureaucracy into civil society – and again this harks back to Weber's observation concerning the rationalisation of modern life. Foucault sees the modern state exercising a particular form of power which is about the control of populations, and the population is controlled through the establishment of surveillance that both observes and defines the population. Moreover, Foucault suggests that increasingly other forms of social power such as the family, kinship, technology 'have come more and more under state control ... one could say that power relations have become more governmentalised, that is to say, elaborated, rationalized, and centralised in the form of, or under the auspices of, state institutions' (Foucault, 2002a: 345). This is an important point because whilst much of the governance literature focuses on the decline of the role of the state, Foucault sees the state as increasing its control on everyday life. Hindess (2006: 116) points out that for Foucault:

> The term 'power' is more appropriately seen as a kind of shorthand, a convenient (if not always helpful) way of invoking 'the total structure of actions brought to bear' by some on the actions of others. Power in this sense is a ubiquitous feature of social life and, for the most part, a relatively unstable and unproblematic one.

When a mother tells a child to wash the action is on one level reproducing the power relationship between parent and child and on the other it is reiniforcing a social commitment to the disciplining of the body – 'cleanliness is next to godliness'. When the child goes into the bathroom and pretends to wash her hands she is resisting parental and social power in her own way – it is micro resistance and an unconscious (or perhaps unknowing) attempt to reshape power relations. For Foucault all power relations involve resistance – relationships and identities are always contested (see Digeser, 1992: 985). We all have power and we are always in relationships of power.

The problem from an analytical point of view is that if power is everything, it is nothing. Foucault defines power so widely that its analytical purchase is diminished. Indeed state power cannot be separated from the general capillaries of power that exist within society. Foucault's definition cannot extract power from any other relationship because power is in all relationships and, moreover, in all identities and roles. We are all involved in the reproduction of power and we are all subject to it. As Hayward says, the teacher is as much constrained by power as the student. Both the term teacher and student define how they act and it just so happens that the definition gives teachers power over pupils. This does not mean that the teacher is outside the field of power but in a different field to the pupil. Foucault, and Hayward, are using the term power to describe what sociologists have for a long time called socialization – the process by which we imbue the values and norms of society and which shape our conception of what is right and wrong and how we act in specific roles. The disciplining of the body is nothing other than the process of socializing the individual (see Lukes, 2005: 97). Foucault is in many ways reproducing the perspective of ethnomethodologists like Erving Goffman (1990), who see individual actors reproducing the social world through their everyday actions (see Hacking, 2004; Jenkins, 2008). For some perspectives this is about making people proper members of the community, for others it is about social control. Foucault and Goffman are both concerned with how we internalize social rules and, through the process of socialization, discipline ourselves. The reason we often don't steal when we have the opportunity or give money to charity is not because of a rational cost benefit analysis but because we have internalized a moral duty and we suffer guilt when we do wrong.

One of the remarkable things about Foucault is that he is often presented by the many commentators on his work as being a relativist in rejecting a notion of absolute truth, of being opposed to the Enlightenment idea of progress, of essentially being idealist in seeing power as exercised through discourse rather than material structures and of seeing power as being in a continual stage of flux and open to continual renegotiation and interpretation. Yet much of his work on power seems to be highly conventional and progressive in that he sees states moving through stages from inquiry-based power to disciplinary power. He states quite clearly (Foucault, 2002a: 64): 'England had freed itself of that absolute monarchy, rushing through the *stage* in which France remained caught for a hundred and fifty years (emphasis added)' and so is clearly suggesting that states have particular patterns of development. Moreover, he also appears to link the development of new forms of state power to economic development (Foucault, 2002a: 69). He rejects the Marxist notion that either knowledge or ideology can be seen solely as epiphenomena of the means of production but he sees particular forms of knowledge as being related to specific forms of production (2002a: 87):

> Those forms of knowledge and power are more deeply rooted, not just in human existence but in relations of production. That is the case because, in order for the relations of production that characterise capitalist society to exist, there must be, in addition to a certain number of economic determinations, those power relations and forms of operation of knowledge. Power and knowledge are thus deeply rooted – they are not just superimposed on relations of production but, rather, are very deeply rooted in what constitutes them.

What Foucault seems to be saying is that knowledge is not just a reflection of relations of production but is part of its constitution.

While Foucault rejects Marxism for its attempt to universalize a theory of power, its belief that there is a real truth that will be discovered through human struggle and its notion that societies go through a progressive development, the imprint of Marxism, remain in his work. Foucault's view that power exists in all aspects of society 'at the factory, in the asylum, in the clinic, in the church, in the family, at school, in the courthouse, and in the army' (Digeser, 1992: 985) has similarities with the views of both Louis Althusser (1971) and Antonio Gramsci (1971) on how state/capitalist power is not only maintained through force but through developing consent. Althusser (1971) maintained that in capitalist societies the state reproduces subjects both through Repressive State Apparatus and Ideological State Apparatus (ISIs) and the ISIs are reproduced in all arenas of society, creating subjects that submit to the power of the capitalist state (Althusser, 1971). Gramsci (1971) also saw power being exercised through the state and hegemony which were the dominant set of moral ideas in a society, thus creating consent for oppression. This link with Foucault is noted by Poulantzas when he suggests that a number of Foucault's 'analyses are not only compatible with Marxism: they can only be understood if it is taken as their starting point' (Poulantzas, 1978: 68). Indeed, Jessop (1990: 245) points out that there are considerable similarities between Foucault and Poulantzas in terms of how they think about power.

One of Foucault's key breaks with Marxism is the notion that societies inevitably go through a defined set of stages of development. For Foucault (2002a: 115) knowledge does not progress smoothly so that there is an accumulation of what we know (although as we saw above, he does talk of stages). Hay (2002: 191) suggests that Foucault rejects 'a process of progress', but offers instead the 'substitution of incommensurate and hence incomparable paradigms'. But it is difficult to read Foucault without a sense that we are witnessing a technological, economically influenced, if not determined, and functionalist change in power relations. The process of disciplining bodies adapts agents to the needs of capitalism and modernism, and the state increasingly takes over the role carried out by the church. However, this process is not undertaken by anyone but is a combination of a whole series of unintended actions and developments that are unconsciously taken by different subjects. How they seemingly combine to form a particular paradigm of discipline is never explained.

It is important to remember that Foucault was a French theorist and that to some degree his analysis of government and governmentality comes from a particular understanding of French absolutism. Daniel Engster (2001) demonstrates how Richelieu saw that the role of the sovereign was to rationally pursue the public interest – reason of state was above all. This point helps us to understand Foucault – he was trying to demonstrate that the state is not rational and that reasons of state/public interest are constructs of particular power interests. His perspective is a critique of the French absolutist state's construction of reason and his critique of sovereignty is a critique of the French notion of sovereignty located very firmly in the king/state.

Digeser (1992: 990) asks:

Is a conception of power that focuses upon the formation of subject and knowledge, that eschews the necessity of intentionality, conflict and harm and that is inescapable, anti-theoretical and productive of resistance power?

The answer is that Foucault provides a very problematic notion of power. It seems to be based on two different conceptions of power First, power in everyday life, what is seen by most as processes of socialization; and second, techniques of power through the process of governmentality, the way that the state organizes society – so it is constitutive in that it creates subjects and it is a mechanism or technique. Power is imprecise for Foucault and in many ways reflective of debates that have continued in social science for many years. However, his notion does sensitize us to the need to see power broadly. That processes of categorization – whether it is calling someone a refugee, asylum seeker, immigrant, or economic migrant – are actually mechanisms of power. What we often see as knowledge may in fact be a power construct that serves a particular interest. The other important point to take from Foucault is that power exists in all relationships; it is relative (in the sense of being seen relative to parts of social relations) and, again, it is not a new idea, but we have to see that all parties to a relationship can have some effect on outcomes.

## Conclusion

Traditional and radical theories of power see power very differently. For pluralism and RCT it is a specific event. For the radical approaches it is a social phenomenon that structures the way the world operates: its radicalism derives from its questioning of the taken-for-granted world as neutral, instead seeing it as an accumulation of past decisions and actions which reinforce the interests of particular groups. In this way, each of the approaches sees what it wants. The traditional positions can look at particular decisions and see a variety of outcomes that support a more pluralist view of power. The radical approaches have little interest in particular decisions, arguing that despite certain favourable outcomes the overall bias of the system favours privileged groups.

Radical theories do sensitize us to the power of the state in ways that the traditional theories do not. They invoke the state either in terms of setting the agenda of decision making as in the second or third faces of power, or in terms of setting the fields of action through the disciplining of the body in the poststructuralist perspective. With these approaches power is complex and, perhaps more importantly as we will see, can be about controlling particular sets of behaviour and determining the nature of particular types of knowledge. From this perspective we can see power in a wider sense; it is about how people understand the world and make decisions, and states can have power through their presentation of knowledge and choices. People make decisions rationally but what is important about power is first understanding what is meant by rationality and then what options are available. Increasingly, as we will see, states have focussed on attempting to shape choices in areas of moral behaviour. If we think of it in terms of traditional welfare policy, states used to be concerned with providing health care but increasingly states are trying to get people to make lifestyle decisions: to stop smoking, take exercise, eat fruit; and operating through very different mechanisms of power. Poststructuralist approaches also make us aware that power is continually contested and that even when people obey the state, we do not always know what resistance and subversion has been involved in enacting state commands. Teachers may attempt to achieve government targets but how do they actually enact that process and how do they subvert the government's aims in doing so? Power is never total; it is always partial and highly variable.

Nevertheless, what all approaches are poor at doing is to relate theories of power specifically to how the state attempts to affect outcomes in society. Traditional approaches see the state reacting, and radical approaches fail to detail the mechanisms through which states can control social groups or individuals. Power is separated from the state despite the recognition of the state as a resource-rich institution that has the ability to use force and to make authoritative allocation of its resources. Radical approaches fail to consider the state as a separate source of power. Indeed, what exists is a separate body of literature on the nature of state power, and in the next chapter we will examine this literature.

# Chapter 3

# The State and Power

Whilst the debate on the nature of power has been almost continuous since the 1950s, discussions about state power have been more intermittent. Conceptualizations of the state and its power can be linked back to the work of Hobbes and Hegel and pluralist thinkers in the late nineteenth century but with the rise of group theory, behaviouralism and comparative politics, discussion of the state went out of favour in mainstream political science, maintained only by some Marxist theorists. Notions of state power can be mapped on to the various perspectives of theories of power – in other words, we can define pluralist, rational choice, elitist, Marxist and poststructuralist conceptions of the state. This chapter is intended to illustrate two points. The first is that there is a lack of correspondence between theories of power and theories of the state; they tend to have developed in separate spheres of academic endeavour and consequently theories of the state often have limited discussions of the nature of state power. Second, and as a consequence, notions of state power tend to be one-dimensional, in the sense that they really focus on the question, for whom does the state exercise power, rather than how. As a result, how the state exercises power is a consequence of definitional fiat rather than analysis of the way that states operate. For example, Marxists see the state exercising power in terms of the economic dominant class and then presume that states can achieve this goal. The argument of this book is that states exercise power in many ways and that we can use theories of power together with understandings of the state to analyse the complex. The point recognized in public policy and development is that states often fail. This chapter is intended to provide a review of the extant theories of the state in order to better develop a framework for understanding state power.

## The liberal perspective: pluralism and rational choice

Approaches that can be broadly based within the liberal tradition have a considerable ambiguity towards the state. The liberal perspective opposes unjustified limitation on freedom of choice and so state power has to be limited and justified. However, from the Hobbesian perspective the state is necessary to maintain order and hence allow people to go about their business. The majority of liberals and early pluralists saw the state as something to be constrained. In terms of state power, the paradox of the liberal view is that the state is necessary but its power has to be restricted. Consequently, liberals focus on the nature of the social contract that sets out the responsibilities of state and citizen. If a contract exists it justifies and legitimizes state power. This view derives from the Hobbesian idea that in order for there to be a stable social order, citizens have to transfer their power to the sovereign who exercises power on their behalf (Held, 1989, 1996). Locke was opposed to the notion that an absolute sovereign would exercise power for the good of all and therefore argued for the need for constitutional limits on what the state could do and proposed a contract between the state and citizen. For Locke, sovereignty remains with the people (Held, 1989, 1996) and the power of the state is limited. Liberalism attempts to reconcile the need for the state to maintain order and the threat that state power represents for individual liberty. The crucial concept is legitimacy. Legitimacy involves

> *constituting and controlling the exercise of power* within the social order, in a manner that simultaneously empowers institutions to perform valued collective functions, and prevents powerful institutions from degenerating into tyranny. (Macdonald, 2008: 548, emphasis in original)

The problem that arises is that for much of modern liberalism Locke's normative prescriptions are taken as given. Legitimacy, once established, becomes an uncontested concept when, as we will see in Chapter 6, legitimacy may be a form of power through the role it plays in justifying state actions. Within the liberal project democracy and legitimacy are taken in good faith rather than contested as part of the process of governing. State power is only malign when it is illegitimate and exercised outside the social contract. Two modern approaches to state power within the liberal tradition are pluralism and rational choice theory.

Pluralism shares the liberal suspicion of unconstrained state power and some early pluralists focussed much more on groups and associations as mechanisms for organizing collective goods (Hirst, 1994).

However, despite the anti-state traditions of pluralism, postwar American pluralists tended to see the state as a benign institution. As Robert Alford and Roger Friedland (1985: 43) suggest, 'In the pluralist perspective, the state's main function is either to serve as a neutral mechanism to aggregate preferences or to integrate society by embodying consensual values'. The key elements of pluralist state theory are well summarized by Robert Dahl (1963: 325):

> Important government policies would be derived at through negotiation, bargaining, persuasion and pressure at a considerable number of different sites in the political system – the White House, the bureaucracies, the labyrinth of committees in Congress, the federal and state courts, the state legislatures and the executives, the local governments. No single organized political interest, party, class, region or ethnic groups would control all of these sites.

For pluralists the state in liberal democracy is fragmented and for Dahl the process of policy making is one of negotiation and compromise (1963: 327). The state is a repository of resources which political groupings can access through the processes of policy making. In this sense the state is almost a vacuum or arena within which groups play out political battles and the state adjudicates between them (Dunleavy and O'Leary, 1985). The state as such is not an input into the policy process but the space in which policy is made. So although early pluralism grew out of a distrust of the state, American pluralism after the Second World War developed a benign conception of the state. Government within a democracy did not exercise power independently but responded to the demands of groups in society. The power of the state is defined constitutionally. The state is limited in what it can do by what J.K. Galbraith called 'countervailing power': the groups, media, parties and citizens that limited what the state could do. The irony of pluralism is that despite the fact that it grew out of a strong distrust of the state and in opposition to Hegelian monotheism, modern pluralism fails to problematize the state. Part of the problem is ontological and methodological (see Holland, 2009). For pluralists political science is about understanding observable political behaviour. Consequently, like rational choice theory, it takes politics and government at face value and pays little attention to the ways in which structural inequalities can distort the principle of political equality (see Marsh, Richards and Smith, 2003).

## Rational choice theory and state power

Rational choice theory exists within the liberal paradigm and hence is highly suspicious of state power (see for example Hayek, 1944). At the same time it sees the state as necessary for resolving collective action problems. The breakdown of cooperation highlighted in the chicken and prisoner's dilemma games can be overcome by state action. As Terry Moe (2005: 223) illustrates, rational choice approaches to the state are faced with the dilemma that the state is necessary to enforce cooperative agreements, but a state that is powerful can be predatory. Rational choice approaches to state power see the state as coercive and see that coercion as necessary for imposing property rights, enforcing contracts and allowing free economic activity (North, Wallis and Weingast, 2005: 2).

The assumption of rational choice theorists is almost universally that a world without the state would be a Hobbesian state of nature. Therefore, the state is necessarily a coercive institution. For Yoram Barzel (2002: 33):

> Power (i.e., the ability to impose costs) can be exercised by the use of violence or by other means. The state is defined by its use of violence to enforce agreements and to resolve disputes. Agreements, however, can also be self-enforced or can be enforced by other third party enforcers. The scope of the state is defined as the fraction of transactions it enforces relative to all transactions within its territory.

Power in the rational choice perspective is focussed either on the rules of the game as we saw in the last chapter, or violence as exercised by the state. Rational choice, being based on an economic theory, tends to see societies as organized on the basis of voluntary exchange; power exists in so far as it is needed to enforce the contracts of the exchange process (see Moe, 2005). Most rational choice analysis of the state is based on modeling state development and state operations rather than analysing the way power affects the state or is exercised by the state. For RCT states develop because of self interest. What North *et al.* (2005) call natural states (which are effectively the types of authoritarian states that exist before free market capitalism and democracy) form through the development of property rights and through the process of ensuring trade. As a consequence, states are able to ensure rents to the dominant coalition: 'the natural state therefore establishes and enforces a property rights system, whereby specific groups with specific ties to the rulers have specific rights and privileges' and the state plays the role of ensuring that these rights are not shared by others (North *et al.*, 2005: 4). For North *et al.* the natural state is limited because the size of the ruling elite is restricted by the need not to dissipate rents. The ruling elite does not have the incentive to provide rights for those outside the elites and they prevent economic development because markets undermine the rents of the elite (through undermining their monopolies) and so the natural state limits access to economic production and trade. North *et al.* maintain that only a limited number of states have developed into 'open access orders' where free political and economic association is predominant.

Rational choice theory models understand state development and organization on the basis of utility maximization assumptions. They see the state as an organization that can use force to ensure contracts. Barzel (2002: 24) believes that it is possible to work out the specific numerical scope of the state because, 'The greater the extent of contract exchange in a state, the higher the ratio, and the greater the scope of the state'. Rational choice theory consequently develops a theory of the state and state power almost without any reference to history, politics or power. States develop teleologically on the basis of self-interests. For Mancur Olson (2000) the state essentially arises out of criminality when the interest of the coercive force within a territory develops so that those with physical power have the ability to prevent crime in their area, because that allows more economic activity from which they can take a proportion. So for Olson (2000: 11) a stationary bandit who extracts money through taxation is preferred by people to a roving bandit because the stationary bandit provides order. States fail to develop when the 'natural state' prevents the development of markets and prevents market prices from coordinating human action (North *et al.*, 2005: 19). (Interestingly, Anthony Giddens (1984: 58) makes a similar point.) The solutions to the problems of governing are economic. For North *et al.* (2005: 22) this explains perfectly why states fail to take advice from 'mainstream economists and donor agencies ... Our theory of the natural state shows that it is a means of promoting order. Controlling markets are a means of maintaining the state.'

For rational choice theorists state power is based on building trust and incentives. Olson (2000) suggests that states have an interest in developing good institutions and good economies because then private self-interest has an interest in limiting crime and corruption. As he points out (Olson, 2000: 105), in a loan contract the lender has an interest in getting repaid and the borrower has an interest in avoiding repayment:

> The lender will try to induce the borrower to pay the loan back by threatening his reputation and access to future credit and, if necessary, by petitioning the courts to seize the borrower's assets. Because lenders, in deciding to whom to lend, favor borrowers with the lowest risks, a higher proportion of loans are paid back than if lenders did not exercise this judgment. That, of course, makes a repayment of loans more common and generates habitual obedience to the private law that grows out of the mutually agreed contract.

For Olson the trust and incentive structures built into the credit system ensure an effective and efficient system with little need for state power. The problem here of course is that often people do not repay loans, banks will lend to high risk borrowers, and enforcement is ensured through the law, state and courts, not private law.

When it comes to specific understandings of the developed state, rational choice theory uses the utility maximization assumption to develop models of state actor behaviour. The focus here is on two political actors – politicians and bureaucrats – who operate within different institutional frameworks, and so self-interest produces different outcomes. Politicians need to be re-elected and so for Anthony Downs (1957) the process of election is a political market. In order to get elected politicians need to attract the greatest number of votes and so they will develop their programmes in a way that accords with the majority of voters. Whilst politicians focus on staying in power, for rational choice theorists, bureaucrats are concerned with maximizing their power and use their control over information to persuade politicians of the need for ever-expanding budgets and programmes (thus explaining the seemingly inexorable growth of developed states) (Downs, 1967; Niskanen, 1973). Of course, this creates a difficult problem within governments because politicians and bureaucrats are not working to the same logic. Unlike pluralists, rational choice theorists do not see either politicians or bureaucrats as working in the public interest (which undermines the assumptions of many existing models of civil service behaviour: see Richards and Smith, 2002; Le Grand, 2003). The constitutional view is that officials service ministers and guard the national or public interest. If they are self-interested, the question arises of how politicians control bureaucrats (Moe, 2005; Horn, 1995). The issue of control is explored within the notion of the principal–agency model where the principal contracts the agents to carry out policy (see Chapter 8) and this approach focuses on asymmetries of information. The information deficit is the fundamental problem of bureaucracy – politicians cannot control bureaucrats and so states cannot achieve their goals.

Rational choice, which like liberal and pluralist theory is concerned with the nature of state power, does not analyse the state or government in terms of power. Whilst it is assumed that the state is coercive, the state is then treated as unproblematic. For many rational choice theorists a state that is coercive in terms of property rights is preferable to Hobbesian anarchy (North *et al.*, 2005; Olson, 2000; Barzel, 2002). Democratic institutions are treated unproblematically and often, as Moe (2005) points out, without any real appreciation of the nature of power. The basis of state power is an acceptance of democratic institutions at face value and a sense that these institutions exist on the basis of cooperation. As Moe (2005: 225) puts it:

> Power has mainly to do with distribution problems, coordination problems, and choices among multiple equilibria, not with nations being forced to do things that are against their interests.

As we saw in Chapter 1, rational choice theory assumes that people are making choices and hence pays little attention to how choices or actions may be shaped by power relations. Relationships are seen as voluntary rather than power relationships. Moreover, rational choice theory accounts are based on stylized models of state growth which see states developing as liberal democratic states because it is in the interests of everyone for them to do so. Consequently, RCT pays little attention to either historical realities or power, nor indeed to the tenuous grip of democracy within many polities.

What is common to the liberal approaches is that power is understood in terms of individual actions (as we saw in Chapter 1) and so very little attention is paid to state power. In effect, power is unproblematic if there is legitimacy; pluralists analyse individual decisions by seeing power as being exercised in a moment by conscious actors and by segmenting power into particular decisions; and for rational choice theorists power is eliminated from the model of decision making. Liberal and pluralist theorists suffer from the paradox that their theories develop from the presumption that state power needs to be limited. Rational choice theorists see states distorting markets and so producing sub-optimal outcomes. Yet none of the liberal theorists seriously tackle the nature of state power. They fail to problematize the state or really focus on how the state operates. They focus instead on a series of individual relationships (the games). The state is seen as coercive, but a fictional contract legitimizes its activities.

## Elitism and neo-Weberian approaches to state power

Elitist theorists do not generally distinguish between the state and power in the way that liberal theorists do. For liberals, power relationships occur within the framework of government or between groups and government; the state is not a structure of power. For elitists, the state is a site of power and within the framework of modernity the state has the ability to control what occurs within its territory. Beginning with Max Weber (1978: 987), bureaucracy provides the state with a unique mechanism of control:

> Bureaucracy is *the* means of transforming social action into rationally organized action. Therefore, as an instrument of rationality organizing authority relations, bureaucracy was and is a power instrument of the first order. (Emphasis in original)

Perhaps most significantly Weber maintains that once administration 'has been completely bureaucratized, the resulting system of domination is practically indestructible'. So whereas liberals elide the question of state power, either through invoking legitimacy or seeing power as a phenomenon external to the state, elitists see state power as the key determining feature of modern societies. Consequently the focus of much elitist work is on the nature of state power, its transformative capabilities and how it is exercised. Nevertheless, Weber was clearly aware of the problem, highlighted by rational choice theory, of the relationship of the bureaucrat to the politician and the difficulty that dilettante politicians could have in controlling professional bureaucrats (Weber, 1978: 993). He also recognized the different types of resources available to actors within the state, and hence the importance of authority to understanding political relations. The power of politicians to an extent depends on the ability to impose authority on bureaucrats. As Alford and Friedland (1985: 169) highlight, 'power derives from the organization of authority in which decisions are made'. States often organize authority in different ways by creating a range of sites of authoritative actions for politicians and bureaucrats, and Weber sensitizes us to the need not to see the state as a monolithic actor but as an organization riven with conflicting interests and with different sources of power.

The fundamental feature of elitist theories, that distinguishes them from Marxism, is the sense that the state has power in its own right and is not solely representing classes or groups in society. According to Theda Skocpol (1979: 22) states are 'organizations geared to maintain control of home territories'; that is, interdependent with but not reducible to world capitalism. Elitism, like liberalism, harks backs to Hobbesian notions of power being located within the state and separated from the rest of civil society. This leads many elitists to focus on the issue of state autonomy. Eric Nordlinger (1981: 1) maintains that the state will often act according to its own preferences 'even when its preferences diverge from the demands of the most powerful groups in civil society'. In a clearly Weberian vein, Skocpol (1979: 29) sees the state as a 'set of administrative, policing and military organizations headed, and more or less coordinated by, an executive authority'. For Skocpol the state may be in competition with dominant classes for resources and so it may not necessarily support class interests, creating the potential for autonomous actions.

Weberian approaches see the state as a distinct institutional ensemble with particular sets of resources which allow it to exercise power within a defined territory and, in some cases, in the international arena: for Skocpol (1979) the state is Janus-faced, looking outwards to other states and inward to its own territory. Having control of financial, military and bureaucratic resources, states are able to exercise power in ways that are unavailable to other groups in society. Hence, this approach is very much an analysis of the modern state (see Chapter 5) and the ways in which it attempts to achieve particular social goals within a given territory. Elitist theories therefore locate power within the state in terms of the resources that are available to transform societies.

At one level these resources are illustrated through the bureaucratic capabilities of the state. Elitist approaches draw directly on Weber's notion of bureaucratic power within a nation state form, with states being national power containers with distinct resources attached to the modern state (Giddens, 1985). For Michael Mann (2006: 352), political power is the 'centralized regulation of social life. Only the state has this centralized territorial spatial form'. So for elitists, the state is very much a distinctive apparatus whose power is based on its centrality within a set of territorial borders. From this perspective, the power of the modern state is based on what Giddens calls administrative power and Mann calls infrastructural power; the ability of states to intervene intensively in society through their administrative capacity. The traditional state was unable to have concern for the everyday activities of its citizens because it did not have the means of regulating everyday life (this to some extent was left to the church: see Giddens, 1985). In the modern era the techniques associated with bureaucracy, the compression of space and time as a consequence of technology, and the development of concepts of citizenship and sovereignty, have enabled modern states to control citizens much more directly. For example, one of the most important elements of the modern state is the ability to collect taxes and, as Hood (2003) points out, the ability of the state to collect taxes is closely linked to its capacities. Without taxation functions the state cannot sustain itself or develop programmes. In addition, Christopher Hood and Helen Margetts (2007) identify what they call the tools of government; the 'effectors' which give states capabilities. These are:

- Nodality – the strategic position to collect and dispense information
- Authority
- Treasure – the ability to raise and spend money
- Organization

It is important to point out that whilst much of the focus of elitist approaches is on administrative resources in relation to the state, Mann and Giddens in particular emphasize other aspects of power – economic, ideological and military – although they discuss these in different terms, which they see diffused throughout society. Mann is conscious of distinct social networks using different types of power. Consequently, and unlike Marxist approaches, elitists do not see states as solely acting in the interest of economic power but instead place the state at the intercies of a set of social powers that may at times support or challenge the state. What is interesting is the way in which the state can use powers that are economic, military and ideological as well as political, but particularly in non-authoritarian states, how it is often faced with alternative elites controlling these other forms of power.

Many elite theorists see military power as the basis of political power, as opposed to the liberal focus on legitimacy as the basis of state power (Poggi, 2000: 38). The state has a monopoly of legitimate violence, although Mann makes the point that military power can be partially independent from the state, or completely independent of it as in the case of paramilitary/terrorist organizations (Mann, 2006: 354–5). In many states in the developing world the military can operate as a separate source of power, either limiting very directly the actions of the state or, at times, taking it over completely.

Work that is broadly within the category of elitism is the most adept at relating notions of the state and power. First, it takes the state seriously as a site of power. Elite theories are on the whole concerned with the role of the state in organizing and controlling modern societies. Second, Weberian and elitist approaches see the state as a distinctive set of organizations and they focus on the resources available to the state in achieving goals. Third, elitism sees the state or state actors as having distinct interests that may not reflect the interests of other powerful groups in society.

The problem with this perspective, however, is that the state is too often portrayed as a separate and distinct actor with internal unity, identifiable goals and strategic intention. Joel Migdal (2001: 250) points out that:

> Theorists, such as those of Weber and political scientists following in his footsteps, created different sorts of problems. Their understanding of the state as a stand-alone organization with firm boundaries between it and other social forces leads to inquiries that zero in on its make up, into how it is constructed. The effect is to essentialise the state and overstate its capabilities.

Writers have long exaggerated the state's strength, assuming that the interests and desires of classes or elites are translated into policy outcomes, and consequently they have overstated its more recent decline in apparent capabilities. It may be that the state has only declined against our expectations of what it should do. For Migdal elites swallow the myth of the state rather than analysing what the state really does. The elitist approaches, especially those focussed on state autonomy, make an unrealistic distinction between state and civil society. Yet Giddens is explicit about the ways in which subordinates are able to subvert the power of the dominant in situations where forms of rule rely on social actors in particular situations to implement decisions (1985: 11). Infrastructural power is dependent on integration between the state and civil society (Smith, 1993) and as a consequence states do not exist above society with a set of unified interests. State actors (a term not easily defined) are involved in complex relationships with citizens so that the boundary between state and citizen is not clear. If a person is a parent, a teacher, a school governor, are they part of the state? The cooperation of parent/teacher/school governor is certainly necessary to achieve the goals of education policy. Goals such as improved examination results may be vital for politicians getting re-elected and for civil servants getting promoted, but they cannot be delivered by them; they can only be achieved if the parent, teacher, governor cooperate and of course the difficulty that Migdal points to is that they may cooperate in some circumstances and not in others.

States are fragmented horizontally and vertically. Different parts of the state such as education and health can have contradictory goals, and senior civil servants have different goals to their juniors and street level bureaucrats. Migdal (2001: 116) reminds us that policies are 'a series of different actions based on particular calculus of pressures that each engaged component of the state faces in its particular environment of action'. This is not a shift from elitism to pluralism because a fragmented state is not a pluralistic state in the sense of the American pluralists; it does not mean that the system is open and democratic (Marsh *et al.*, 2001). The state–society nexus is much more complex than elite theory allows and the processes of state reforms over the last twenty years have made the relationship more intricate. Increasingly, state policies are delivered not by traditional state bureaucracies but through a myriad of actors. In delivering policy state actors are often integrated into complex networks of organizations (e.g. multi-level governance). Groups and actors within civil society are able to frame state decisions and policy because states need social groups – non-state actors – to deliver goals, and states dependent on coercion cannot achieve complex policies. This is a point picked up by more radical, post-modern notions of the state which are discussed below (Miller and Rose, 2008: 26).

A second problem with elite approaches, especially the work of some of the leading figures such as Skocpol, Mann, and Giddens, is that they focus their explanations around grand historical narratives which simplify the development and nature of the state by avoiding the analysis of detailed and particular events (Migdal, 2001; Stones, 1996). For Rob Stones (1996: 198) the work of Mann uses narrative to construct sets of causal explanations which are arbitrary. This is an important point, and it is a criticism that can be leveled at much of the political and sociological analysis and international political economy that focus on issues such as the changing role of the state, globalization and neo-liberalism. Often the analysis is at such a level of generalization that sweeping statements can be made about the impact of neo-liberalism or globalization which appear plausible, but when investigation turns to particular cases and contexts, the assumptions unravel fairly rapidly. For instance, claims about how neo-liberalism has reduced the role of the state have little empirical support when analysis of reform processes in particular countries is undertaken. This point resonates with the first criticism that states are complex organizations and relationships and generalizations about the nature of state interests and state powers are difficult to sustain.

Concepts of state power within the Weberian tradition undoubtedly take the state and its resources seriously. The state is seen as a unique organization with the ability to impose its authority on a society. It is not a coincidence that many writers within this tradition have been critical of the strong globalization theories which see the nation state disappearing. Moreover, the most useful element of Weberian approaches is the focus on state resources as a mechanism for achieving particular goals. However, these approaches are not able to deal with the paradox of the modern state; the state has tremendous reach and resources but often fails to achieve relatively simple goals. Migdal's focus on the more particular complexities of state–society relations is more able to deal with the vagaries of state performance.

## Radical approaches to state power

Radical approaches include two very different views of the nature of the state, Marxist and poststructuralist, and, in particular, the work of Foucault. Marxist approaches in relation to the state have received considerable attention (see Dunleavy and O'Leary, 1985; Alford and Friedland, 1985, Jessop, 1982, 2008) and therefore the discussion within this chapter will be fairly brief. In terms of poststructuralism, the discussion of the state tends to be implicit rather than explicit and poststructuralists generally oppose the idea of seeing power located within the state (Dryberg, 1997: 185–6).

Marxist theories of the state have moved a considerable way since Marx's aphorism that the state is nothing but the management committee of the bourgeoisie. Marxist theorists have paid considerable attention to the nature of the state but less to the way in which states exercise power. To summarize Marxist state theory is necessarily to distort it. Nevertheless, the essence of Marxist understandings of the state is formed of two key pillars: one is as a coercive institution that affects (in different ways according to different theorists) the interests of the capitalist class; the second is a set of ideological mechanisms which ensure that particular capitalist interests are presented as general or national interests and hence ensure the acquiescence of subordinate classes. For Jessop (2008: 9):

> The core of the state apparatus can be defined as a distinct ensemble of institutions and organizations whose socially accepted function is to define and enforce collectively binding decisions on a given population in the name of their 'common interest' or 'general will'.

What is interesting about this definition is that at one level it is general enough to be broadly acceptable to most traditions for understanding the state but at another level, despite the attempts to move away from the classical Marxist tradition of the state as an essentially economic organization and politicizing the understanding of the state, the definition contains an implicit view that the state is sufficiently reflective to define a collective interest. Bob Jessop, following the work of Nicos Poulantzas, aims to politicize the state, seeing it as reflecting political battles and conflicts rather than determining, and pursuing in some vague manner, the interests of the dominant economic class. Poulantzas speaks obtusely of the state as the condensation of class forces and so like a pluralist sees the state reflecting the balance of forces in society but without explaining the mechanism by which this process occurs. Also, of course, he does not really see the state as directly exercising power. From this Marxist structuralist perspective the state's power is about ensuring capitalist accumulation and state policies can be seen as fulfilling this goal (such as an education system that produces factory workers). Where this does not occur, state policies are responding to class pressure that has forced concessions (Jessop, 1990: 29–38). Consequently, the postwar social democratic state can be seen as a mechanism for ensuring the sustenance of capital both through economic and social intervention, but also one that has had to respond to the political demands of a powerful labour movement.

The irony of Marxist analyses of state power is that whilst the basis of Marxism is a strong critique of liberalism – and indeed it is an attempt to undermine the liberal ideology of the state – it does in fact treat aspects of the liberal state unproblematically. For instance, the Marxist critique of law is that the law is not neutral but is there to serve particular interests; law is often biased against the interest of workers, for example in the way that industrial relations legislation makes it difficult for unions to strike. According to Jessop (1990: 57): 'Hirsch agrees that the bourgeois state codifies the norms of commodity exchange and monetary relations, and ensures their clarity, stability and calculability'. Moreover, it uses executive power and force outside the rule of law to maintain the capitalist order. What is interesting is that it is presumed that law and force act as simple and effective instruments for achieving state goals. Law is seen as serving particular interests but, more importantly, it is seen to work; the state has power because it can make law (and it controls the apparatus of force – something disputed in the Weberian accounts) and therefore state power is not a problematic concept. The state is a source of power and it controls society; unlike the poststructuralist position discussed below, the nature and effectiveness of law is not something that needs to be discussed and consequently Marxist theories do not really grapple with how states try to achieve their goals. As Jessop (1990: 238–9) points out, Poulantzas focuses on class power and not state power and this is a fundamental aspect of all Marxist state theory; it is not really concerned with the state as a source or mechanism of power but either the power of classes in relation to each other or how classes use the state. This then leads to the criticisms raised by Skocpol and Migdal that Marxists have a simplistic understanding of the state by seeing it as reacting to social forces and creating a false unity.

These criticisms of the Marxist theories of the state are ones that Jessop consciously tries to avoid in his strategic relational approach. Jessop makes a number of interesting and important points. First, he does not see the state as exercising power – because the state cannot act – but as the site of strategies:

> The state is an ensemble of power centres that offer unequal chances to different forces within and outside the state to act for different political purposes ... In short, the state does not exercise power; its powers are activated through the agency of definite political forces in specific conjunctures. (Jessop, 2008: 37)

For Jessop, the state does not act; rather, it is always politicians and officials in particular situations. Of course, this must be true (and indeed is very close to the Weberian tradition) but the crucial question is: what are the tools, techniques and technologies that state actors use? Jessop acknowledges the existence of specific capacities and that the exercise of these capacities may face conditions that affect their success or failure, but he does not pay attention to the capacities. However, when discussing the gender selectivities of the state, Jessop (2008: 171) does identify force, law, money and knowledge as the mechanisms of state intervention, and in doing so provides a list very similar to that of Hood and Margetts (2007) outlined above. Jessop defines these mechanisms as the media of intervention and points out that they can be combined to 'support specific interventions' (2008: 172). Whilst he clearly says more about the nature of state capacities, he identifies a fairly traditional liberal/elitist conception of state power.

Poststructuralist accounts resist linking the state to power whilst at the same time extending the remit of the state to nearly every aspect of life. Torben Dryberg criticizes Marxist and liberal approaches for confining political activity within the state. (Although with many Marxists and liberals, particularly pluralists, this is not the case, with both explicitly examining political activity outside of the state and both pluralists and Marxists having a normative desire for a very limited state – both seeing it as antithetical to true democracy.) In Dryberg's view, politics is reduced to a 'subsystem within society with a more- or less- specific location'. (Dryberg, 1997: 188). Moreover, both Marxists and liberals essentialize both the state and its *modus operandi*. For Marxists and liberals a dominant state is an essential aspect of a capitalist political order – without the state guaranteeing property rights and markets there could be no capitalism and no development. Moreover, the reason for the state's dominance are self-evident. For Marxists it is to ensure the continuation of capitalism and for liberals it is to maintain order. In effect they both see the state as the key institution within society existing in order to maintain the principles that underpin the market economy. Their differences are normative; for Marxists this is undesirable but for liberals it is the route to freedom and prosperity.

However, poststructuralists dispute both the nature of the state and, as we saw in the last chapter, the nature of power, seeing it as being dispersed and existing in all types of relationships – not solely possessed by a container such as the state. From the poststructuralist perspective there is an attempt to 'ignore the distinction of the domains, of personal, economic and social life' (Miller and Rose, 2008: 19). Building on Foucault's notion of governmentality, political power is not reduced to the state but is an 'ensemble formed by the institutions, procedures, analyses and reflections, the calculations and tactics that allow the exercise of this very specific albeit complex form of power' (Foucault, 1979, quoted in Miller and Rose, 2008: 27). Despite the poststructuralist emphasis on the indeterminacy of power, its existence outside the institutional forms of the state and its presence in all relationships (see for example Flyvbjerg, 1998), poststructuralism actually contains a more all-encompassing view of the state than it might care to acknowledge. In many ways the poststructuralist notion of state power is little different from that of Althusser's in the sense that it sees state control operating through all aspects of the social structure. This actually seems to create a very deterministic and all-controlling state. For example, Peter Miller and Nikolas Rose (2008: 48) maintain that:

> The forms of political rationality that took shape in the first half of the twentieth century constituted the citizen as a social being whose powers and obligations were articulated in the language of social responsibility and collective solidarities. The individual was to be integrated into society in the form of a citizen with social needs, in a contract in which individual and society had mutual claims and obligations.

From this perspective the various aspects of the welfare state are seen as a mechanism for creating the social citizen which fits into this contract. Consequently, the poststructuralist view has shifted from a notion of power as open and contested to a situation where states seem to have a considerable ability to mould citizens into particular patterns of behaviour. Without a notion of an intentional agent who can direct the state or society, the poststructuralists see the micro-struggles of power as leading to a fairly consistent set of policies that have a totalizing effect on the individual. In a sense, the poststructuralist position focuses on the question of how government delivers its goals. As Miller and Rose (2008: 51–2) suggest, 'Individuals themselves, as workers, managers, members of families can be mobilized in alliance with political objectives, in order to deliver economic growth, successful enterprise and optimum personal happiness', and they point to how government can use a wide range of technologies to 'educate citizens in governing themselves'. Politicians and officials may say, 'if only we were so lucky'. The reality of states is much more about governments developing programmes – that are often incoherent and contradictory – and continually searching for mechanisms to ensure that these programmes are delivered.

The irony of the poststructuralist position is that it opposes locating power within the state, but it extends the state into most activities of society. At the same time, behind the complex language the analysis has similarities with pluralist positions of policy making. For Miller and Rose (2008: 63), in implementing policies the state relies on a complex range of organizations and professions and has to develop relationships with groups and individuals in order to make difficult and incremental changes; this highlights the degree to which poststructuralism shares assumptions with pluralism about the openness and indeterminacy of the state. At the same time, the emphasis on the modern state's attempts at organizing, auditing and recording chimes with the elitist notions of the state infrastructure. The poststructuralist desire to avoid essentializing the state leads to a considerable ambiguity about the nature of state power. It is powerful and powerless at the same time. It is able to engage a whole set of organizations in its ends but it is also a 'congenitally failing operation' (Miller and Rose, 2008), a notion that would have sympathy with conservative writers such as Friedrich Hayek and Michael Oakeshott. Like pluralists they are not clear whether the state is a threat or a benign institution.

## Conclusion

The reason for reviewing the various theories of state power is to demonstrate two points. First, whilst these theories focus on aspects of state power, there is little theoretical engagement with concepts of power and, as a consequence, they do not really engage with the ways in which states exercise power but focus instead on who is successful: is it a group, an elite or a class? How these interests use the state to achieve goals is not examined and, as we have seen, there is an assumption that the state is a unified instrument able to deliver goals. There is a need to qualify this statement. Whilst pluralist, rational choice and Marxist theories pay little or no attention to the techniques of power, elitists and poststructuralists focus on the mechanisms and capabilities available to states. This failure to engage with the mechanisms of power is intriguing. It is curious that for Marxists, if the state exercises power in the long term interest of capital, there is an assumption that the state can deliver on this goal. Marxist theories, particularly within the framework of Poulantzas, would suggest that there is no simple translation from the interests of capital to policies, but rather that there are often prolonged conflicts which limit the state's ability to deliver. Yet their focus is on the processes of conflict and not on delivery. As Colin Hay (2006b) points out, the classical Marxist tradition locates power in the coercive apparatus of the state; but Gramsci's notion of hegemony is interested in the translation of a certain set of moral, political and cultural values into the norm, thus enabling the state to ensure a consensual subordination. Hence, like the neo-structuralists, this position is concerned with how a wide array of institutions becomes engaged in state projects. Nevertheless, both Lenin and Gramsci in their differing conceptions of power focussed at a very abstract level and they paid little attention to the particular mechanisms of state power. Pluralists at one level are not really concerned with state power, seeing the state more as a reflection of social pressures. However, much work on public administration and public policy within the pluralist tradition is concerned with how states deliver policy (see Pressman and Wildavsky, 1984 ; Lipsky, 1980) but does not address these problems as issues of power. Rational choice theory, as we saw, does not directly address the question of power in terms of states, beyond seeing the state as a coercive institution. The state is set up as a solution to problems of collective action but this process of resolution creates a rent-seeking state. However, rational choice theorists are curiously quiet on the actual nature of state power beyond its philosophically defined coercion.

Elitism and poststructuralist accounts of the state are concerned with techniques of power and the ways in which states attempt to achieve their goals. From Weber onwards, elitist approaches focus on the development of state capabilities and the ways in which modern states have developed mechanisms for controlling society. Poststructuralists implicitly criticize this approach, whilst also explicitly criticizing Marxist approaches, by suggesting that a focus on the state limits the sort of mechanism available in terms of processes of governmentality. For elitists this discussion is rarely located within conceptual discussions of power, but for poststructuralists the conception of power cannot be separated from their understanding of the state, although this does, as we saw above, produce a somewhat contradictory conception of the state. Poststructuralists effectively define the state out of existence (see Jessop, 1990: 292–4) and so, like pluralists, fail to deal with the way it affects society.

The central point is that theories of power and theories of the state rarely meet. Notions of the state and notions of power are not integrated and, perhaps more importantly, the philosophical underpinnings of the approaches mean that they tend to see state power as unidimensional. This leads to an assumption for some theories that the state is a relatively unified and distinct set of institutions and that the state exercises power in relatively consistent ways. However, one of the aims of this book is to demonstrate that state actors do not have philosophical consistency and that they have a range of mechanisms for attempting to affect society. States can use coercion, incentives and ideologies and respond to groups or class pressure. There is no single mechanism of state power. Theories of the state pay little attention to the variability of state power or to the actual impact of the state's capabilities. So whilst theories of power pay little attention to the state, theories of the state pay little attention to power.

## Chapter 4

# A Framework for Analysing Power and the State

In the preceding chapters the book has highlighted the ways in which theories of power do not engage with each other and how theories of the state have failed adequately to deal with the nature of state power. The absence of dialogue means that there is little attempt to analyse the nature of state power and it is this failure which has often led to debates about the nature of the state being simplified. So, for instance, the contemporary debates on governance and globalization can quickly dismiss the state and then reassert its importance by extrapolating from particular events, rather than analysing the ways in which states exercise power. It should be recognized that states are imperfect institutions varying across space and time in their ability to affect outcomes. To talk of the decline of the state makes little sense when states as institutions are robust and central institutions in all modern societies. What does constantly wax and wane is the impact they have on the societies they govern. As such, this chapter develops a framework for analysing the variability and changing nature of state power. In order to understand the state we need to see that it is an organization dependent on the decisions of reflexive actors. Its capacity to affect outcomes, therefore, depends on its ability to obtain the compliance of individuals. Consquently, power is not a single concept or thing but a way of understanding social relations.

## Power, capacity and agents

We have seen in Chapters 2 and 3 that there are many ways of understanding power. These conceptions of power cannot be separated from understandings of the social world. Different approaches to power conceive of human behaviour and action in a range of ways. A number of approaches to power begin by focussing on the agent but when it comes to analysing power they remove agents from the equation. Some see agents as essentially passive – as in rational choice theory – and others are concerned about individual behaviour but not individual perceptions – as in behaviouralism. For behaviouralist approaches and rational choice theory power is intentional – it occurs when someone chooses to exercise power – and they focus on the behaviour of individuals in determining how power operates and who has power. Nevertheless, they pay no attention to the perceptions of individuals – in understanding power it is actions not beliefs that are important. Postmodernist, constructivist and ethnomethodological theories focus directly on the perceptions of individuals – how they interpret the world and how they create the world is central to the understanding of power. Nevertheless, in the case of Foucault, whilst we cannot say that one interpretation of the truth is more accurate than any other, it turns out that individuals have little possibility, if any, of breaking out of their particular episteme and therefore the agents have no control over their situation. Structuralism in its purest form from Marxists such as Althusser, and some of the work of Poulantzas, eliminates the human subject from reality and thus sees individuals as nothing more than bearers of structures (which in some ways brings them round to the same position as Foucault).

However, if we are to understand power, and indeed the nature of state power, we need to follow Anthony Giddens (1984) and Pierre Bourdieu (1989) and avoid the traps of 'objectivism and subjectivism'. We need to sustain a role for agents, their perceptions, their choices and their reflexivity. As Rob Stones (2005: 14) clarifies:

> The first, objectivism places all the emphasis on impersonal forces and subject-less structures in which agents, if they are considered at all, are no more than playthings or puppets of reified social systems. The second, subjectivism, reduces the whole of social life to the actions of individual agents or groups, their actions, interactions, their goals, desires, interpretations and practices.

As Stones demonstrates, Giddens attempted to develop a theory which takes account both of the existence of social structure and the notion of interpretive agents. Likewise, Bourdieu (1989: 16) calls for a 'constructivist structuralism or structuralist constructivism':

> By structuralism or structuralist, I mean there exists within the social world itself and not only within symbolic systems, objective structures independent of the consciousness and will of agents, which are capable of guiding and constraining their practices or their representations. By constructivism I mean a twofold social

genesis, on the one hand schemes of perception, thought and action which are constitutive of what I call habitus, and on the other hand of social structures, and particularly what I call fields and groups.

Humans are complex social beings that are able to exercise choice and perhaps reflect on their social situation. People faced with similar social situations can develop very different perceptions of their situation. A person brought up on an inner-city estate surrounded by unemployment and dysfunctional families may think, and may be right, that she has limited choices and have limited horizons about what she can achieve. In most cases she will reproduce the behaviour of her parents.

However, another individual, for example someone called Christine, may see that she must escape from her background 'and make something of herself'. Whilst there may be many more who are limited, some do make an escape – this does not demonstrate that we live in a land of opportunity but it demonstrates the human ability to make choices outside the social framework within which we exist. So Christine works hard, goes to college and learns a skill that is in demand, earns a decent salary and buys her own home and breaks out of the social structure into which she was born.

Ed, on the other hand, has a parent who is a lawyer and another who is a university professor. He does what is required of him at his private school, gets 4 As at A level and goes to a top university and follows his mother into law. By the age of 35 he has a large salary and decides to go into politics; within five years he is a Cabinet Minister. Ed gets a good job without trying too hard but works hard to get into Cabinet by the age of 40. Christine gets a good job through struggle and hard work and making the best of her situation and achieves an income well above that of her parents. Both Ed and Christine exercised choice and both did better than their contemporaries but the range of choices available to Ed and Christine are very different (and the ease by which they can achieve them) because of the variation in their social situations. If we look at the majority of Christines they will have low paid work and the majority of Eds will be in secure middle class occupations. Ed and Christine could reflect on their situations and do something differently but the majority of Christines are held back by the social situation and the majority of Eds are advantaged by their social situation. Such issues are raised in relation to the issue of teenage mothers. For some, teenage mothers are a consequence of deprivation and to an extent structurally determined. However, Helen Wilson and Annette Huntington (2006: 64) argue:

The idea that teen motherhood is problematic ignores the possibility that teenage women weigh up their opportunity costs when they continue a pregnancy to term (Geronimus, 1997), no doubt in much the same way as older women who opt for later parenthood.

This raises the question of how we frame and understand choices within social structures. Are teenage mothers making choices or are their actions a consequence of restricted choice?

Yet this analysis is sociological and does not necessarily focus on the question of power. Power arises as it relates to the resources available within a particular structural context – working class teenage mothers and professional women who choose to have babies later have different resources and so have different abilities to affect their life chances. What we can see here is that the social structure acts as a mechanism for restraining and enabling behaviour. The social structure ensures that deprived women are more likely to become pregnant young, and that professional, middle class women have a range of choices. This does not mean that the structures are determining, but they provide the framework of choice. This is similar to the way institutional rational choice theorists see structure providing a particular set of preferences. However, the problem with the rational choice approach is that it sees the set of choices as external to the actor whereas in reality they are embedded in the particular situation within which they exist (or in Foucault's sense how the body is constructed). For example, in certain deprived communities it is the norm for teenagers to have babies and in the professional middle classes the social pressure for women to settle down and become 'homemakers' has reduced; thus how actors define themselves affects choices. These may not be conscious choices but expectations as a consequence of social position. This sense of power resonates with Amartya Sen's notion of poverty as 'capability deprivation' (Sen, 1999). Capability is the ability to do something and so central to a conception of power.

An important question is how people reproduce and change the structures they face. For a poor woman to have a child at 16 who is born into a low-income world and is poorly educated reproduces the capability deprivation that the mother faced. However, there are some young women who reflect on their position and make different choices from their peers, deciding to go on with school, training or work. Moreover, the state can play a role. It can create schemes of work, support or training that allow women greater opportunities whether or not they have children.

It is important to illustrate the role of government in this process. The inequalities, and the mechanisms for breaking out of them, are not a consequence of luck. They are a consequence of power struggles and policies developed within and without the state and implemented through government policy. Governments are central to sustaining and, at times, challenging the structures of privilege that ensure that resources are more easily available to some groups rather than others. Indeed, Barry Hindess (2006) makes a very important criticism of Lukes and those involved in the power debate when he suggests that they pay insufficient attention to the role of government in the reproduction of power in social life. As he points out, Foucault suggests that: 'To govern ... is to structure the possible fields of actions of others' (Foucault, quoted in Hindess, 2006: 118). As Hindess (2006: 118) argues:

> Government is relatively stable but while it sometimes seeks to determine the behaviour of individuals, it normally aims to influence them indirectly by acting on the manner in which they regulate their own behaviour and the behaviour of others.

So government, or the state, occasionally directly enforces particular forms of behaviour – usually through laws and sometimes by coercion. More often it enables the reproduction of certain forms of behaviour. Low levels of expenditure in social housing schemes means a high concentration of poor people with a range of social problems; consequently, the life chances of people in that situation are low. Expensive private schools are given charitable status and therefore are subsidised by the state because they do not have to pay taxes. The key point is that government – often, as Hindess reminds us, operating with other social actors – can maintain patterns of social behaviour that reproduce existing social structures. These social structures define the 'possible fields of actions' of individuals.

If we are to understand power we need to take account both of structures and of how they distribute resources – whether these are economic, social (cultural capital in Bourdieu's terms), information or relationships – and how those resources are accessed by actors. As Giddens (1984: 15) argues:

> Resources ... are structured properties of social systems, drawn upon and reproduced by knowledgable agents in the course of interaction. Power is not intrinsically connected to the achievement of

sectional interests. In this conception the use of power characteristizes not specific types of conduct but all action, and power itself is not a resource. Resources are the media through which power is exercised, as a routine element in the instantiation of conduct in social reproduction.

The problem with the theories of the state, as discussed in Chapter 3, is that whilst they are interested in state power, they actually pay little attention to the way that states exercise power. It is seen as a generalized capacity; there is an assumption that states can do things, that they can achieve goals, and in a sense the focus is on who has power within that framework, whether it is classes, groups or state officials. They have power if the state adopts their goals, but the actual implementation of those goals is seen as unproblematic. It is, as Bourdieu says, (1999: 53):

To endeavour to think about the state is to take the risk of taking over (or being taken over by) a thought of the state, that is, applying to the state categories of thought produced and guaranteed by the state and hence to misrecognize its profound truth.

In other words, many people study the state and accept the way states are presented constitutionally as the reality and in doing so misunderstand its real nature. However, what we are interested in is the way that state institutions achieve their goals and not how groups or individuals influence what those goals are (although of course there is an important relationship between them).

In order to understand this process there are two important factors that we need to take into account. First is the point that Joel Migdal makes: the distinction between state and society is artificial. The state and society are not separate spheres but continually integrated. The boundaries of the state are permeable – and this is not a new development. This is because states do not have the ability to control everything. As we will see in Chapter 7, even authoritarian regimes rely on building social relations beyond the state. The point that comes from the elitist literature is that if the state is to be effective it needs to build infrastructural power by developing relations with social groups. As soon as states want to achieve specific social goods they need support and delivery mechanisms in civil society (or organizations that integrate states and society). For instance, governments cannot have a health policy without working with doctors, and with any public health policy doctors become closely integrated into processes of making and, particularly, delivering policy (the question of whether doctors are state actors becomes a complex one). There has to be cooperation because such a technical policy cannot work effectively through coercion.

This highlights a second point. State goals depend on the actions of thousands or millions of individuals. If the government is going to deliver education it needs people to train as teachers and once trained to teach in ways that are consistent with government policy. This raises an important point: if states are to exercise power in order to achieve goals they need a whole series of agents to act – agents who have shared and conflicting interests and motivations. Some of these agents will work directly for the government such as civil servants, others may have a more indirect relationship such as teachers, and others are citizens. Moreover, government aims may be contradictory or difficult to achieve. It may be that the highest education standards are achieved when teachers have the most autonomy. Hence, as we will see in Chapter 11, when governments attempt to control obesity they have to affect the behaviour of a range of individuals from civil servants to the action of a child in eating. The problem for the government is how to motivate individuals to act in specific ways that are consistent with government goals. Traditionally modern states have attempted to control predominantly through law based on authority, bureaucracy and force. These offer generalized forms of control in that they are targeted at citizens in general. However, more recently in order to control individual behaviour governments have developed mechanisms that assume more direct control over agents: regulation, rationality, surveillance and risk assessment. Within this context the next section will develop a framework for understanding how states exercise power rather than how groups affect the state.

To conclude, in order to understand the state we need to take account of a number of factors:

- State power is always partial – states never have complete success for their policies and some policies are not implemented at all. State power varies across policy, state and time – making arguments about the decline or increase of state power inappropriate because states as a whole do not gain or lose power and even the most powerful states will fail in some areas.
- The state is not unified; all states are made up of numerous bodies that include formal governing bodies but also a range of quasi-,

para- and non-state bodies (Flinders, 2008). For instance, in most continental European countries university lecturers are employed directly by the state as bureaucrats, whereas in Britain universities in principle have independence from the state, although the majority of their funding is public funding and government control of universities is relatively high. Are British universities part of the state?

• The state is not separate from civil society. The state cannot execute policies. Primary health care will not occur without the cooperation of medics and therefore the line between the state and civil society is blurred. For governments to achieve goals they are involved in complex processes of interaction in order to achieve these goals and therefore state power depends on the mechanisms outlined in this book and which are often intangible, such as persuasion (although persuasion could be seen as a facet of legitimacy).

• State power in the sense of achieving outcomes (in terms of implemented policies and changes in behaviour) is a process involving complex patterns of dependence and negotiation. States rarely act through fiat. They rely on convincing people through force, legitimacy, bureaucracy, regulation, incentives or surveillance to act in specific ways. Citizens as either bureaucrats or actors in civil society are often able to subvert the intentions of government, meaning that governments are often continually trying to 'patch up' governing failures (this may account for why, despite governments supposedly reducing their role, they introduce increased amounts of legislation and regulation).

## A framework for understanding power

The traditional arguments about power are framed in terms of whether power resides within an elite or is constrained by groups and processes of democratic accountability. Power is thus conceived of as an identifiable object. The state in much state theory is assumed to be a distinct organization exercising power over society. In radical approaches, Foucault and others see power as operating in a much more diffuse manner through the controlling and creation of the individual body or social category. This book works on a different assumption. It assumes that power as a philosophical concept only takes us so far and that in order to understand the impact of the state we need to examine the mechanisms of power. Consequently, power is multidimensional; it operates both directly and indirectly; observably and through mechanisms that are difficult to observe directly. It can exist in direct forms of observable power such as force, but also through processes of social organization. State actors are not fussy; they can arrest people who drink-drive and they can try to manipulate our wants so that drink-driving becomes socially unacceptable. How state actors exercise power does not have to be philosophically consistent and hence they can use a range of tools to achieve their goals. The focus of the book is on power and the state and the assumption is that the state as a set of institutions has resources which actors can draw upon in order to exercise power. Power, as Lukes (2005), Dowding (1991) and Morriss (2002) recognize, is a capacity. Having resources and capacity does not mean that the state is always successful in changing behaviour or achieving desired outcomes (all governments want to eliminate crime but are unable to do so but they also fail at simple goals like improving standards of reading or stopping people breaking the speed limit), but sometimes the state is successful (in collecting taxes from most people) and sometime the state is difficult to resist. The book intends to examine the mechanisms the state uses to achieve its goals and the cases when it fails. In order to do this the book will first look at the way the state has changed.

The debate on power is endless and interminable, and it has no resolution. No one will learn the secret of power, nor will academics agree on a set of definitions of power because, as we have seen, power is not linked to an 'objective' definition. It is not possible to pin power down; it is linked to how social scientists understand the nature of human beings, knowledge and methodology. However, what we can do with power is be sensitive to the different ways that it is defined and exercised, and see that power is multifaceted and works through different processes. Power is not some social object but a heuristic for helping us to analyse social and political relations within complex societies. If we think of power as a tool, we can use power in different ways in order to unpack the complex nature of state–society relations. Sometimes power is overt and measurable and at other times its source and mechanisms cannot be easily determined. The literature discussed in this and the preceding chapters does, however, indicate some of the key elements we need for understanding power:

## 1. People are agents

People are agents who exercise choice. However, their motivations for choices are complex as Weber, amongst many others, recognized.

Stones (2005: 102) uses Ian Craib to illustrate that an 'agent's conduct will often be characterised at its core by a lack of conceptual clarity and even by flat contradiction'. Choices cannot be reduced to utility maximization and they are often not transitive. Moreover, choices are not free in the absolute sense but are conditioned by social structures. What we believe is linked to the power structures of a particular society. If a woman lives in a rural society dominated by the Catholic church she is likely to believe that abortion is wrong and if she becomes pregnant she is more likely to choose to get married than have an abortion (of course the facilities for abortion are unlikely to exist even if she wanted it). The choice of marriage is a rational choice on the basis of her beliefs. Rational choice theorists could defend it as a utility maximizing choice – however the choice would be made because she believed abortion was wrong, not because she is a utility maximizer. For example, if she had the money to go abroad for an abortion and could go away without her family knowing then the utility of abortion may be high but beliefs may prevent that choice. There are, as Stones (2005: 84–5) demonstrates, external structures – laws that make abortion illegal and the lack of abortion services, the wrath of the Catholic church – and internal structures. Internal structures refer to the skills to reflect on the external structures – what Stones (2005: 85) calls the 'contextually specific knowledge of external structures' and 'the general dispositional'.

Contextually specific knowledge is important in understanding why agents act differently when faced with the same external structures. Maria and Dolores may both have been bought up in the same rural community, attended the same schools and the same churches. However when Maria gets pregnant the idea of abortion abhors her and she quickly marries the father. Dolores on the other hand had a religious mother who married an outsider, sceptical of the church's teaching and who encouraged Dolores to question the church. When Dolores gets pregnant she talks to her father who, despite disapproval, funds her to go abroad for an abortion.

The general dispositional, according to Stones (2005: 88), refers to

Generalised world views and cultural schemas, classifications, typification of things, people and networks, principles of action, typified recipes of action, deep binary frameworks of signification, associative chains and connotations of discourse, habits of speech and gesture, methodologies for adapting this generalised knowledge to a range of particular practise in particular locations of time and space.

The general dispositional is how we internalize social rules and turn them into the taken-for-granted aspects of our daily life. It is similar to Foucault's notion of social discipline – the way in which the social self is created.

In terms of power, the important question is the relationship between the external structures, the internal structures, and an agent's capacity for choice. So when faced with a forceful external structure like the state most people, as Stones (2005: 114) points out, 'will feel the need to comply', often because they lack an alternative mechanism for achieving their goals. But as Stones (2005: 115) argues, the possibility to resist exists if an agent has:

1. adequate power to resist without endangering the conditions of possibility for the realisation of core commitments;
2. adequate knowledge of alternative possible courses of action;
3. adequate critical distance in order to take up a strategic stance in relation to a particular external structure and its 'situtational presence'.

When states attempt to achieve social goals they are challenged on one side by a whole series of factors they cannot control (for instance, crime rates often vary according to economic conditions, not government policy) and on the other side by actors who are reflexive and able to exercise choice. This is where the rational choice framework is problematic because it assumes people will act in a certain way when faced with certain choices. The reality is that people can act in a 'perverse' manner because they interpret situations and choices in particular ways. Governments are constantly thwarted by people acting unexpectedly. However, state actors as agents are an important element in the process of understanding state power. States have a series of resources – including money and the bureaucracy – and a range of mechanisms and control of particular institutions such as the police, army etc. The sorts of resources that state actors choose for developing and implementing policy are crucial to whether the policy is a success or not. Increasingly, governments see leaders in the public sector as individuals who are able to pull together the right tools for successful implementation. However, the flip-side is that citizens are reflexive agents who have the ability to resist and subvert and so whilst people may at one level be obeying the state, they can often find ways of resisting. This is the paradox of state power; it ultimately relies on people to deliver goals but people can subvert the delivery; this explains the continual search for new mechanisms of power. Moreover, many of the new forms of state power, which are discussed in this book, are concerned not with ordering people to act in certain ways but with attempting to change their contextual knowledge and their general disposition so that they think about choices in different ways. To take a simple example, governments attempt to make people stop smoking not by banning cigarettes but by making people aware of the health consequences of smoking.

## 2. Structures provide resources for power

Structural power is not a useful concept but the notion of structure is essential to understanding power. Structures are the institutionalized distribution of resources within a society or organization that ensure that certain agents or groups have greater resources than others (and often reflect historical outcomes as the result of choices by powerful actors). Structures, as we saw above, exist independently of individual human beings but not of humans. As Mark Haugaard (2000: 65) reminds us:

> Social structure does not exist materially outside its moment of reproduction. What gives structure its permanence is the fact that there exists a system of ideas and beliefs which actors use to reproduce those social structures as a matter of routine.

In exercising power actors draw on resources that may be embedded in organizations. Resources refer to a wide range of material and ideological benefits. The prime minister can draw on the authority of his or her position as a mechanism to get people do what they want. Resources may be material as in the case of economic resources and they can be organizational. The reasons why governments in the developed world can achieve goals is because they have the organizational mechanisms to do so. Modern states are in a structurally privileged position compared to other actors/institutions. They have access to resources: money, authority, force, and ideas, that are not available to such an extent to any other interest. For example, despite the extent of the global economic downturn, developed states are able to subsidize banks with billions of dollars. Consequently, within modern societies states have a singular ability to affect events within a given territory. This does not mean that they are all-powerful because power depends on the ability to use the resources for a particular end and many factors constrain their use. In this sense the mechanisms of power identified in this book are ideally seen as resources that are available to the state. What is clear is that not all states have the same resources and states cannot always use the resources they have in all situations. For instance, legitimacy as a resource waxes and wanes. George Bush had much greater legitimacy on 12 September 2001 than on 12 September 2008.

## 3. Power exists in all relationships

All relationships are power relationships. As Foucault argues, power is relative and one's position or power is defined only in relation to another. In addition, power is based on dependence. When the state exercises power it depends on people responding to its authority or financial resources. If they do not the state cannot deliver. Therefore even in relationships with a significant imbalance of resources, the resource-rich will have some dependence on the resource-poor. As Stones points out, even when we comply we may be doing so in a way where we are conscious of opposition (see also Scott, 1990). In addition, in many situations those who are weak have opportunities, as Foucault observed, of micro-resistance: the put-upon secretary can find little ways of making life difficult for the boss; the production line worker can find small ways of disrupting the production process. It is interesting how powerful organizations are constantly on the guard against micro-resistance. For example, in call centres – where very alienating labour practices often exist – call centre managers have developed processes to counter micro-resistance (Van den Broek, 2003).

Power is everywhere and power relationships are relationships of dependence. This means that power is not, as suggested by Robert Dahl and the behaviourists, a zero sum. If A gains power B does not lose it. Power is a way of understanding relationships that are often based on dependence. If A wants to achieve something, then A is dependent on B doing it. In having this dependence power will always be two-way. However, A may have more resources than B, but whether A can get B to do something is not a theoretical question but an empirical one.

## 4. States are always dependent on other actors to achieve their goals

Because states rely on people acting to fulfil their goals, they cannot do anything without the cooperation of other actors and hence power is based on exchange relationships. The nature of power is not one-way. If the state is going to achieve goals it will rely on actors cooperating and it often has to make concessions in the process. Consequently, states are constantly engaged in processes of exchange relationships. The problem for democratic governments is that they cannot afford to forego their legitimacy and so to retain support they will often make considerable concessions. This is why it is so difficult to deal with a problem such as global warming. The policies that are necessary to tackle climate change are unpopular with a range of constituencies and so governments are reluctant to undertake strong measures. The necessary concessions undermine the policy.

## 5. States are continually exercising power in contexts they do not control

States are frequently affected by a series of economic, social and political contexts that they cannot control. The collapse of the authoritarian states in Eastern Europe was a consequence of the failure of governments to produce sufficient economic growth to satisfy the material needs of their populations. In the West governments' economic choices were greatly constrained by the end of the postwar boom. Similarly, social changes such as the breakdown of the traditional family create a series of issues for governments that are very difficult to control. In understanding state power, we can only play limited attention to the role of elites. They face a whole series of constraints from the capabilities of the state, to other powerful groups in society, to the need to retain legitimacy, to the impact of the international political and economic order. The Bush administration had little choice but to underwrite the mortgage agencies Fannie Mae and Freddie Mac because of the impact of their collapse on the banking system. So whatever the ideology of the Bush administration, they were left no option but to intervene. States are as much done to as doing. They are often reacting to situations beyond their direct control.

If we are to understand state power we have to understand that it is flawed and limited. States attempt to effect change within the context of external structures that they do not control and through reflexive agents that have the ability to subvert state intentions and commands. If states are to be successful in achieving their goals they need to be able to change the way individuals behave because the enactment of decisions is dependent on their cooperation. If governments are going to outlaw drink-driving they have to do more than introduce legislation. They have to ensure that the police and law courts enforce the law but ultimately that drivers do not drink. This requires a change of behaviour which could be a consequence of the coercion of law – but if this was the only mechanism then it would take tremendous police resources to catch only a small percentage of drink-drivers. Rather, governments rely on the fact that some people will accept the authority of the law and others may gauge that the risk of getting caught is too great and so desist. Eventually, it may be that social change occurs so that drink-driving becomes socially unacceptable; that the contextual knowledge changes. However, this new social understanding is difficult to achieve. It depends on a police force that is cooperative and on the nature of the particular concepts. Societies where drinking is seen as part of everyday life (and distinct from drunkenness) may have great difficulty getting the police to enforce a strict policy or the citizens to take them seriously. So modern states, despite their considerable resources, rely on a range of mechanisms to achieve their goals. These can range from the traditional such as authority, to the new such as surveillance.

## Conclusion

A single definition of power is impossible because of ontological and epistemological differences but also empirically – power operates in different ways in different circumstances. Consequently we can only provide a framework for analysing power and not a definitive conceptualization of power. It is a heuristic for understanding social relations. We need to see power as relational and multidimensional. Power is a capability that is expressed in a relationship. Sometimes power is observable. If someone holds a gun to a soldier's head and says 'go to the front line' and he goes, it is clear who has power and how it is exercised. But if a solider volunteers to go to the front because he is imbued with a sense of nationalism, then the processes of power are much more complex and difficult to discern. However, we can see that nationalism has been used as a structural resource to ensure a soldier takes a particular course of action. Nationalism is a resource that states can use to legitimize their actions and it increases the ability to achieve particular goals. So power is not structural but resources are distributed by structures and those resources are used in the exercise of power. States are in vulnerable positions because control of their societies is difficult – and often ends in failure. Therefore, states depend on building relationships with society – the state/society dichotomy is not a clear divide – and using a range of mechanisms to attempt to affect social outcomes. In the next chapter we will examine how the modern state developed before examining the various ways that the state exercises power.

# Chapter 5

# The Development of the State from Modernity to Past-modernity

Since the 1970s there has been a sense in academic and political writing that the state is in crisis. The modern state as it exists in the industrialized West has reached the limits of it capabilities. The state has been hit by a series of crises from the economic crisis of the 1970s to the problems of global warming, intractable problems in relation to conflict in various parts of the world and a growing awareness of the impact that finite resources have on social relations between and within nation states. The economic crisis of the 1970s raised the prospect that the modernist project could not be fulfilled (see Offe, 1984) and the end of the Cold War and the rise of Muslim extremism created instability in the international order. This has led a number of authors to suggest that we now have a postmodern state – one that is fragmented and that has abandoned the Enlightenment project of continual progress (Sorenson, 2004). The literature on globalization and governance has questioned both the context and organization of modern states, and they highlight the limits of its capabilities in what appears an increasingly complex world.

The debate about the state reflects both changes in the way the state is perceived and what the state is in empirical fact. Much of the literature on the state assumes, either implicitly or explicitly, that the twentieth-century state was a modernist state with the capability to intervene and effect change in society. The nature of state power is based on an assumption that states were in some ways able to control the societies within which they operated. Consequently, much of the argument in the literature is suggestive of a qualitative shift in the nature of the state as it moves from one of modernity to postmodernity and consequently what we see is a decline in both the ability and desire to control society. However, states have clearly had modernist projects (and the recent focus of international agencies on state capacities suggests that this is seen as a universal, normative good) – they have attempted to modify in a rational way the nature of society but they have often been unsuccessful. Consequently, states have attempted to develop new forms of control. So whilst states may have abandoned the types of interventions associated with modernism, they are still trying to develop mechanisms to change societies. The argument of this chapter, and the book, is that notions of the postmodern state overestimate the degree of change and that in fact what we see is very considerable changes to the modern state which do not undermine, and may even enhance, its power and centrality. In the next section the chapter examines the key features of the modern state and highlights how the teleology of the shift from modernism to postmodernism is too simple for understanding the complex phenomenon of the state in the developed world. Rather, the *past*modern state sees new forms of state power developing on the existing structures and institutions.

## The development of the modern and pastmodern state

### The problem of modernity

The twentieth century saw the establishment of the modern state in the developed world. The modern state was seen as unified, purposeful, bounded and hierarchical. Its power was based on its growing authority and the development of bureaucracy. There is a growing argument that the modern state has now fragmented and that it has lost its single purpose and method. No longer is the core mechanism of the state the uniform, hierarchical, line-bureaucracy directed at social progress (what Weber saw as the defining feature of the modern state); it is now post-bureaucratic. The aim of this section is to analyse the key features of the modern state and to assess whether they have been undermined. The purpose is to demonstrate that the modern state was never as fixed as often supposed and therefore to talk of a postmodern state makes little sense. Indeed, the suggestion is that in understanding modern states in the twenty-first century we need to see states firstly as subject to considerable variability. States impact differently across time, space and policy area and the notion of a lineal progression from pre-modern, to modern to postmodern does not, as Foucault suggests, makes sense. Consequently, it is useful to think of states in terms of Stones' (1996) notion of *past*modern rather than postmodern. In other words, states have developed from the modern state and developed new forms and mechanisms but without losing the key features of modernism. States may be more fragmented and permeable but they are also concerned with progressive policy and the control of their populations in alternative ways. As we will see in the course of the book – we have not seen the eclipsing of the modern state but the development of states in different ways through the use of a range of mechanisms to exercise power.

The key features of the modern state which developed in the twentieth century are what Weber sees as a monopoly of violence, legitimacy and bureaucracy combined with control of territory based on external and internal sovereignty. The point is that all of these are presented as having been absolute, when in reality they were for all states – and for some more than others – only partial. For instance, and ironically, the sovereignty of states in Western Europe after 1945 was highly dependent on the military and economic support of the US. More importantly, these elements of the modern state, whilst important, are perhaps epiphenomena of the underlying feature of the modern state: rationality. The modern state is part of the Enlightenment project and the general acceptance of the terms of modernity. Modernity is based on the notion that there is a truth that is knowable and that through rational procedures we can identify that mechanism for achieving the true path to progress. Consequently, the modern state becomes an organization developed on rational lines which controls a society in order to achieve social progress, often based on a set of collective goods (such as clean water or education) . The state is legitimized because its end is the general good of social improvement and this process of improvement is delivered through the rule of law and a bureaucratic process that reaches all and treats all equally.

For many, particularly social democratic parties but also authoritarian parties on the left and the right, the state has been seen as a mechanism for achieving a whole series of social goals. Yet there have been a large and growing number of critics of the modern state. From once being the hope of humanity, the modern state (and modernity) is increasingly blamed for all that is wrong in the world. For instance, John Gray (2003: 2) claims:

> The Soviet Union was an attempt to embody the Enlightenment ideal of a world without power or conflict. In pursuit of this ideal it killed and enslaved tens of millions of human beings. Nazi Germany committed the worst act of genocide in history. It did so with the aim of breeding a new type of human being. No previous age harboured such projects. The gas chambers and the gulags are modern.

Gray is building on an argument that is developed with much greater subtlety in the work of Zygmunt Bauman. For Bauman (1989) the Holocaust is not a failure of civilization but the ultimate expression of the modernist project. What made the Holocaust possible was that the techniques of the modern state were applied to genocide. Bureaucracy is amoral. What is important is the end, and the rationality of the modern state is applied to achieving that end. Bauman (1989: 23) highlights how Jews were incorporated into their own destruction through the bureaucratic method:

> This astonishing effect of successfully extending the rules of bureaucratic conduct, complete with the delegitimation of alternative loyalties and moral motives in general to encompass the intended victims of bureaucracy, and thereby deploying their skills and labour in the implementation of the task of their destruction was achieved.

Moreover, it was the nature of bureaucracy that ensured that ordinary and decent Germans were prepared to become part of the machinery of genocide:

> The increase in the physical and/or psychic distance between the act and its consequences achieves more than suspension of moral inhibition; it quashes the moral significance of the act. With most of the socially significant actions mediated by a long chain of complex causal and functional dependencies, moral dilemmas recede from sight, while the occasions for more scrutiny and conscious moral choice become increasingly rare. (Bauman, 1989: 25)

For James Scott (1998, 2006) the modernist appeal to science and social improvement has led to the state undertaking tasks which, whilst aimed at improving the human condition, have produced disasters. 'Society became an object that the state might manage and transform with a view towards perfecting it' (Scott, 2006: 5). Scott sees modernism's appeal to science as a mechanism for depoliticizing and legitimizing ruthless interventions into people's lives in the name of progress without taking account of their local knowledge and experience or interests. These perspectives on modernism define the state as all-powerful and so allow later analysts to illustrate the decline of the state. However, as Scott is well aware, modern states often failed and, as we will see, even the most powerful did not have total control.

## Territoriality, Borders and Sovereignty

One of the defining features of the modern state, and the state in the modern world, is the notion of territoriality: modern states control a distinct and identifiable area. States are defined by their territory and the development of borders was essential to the establishment to the modern state. Peter Taylor (2003) argues that the power of the modern state is a consequence of the fusing of nation and state. For John Ruggie (1993), one of the central features of the modern state is that it 'differentiated its subjects collectively into territorially defined, fixed, and mutually exclusive enclaves of legitimate domination' (quoted in Ansell, 2004: 3). He then suggests that this exclusive and fixed territoriality is breaking down, in the so-called post-modern era. Writers such as Ruggie see in the late twentieth century the weakening of borders and the undermining of traditional conceptions of sovereignty. The argument of, for example, Martin Shaw is that the state is being considerably reformed in its territoriality and sovereignty by the processes of globalization. For Shaw (2003: 120), we no longer have nation states but the 'western state' which

> has developed into a massive, institutionally complex and messy agglomeration of state power centred on North America, western Europe, Japan and Australasia ... The western state can be defined as a single state conglomerate because borders of violence have been largely abolished within, and have shifted to the edges of this bloc.

Territoriality and sovereignty are being transformed by globalization, immigration, technological and environmental change, and the development of global and regional institutions. Taylor sees the futility of territoriality in the future and believes that, 'the state as a container is ultimately doomed'. Consequently, it is suggested that economic activity and social relations are occurring through 'trans-border spaces' which redraw the relationship between time and space (Sum, 2003: 209). Neil Brenner (2004: 44) states the argument forcefully:

> [T]he contemporary round of global restructuring has radically reconfigured the scalar organization of territorialization processes under capitalism, relativising the primacy of the national scale while simultaneously enhancing the role of subnational and supernational scales in the process.

These arguments about the rise and fall of sovereignty create a false linearity to sovereignty and borders. The arguments concerning the end of territoriality both over-estimate the strength of sovereignty in the past and underestimate its continuing importance. There can be little doubt that notions of sovereignty and borders are central to the idea of the modern state, but that idea has always been contested. Sovereignty has both internal and external dimensions (Aalberts, 2004: 24). The external element is the recognition that other states will not interfere in the internal affairs of a state. As Paul Hirst points out (2005: p.37), 'When States accepted the legitimate existence of others as exclusive governing powers, it mattered crucially where the rights of each began'. Modern states came into existence on the basis of mutually recognized borders and the understanding that states could not, in normal circumstances, intervene across those borders.

The second element, however, was that within those borders there was internal sovereignty. Essentially derived from the Hobbesian notion of state power is the idea that states control what goes on within their territory and consequently the state is the ultimate authority. The reality is that few states have exercised internal sovereignty in the way that theories suggest. The Westminster model in Britain and authoritarian regimes have tended to locate power clearly with a central state authority. However, as pointed out by George Sabine (1974) long before the debate on globalization the notion of internal sovereignty 'does not precisely fit any government in the world except Great Britain, not even the British Empire; the authority of Parliament, though theoretically intact, is quite shadowy as applied to the self-governing dominions'. Many nations have federal structures where power is shared between the centre and the regions. Moreover, even in authoritarian regimes of the past, power was often within the party rather than the state, or divided between state and party rather than located simply in the state. Likewise a number of authoritarian regimes, for example the Soviet Union and Argentina, had federal systems which granted considerable autonomy to the regions. Therefore, highly unified and indivisible internal sovereignty is relatively rare. There are liberal states such as Britain and France that have a tradition of strong state sovereignty, and authoritarian regimes which have divided sovereignty.

The suggestion from the postmodernist perspective is that states once had borders, exercised politically through sovereignty, and that the notion of fixed borders and indivisible sovereignty is now disappearing. However, borders and sovereignty have always been both metaphorical and real. Borders are obviously metaphorical in that they do not really exist, they are lines on the map. However, many borders are real because they are maintained by fences, armed guards and check points. Within the European Union different types of borders exist within one country. Following the Schengen agreement Spain's border with France exists purely as a line on paper. Hirst (2005: 37) suggests that:

> [B]orders now matter less and less, in some cases less than the borders between US states. Once such frontiers were closely guarded: now they are often imperceptible. The reason is not merely because the states in question are no longer in conflict, but because it is increasingly difficult to tell the peoples of adjacent states apart.

Despite the fact that for hundreds of years blood and ink was spilt creating this border through the Pyrenees, today the external signs of the border have disappeared. In many parts of the crossing there is nothing more than a battered sign saying 'France' or 'Spain'. However, it is not true, as Hirst implies, that the people are the same. Rather, the border is inculcated into the lived experience of those who cross it. We know when we are in France or Spain without a physical border. On one side they speak French and on the other they speak Catalan or Basque or Spanish. As Foucault would say, we carry the border within ourselves. But the border does not exist in this way because of 'biopower' and self regulation. It exists this way because of geo-politics. After hundreds of years of war the French and Spanish states are secure enough to know that they are not threatened by the other. Just over the French border there exists for strange reasons of history the Spanish enclave of Llívia. This small enclave lives the Spanish way inside France. For a long time France would not allow direct travel from France into Llívia, it was necessary to go into Spain and then take a particular road to Llívia. Now travel is free, the borders are open, but Llívia remains Spanish (or Catalan) speaking and Spanish in its way of life.

At the other end of Spain inside Morocco there are two very different Spanish enclaves: Ceuta and Melilla. These are remnants of the Spanish empire but today are treated as part of the Spanish mainland. To the Spanish they are never thought of as Spanish colonies, they are as much part of Spain as Seville. However, the nature of their borders with surrounding Morocco is very different to the border with France. These are real borders with high fences, barbed wire and armed troops. People who cross the border from the rest of Africa are often sent back.

With the changing forms of the state borders have not disappeared but they have become complex and multivariate. Those in the developed West can move freely across borders, those in the developing South are continually constrained. Governments faced with more mobility are reinforcing borders but borders are stronger for some people than others. Spain has no limits on the Germans, Dutch and British who move to live on the Costas but tries with all its power to prevent movement from Africa.

However, the nature of borders has always been relative. For many Africans borders have no meaning. Even in China and the Soviet Union with strong states and a clear sense of their borders – often involved in skirmishes – many nomads had no sense of the existence of defined territories. Borders exist in relation to others and social structures. If you are white and middle class it is easy to cross national boundaries but if you are poor and black it is extremely difficult. If you are an economic refugee from Africa you are a danger and need to be discouraged or prevented. If you are a political refugee from North Korea you are a hero to be welcomed.

Consequently, the sovereignty of states has been the exception not the norm. Most states have had sovereignty in the legal sense but not in the empirical sense. For instance, most of the states in Eastern Europe in the period following the Second World War had legal sovereignty but they did not achieve 'real' sovereignty until the collapse of the Soviet Union. At the point when commentators were seeing sovereignty disappearing, they were gaining independence for the first time. However, many of the former communist states quickly joined the European Union, dissolving again their national sovereignty in order to protect their borders from future encroachment from Russia.

National borders and sovereignty are key elements of a modern state but their existence has always been exaggerated and so again the sense that they have disappeared is exaggerated. As part of this process of developing modernity, states often try to impose a uniformity on peoples within a territory, enforcing a single language and way of life – something done relatively successfully in France but poorly in Spain and the Soviet Union. The point is that borders and identities are mythical mechanisms that legitimize the expression of state power over a particular space without external interference. Without the borders and sovereignty there would not be a conception of a nation state. Therefore, the apparent debate about borders and their growing permeability and declining sovereignty is, in a sense, crucial to the future of the state. However, it is important to understand that borders have always been contested and permeable with high levels of migration a constant feature of the twentieth century (even between the borders of East and West Europe). Modern states never succeeded in their goals of imposing a single, uncontested national identity behind clear and unquestioned borders. It is a mythical part of the state.

## States and civil society

The other important boundary in terms of understanding the capability of the state is the boundary between the state and civil society. How does the state relate to individuals in society? This is often seen as a way of distinguishing between so-called totalitarian regimes and liberal societies. At the totalitarian end of the spectrum there is no distinction between the state and society. The whole of life is politicized and effectively controlled by the state. In a liberal society the role of the state should be limited with individuals free to make as much choice as possible. Theda Skocpol's notion of state autonomy posits a distinction between states, that have distinct interests, and civil society, which may have a range of conflicting interests. However, as Timothy Mitchell (1991: 88) points out: 'the edges of the state are uncertain; societal elements seem to penetrate it on all sides, and the resulting boundary between state and society is difficult to determine. They respond by giving the state a narrow definition, personified as a policy making actor'. As Mitchell notes:

> [T]he boundary of the state (or political system) never marks a real exterior. The line between the state and society is not the perimeter of an intrinsic entity ... It is a line drawn internally, *within* the network of institutional mechanisms through which a certain social and political order is maintained.

The relationship between the state and society is rarely fixed or even clear (Migdal, 2001). Many organizations have ambiguous relationships with the state – are they part of the state or separate entities? If the state privatizes the railways but heavily regulates them are they in the private or public sector? In reality a range of policy networks exist which embed social actors within the policy-making processes of the state (Smith, 1993). The *past*modern state, which shifts away from the modernist focus on the state, does not see the state disengaging but becoming integrated within civil society in more complex ways. The point about the new forms of power is that they create ways of modifying behaviour without direct state intervention. The state exchanges bureaucracy for other mechanisms of intervention which continue to be about the state having a central role, but working in more complex patterns of dependence with civil society. For instance, when states use regulation and targets in terms of control they are trying to get groups and organizations to control themselves rather than be directed by state bureaucracy, hence making the boundaries between state and society more complex. Regulation places the burden of delivery on groups within civil society and not the state bureaucracy and yet the state controls delivery through the regulatory process. In addition, the state continues to exist as a distinct authoritative allocator of resources, but the mechanisms of control are more varied and increasingly developed through embedding relations within civil society.

## From extensive to intensive to fragmented power

The other important element in the development of the modern state is the extension of capabilities through the growth of legitimate, bureaucratic power. Bureaucracy, as we will see in Chapter 6, is the basis of the modern state's power. As Michael Mann (1984: 185) reminds us, the modern state is based on 'a monopoly of authoritative binding rule-making, backed up by a monopoly of the means of physical violence'. A crucial aspect of the development of the modern state is the creation of bureaucratic power, which means that the state can shift from despotic to infrastructural power. Despotic power is the form of power that belongs to absolutist and authoritarian pre-modern states. It is 'the range of actions which the elite is empowered to undertake without routine, institutionalised negotiation' (Mann, 1984: 186). Within this context states often act with little constraint and their power is either force or the fairly immediate threat of force. Whilst the power of despotic power may be fairly extensive, it is not intensive, and it only extends as far as the central state can extend its force (Mann, 1984, 1986).

Infrastructural power is 'the capacity of the state to actually penetrate civil society, and to implement logistically political decisions throughout the realm' (Mann, 1984: 186). It is important to understand that the process of state modernization has seen states developing more and increasingly complex mechanisms for controlling populations and achieving state control. Scott (1998) demonstrates how this process of building infrastructural power begins with the process of naming. If people are to be controlled and taxed effectively, they first have to be named. Of course, this process cannot be separated from the need for borders. It is the process of control within a specified territory that makes states so effective (Jackman 1993). The basis of the modern state is having control over a named population, who identify with the state, and of course, it is a degree of commitment to the state that enables governments to get people to do things that they would not otherwise do (such as joining armies and going to frontlines or killing Jews in gas chambers). Central to the modernist project is the development of bureaucracy because it is an institution for focussing considerable resources on the need to achieve a specific and pre-planned goal (Bauman, 1989). For Bauman, bureaucracy provides technical, not moral, responsibility. The point is that the bureaucracy should be able to achieve whatever goal is prescribed. Its purpose is effectiveness and not making moral judgements. One of the key principles of the British civil service is neutrality, and this evasion of moral responsibility is what many bureaucracies throughout the world have attempted to emulate. As Bauman (1989: 101) illustrates, with a bureaucracy

> the skills, expert knowledge, inventiveness and dedication of actors, complete with their personal motives that prompted them to deploy these qualities in full, can be fully mobilized and put to the service of the overall bureaucratic purpose even if (or perhaps because) the actors retain relative functional autonomy towards this purpose and even if this purpose does not agree with the actors' own moral philosophy.

Central to the development of infrastructural power is the building of consent and cooperation. The activities of the modern state are based on agreement, or at least willing compliance, rather than force (although, as writers from Gramsci to Weber realize, legitimate authority is backed by force). Some degree of cooperation is necessary for a bureaucracy to work. If the government decides that it wants a national curriculum, this will not work if teachers continue to teach what they choose; it can only work if teachers cooperate. This point is again well illustrated in Bauman's (1989: 118) study of the Holocaust:

> It seems, however, likely that, were the co-operation not forthcoming, or not available on such a large scale, the complex operation of mass murder would confront the administrators with managerial, technical and financial problems of an entirely different magnitude.

Bauman illustrates that bureaucracy can induce actions by individuals which fulfil the purpose of the bureaucracy but are against the interests of the actors involved. He sees this as a consequence of specialization, but in reality bureaucracies often have considerable legitimacy and, of course, in bureaucratic processes, force is relatively close. The principle of bureaucracy is hierarchy and so each part of the chain follows the orders from above.

Mann emphasizes a fundamental issue in terms of how we understand state power: how are states able to implement their policy goals? In despotic regimes it is through force and in modern 'democratic' states it is usually through some process of negotiation or interaction with civil society. Whilst despotic powers may seem effective, they are limited to the reach of force. Franco used despotic mechanisms to try to impose Spanish on Catalan speakers including arresting nationalist leaders, but he did not sufficiently control local despotic powers and so failed to implement the policy comprehensively. Infrastructural power is based on having administrative mechanisms for the delivery of public goods. For example, states might work through a complex administrative mechanism whereby they develop a bureaucratic process to ensure the delivery of public goods on the ground. This is usually the case in terms of policies such as the distribution of welfare benefits. In other examples, states usually have to develop complex networks with groups in civil society to deliver public goods.

However, as we will see in the course of this book, the question remains of whether states can actually control citizens even when they have complex mechanisms of infrastructural power. Michael Lipsky (1980) demonstrates that often street level bureaucrats such as police officers, teachers and doctors have considerable autonomy and they may not ultimately deliver what state actors want (see Geddes *et al.*, 2007). Moreover, in terms of reforming policy it is often the case that the central state is dependent on the bureaucracy to deliver change but a bureaucracy opposed to change may prevent rather than realize it. The fundamental problem is that government ministers and senior civil servants cannot see what happens on the ground. Information systems are used to try to increase the control of the central state but the veracity of the data is hard to gauge. As a consequence change may only be effected as a result of the development of new actors or institutions.

It is difficult to account for state power without examining the wider context of the general economic conditions (González Rossetti and Mogollón, 2002). The idea of the modern state, bureaucracy and infrastructural power imply states that are effective. Yet state power is constrained and partial, even in well-organized modern states. As Alejandra González Rossetti and Olivia Mogollón remind us, the ability to achieve change may not depend on the existing infrastructural power but on the institutional context within which policies change. This is perhaps the problem with Mann's account. Infrastructural power is presented as static. States shift from having despotic power to infrastructural power. But power is here, as elsewhere (see Chapter 4), a capability that may not be realized and whether infrastructural power works will depend on the particular situation and the balance of forces at that time. Similarly, writers like Bauman and Scott almost reify the modern state. They describe the modern state as an indefatigable behemoth able to direct every aspect of society and to achieve its evil ends (almost the sort of state that exists in George Orwell's *1984*). However, what is remarkable about states is how often they fail to achieve their goals, even when they seem to be relatively simple, and how even within authoritarian regimes there are numerous sites of resistance to the state. Both developed and under-developed states can have considerable problems in dealing with issues such as literacy, teenage pregnancy, introducing new IT systems or controlling inflation. Bauman emphasizes the role of bureaucracy and modernity in the scale and thoroughness of the Holocaust, but on a whole range of tasks bureaucracy often fails; the Holocaust bureaucracy was one backed by tremendous force and fear and it is possible that these were key factors, not the bureaucracy. Likewise, in his critique of modernity Scott focuses on authoritarian regimes and the costs of their modernist projects. It is also possible to point to democratic regimes where modernist projects such as the establishment of clean water and sewage, public education and free health care were successful and highly approved of by those who received the benefits. So infrastructural power helps us to understand the way modern states operate but it does not mean that modern states have complete control of their societies. To a degree success requires working through the many and ill-defined layers of state and civil society.

## Postmodern delivery

The modern state is built on the notion of a hierarchical and centralized state delivery of standardized goods in standardized ways. This, of course, was never the reality. Many states were always highly fragmented; the United States is one example. Often complex and multiple ways of delivering services existed. In Sweden, agencies have always been used for service delivery and in France and Spain, health services have long included a combination of private and public services. Frequently, public goods such as pensions have been provided differently in the public and private sectors (as in the case of Mexico).

The postmodern state is presumed to be fragmenting and decentering the state. Central government is no longer seen as a suitable mechanism for delivering public goods. The new public management literature points to the role of markets, the private sector, voluntary goods and citizens in the development and delivery of public goods. Pressures are developing both for the decentralization of democratic processes and for service delivery through regional, local or even neighbourhood structures.

It is in response to the issue of delivery and effectiveness in central government that much of the new public management and governance literature describes the state as losing its control over the process of delivery; and suggests normatively (in the case of much public choice literature) that services are much better delivered by non-state actors. (This of course sets up new sets of relationships in terms of infrastructural power. In its bureaucratic mode policies are converted into public goods through authority, legitimacy, negotiation, duty and direction, while relationships with non-state partners have to be based on exchange, contract, and possibly persuasion.) The argument, as outlined above, is that the shift to new public management – privatization, the use of agencies and an increased role for the private sector – has led to a hollowing out of the state. The argument put forward by Rod Rhodes (1997) is that the state has hollowed out upward to international bodies, outward towards the private sector and downward to local and regional bodies and semi-autonomous bodies. Power is seen as shifting away from the state to new arenas.

However, whilst the role of the state has changed it has obviously not disappeared. As Jon Pierre and Guy Peters (2000: 94) clarify: 'the emergence of these patterns of governing should not necessarily be seen as indications of weakening of the state but rather as transformations of previous models of governance into new ones which are better geared to the politics and political economy of the late twentieth century'. Likewise, Bob Jessop (2004) talks of governance occurring in the 'shadow of hierarchy'. In other words, although governments may set up new patterns of delivery where the state has a less central role, this is conducted within the remit of the state and with the state willing to re-impose control at times of crisis or political necessity. The clearest example of this is the case of Railtrack in Britain. The government privatized the rail industry in 1992 but, faced with poor services, rising prices and a number of rail accidents, the government then retook control of the track operating company, Railtrack. However, it seems increasingly to be a response of states when faced by economic crisis since Autumn 2008.

Georg Sorensen (2004: 5-8) rejects the idea that the state is in retreat but also importantly highlights how the notion of whether the state is in retreat or enhanced is a simplistic argument because it is based on zero-sum notions of state power. For Sorensen (2004: 6–7) we need to move away from

> a zero-sum game of 'winning' or 'losing' and instead accept a more theoretically open view of transformation. Starting from the idea of 'transformation' makes it possible to study the changes which states undergo, both in their internal make-up and in their relations with other actors, without making the false assumption that this is a game of only 'winning' or only 'losing'. It is a game of change, of transformation, which is almost always complex.

The point is not that the state is in retreat but that it is developing new forms of power which change the way it operates, how it affects citizens, and how it delivers policy. The foundations of the modern state are still in place but states are operating in new and diverse ways which create complex relationships with civil society.

## The partiality of the modern state

Modern states are based on an idea of the visibility of the state through the fact that it continually impacts on the lives of its citizens. Indeed, the notion of modern states as practically ubiquitous organizations may partly reflect their presentation by politicians and bureaucrats. However, the assumption of the all-powerful modern state may be overstated. Even in authoritarian states: 'The difficulty of maintaining the visibility at all times of the behaviour of all the subtests sets limits to the comprehensiveness of totalitarian power' (Wrong, 1988: 19). Equally (as we will see in Chapter 12) states have considerable spaces where they do not control what occurs; most obviously the criminal world but also issues of the black economy, people who leave their homes without trace, the treatment of abused children in families – the list is as long as can be imagined.

The point that Corbridge *et al.* (2005) make is that the absence of the state is not unusual, but the norm in developing societies. They demonstrate that in parts of India the state does not appear for many people. Where there is no welfare state, the poor often have little or no contact with the state. This problem is more acute, for example, in mountain areas of Pakistan where the state rarely, if ever, enters and consequently it is ruled by tribes who collect taxes, maintain law and order, deliver public goods and administer justice. Tasneem Siddiqui (2006: 173) points out that in Pakistan:

> If you go to low income areas, you can see that the state hardly exists there. From solid waste management to road maintenance to water supply to sewerage and street lights, nothing works. This is the state of affairs as far as low-income people are concerned. When conditions become unbearable, poor people organize themselves and try to solve some problems.

Even in developed societies it is possible, for example, to see that local parks in middle class areas receive more attention than those in the poorer parts of a city. However, whilst it may be the case that the poor in developing and developed countries may receive little in terms of public goods from the state, it is the case that in many states, except where the state has almost completely collapsed, the poor receive considerable attention from the state in terms of public order. For example, in Brazil the gaze of the state falls more on the poor than the rich. The wealthy in Brazil have little experience of the state, they have private health care, private education and often live in gated communities with private security. Apart from providing the legal framework, the state plays almost no role in the organization of gated communities. Indeed, as Atkinson and Blandy (2005: 182) demonstrate, governments have great difficulty in controlling gated communities. This means that state organizations are then focussed on maintaining social order (or perhaps more accurately containing social disorder) within the poor parts of a city such as Rio de Janeiro or Johannesburg (see Paes-Machado and Noronha, 2002).

The notion of private security raises a whole range of issues in relation to the power and role of the state (see White, 2009). However, two important points emerge from this discussion. The first is that, despite the arguments concerning sovereignty, the remit of the state is not comprehensive within a territory. There are sectors, areas and people who – even in well-developed states – have little direct contact with the state (although it is true that activities still take place within the context of a legal and moral framework determined and regulated by the state). Second, this leads to an important epistemological point: that experience of the state is in many ways subjective (Rudolph and Jacobsen, 2006: 343). How one person reacts to the state is different from another and so perceptions and experience of the state are different. In Britain black men are six times more likely to be stopped and searched by the police than whites and so their perception of the state is likely to be very different.

This notion that the state is experienced differently highlights the idea that states are always partial and variable institutions. This is reflected not just in how they are experienced but also in their capacities. Francis Fukuyama (2005: 12–13) suggests that some states have more capacity in some areas rather than in others:

> A country like Egypt, for example, has a very effective internal security apparatus and yet cannot execute simple tasks like processing visa applications ... Other countries like Mexico and Argentina have been relatively successful in reforming certain state institutions like central banking but less so at controlling fiscal policy or providing high quality public health or education.

The issue of capacity is in some ways oversimplified because it is linked to notions of legitimacy (Jackman, 1993) and to the size of the state and the range of its functions. To relate state capacity to function, legitimacy and size is understandable because it make capacity relatively easy to measure. Yet capacity is not about what states do or how much of it they do but really what impact they have. When they set out to do things, do they deliver the things they want to achieve? States may have legitimacy but still not achieve all their goals, or lack legitimacy and achieve their goals. Even within highly developed and well organized states they tend to limit what they intend to achieve. The United States maintains social order for the majority of people but many live in situations of considerable disorder. Over 1000 children under 18 are killed by guns in the United States every year and about 80 people a day die as a result of gun use. The issue is that it is not the existence of institutions, money, legitimacy and policy that matters, but the ability to control what happens. If a state spends billions of dollars on social security does the requisite amount of money go to those for whom it is intended? If social security policy becomes more complex and is related to goals of getting people back to work and reducing poverty, does it achieve its goals? As Scott (1998) has illustrated, the hubris of the modern state is the belief that it can improve people's lives, but consequently it has impacts that may make their lives worse. There is no doubt that states can do things but can they do the things they intend to do? How do they deliver intended public and selective goods? The argument hitherto is that the modern state had the mechanisms – the capacity – to deliver, but the development of globalization, new public management and changing demands of the people have undermined the modern state and we are seeing the development of *past*modern forms of the state which recognize the limits of the state and are more fragmented and flexible in the processes of delivery.

## Conclusion

Many authors from a range of different disciplines and sub-disciplines suggest a teleological development of the state from an authoritarian to modern to postmodern state. Marcelo Escolar (2003: 30) provides a useful summary:

> [T]he building of state power in the absolute states of Western Europe entailed five basic aspects: the institutional consolidation of a centralized political and administrative apparatus; the organization of bureaucracy and infrastructure within the territory ruled by the monarch; the projection and assessment of alternative strategies for the expansion of the state; the implementation of alternative offensive and defensive tactics launched from the territorial base; and the legitimization of the political rights of the people both within and beyond. Although these factors were formulated during the Renaissance and generally incorporated into the organization and style of state management during the seventeenth and eighteenth centuries, they were inherited by the democratic states which were to follow.

However, as we have seen, a range of factors have led to the suggestion that states have lost many of the features of modernity. The state has lost control over its boundaries, sovereignty has declined, bureaucracy has been replaced by other mechanisms of service delivery and the state's relationship with civil society has been transformed. However, the view of the modern state outlined by Escolar is an ideal type that little reflects what has occurred for the majority of states. Sovereignty was always limited, boundaries contested and bureaucracies partial in their effectiveness. States aspired to these features but rarely achieved them. Consequently, the arguments from governance and postmodernism about the decline of the state simply reflect a recognition that the empirical reality does not match the ideal rather than proving any real decline of state power (which may or may not have happened).

States are, in general, different now from what they were thirty or fifty years ago – it would be strange if they were not. The environment within which they operate has changed as a consequence of international and domestic economic change (whilst much attention has been paid to the impact of globalization, few writers focus on how domestic economic change has affected the state). In the twentieth century many states were concerned with promoting industrial development. With the decline of manufacturing and primary industries, states have in general moved away from a direct development role (see Castells, 1996; Hall and Soskice, 2001). The expectations and interests of citizens have changed, putting new demands on states. In the 1970s there was much discussion of overload with the suggestion that people were making too many unrealistic demands on the state in terms of resolving both personal and societal problems (see King, 1975; Birch, 1984). However, if anything, the demands of citizens are greater now than ever. In the period after the Second World War considerable numbers of people in Western Europe lived in poverty, they had poor housing and were recovering from the insecurities produced by the economic crises of the 1930s and the many insecurities of the Second World War. Consequently, their expectations of public services were low. In the twenty-first century many people live in decent housing and are very well clothed and fed and so when they confront run-down public services and standardized public goods they are disappointed. People have high expectations in the private sector and they are demanding similar levels of service in the public sector.

The point that Stones makes is extremely pertinent. The twenty-first century society and state (in the developed world) is built on modernity – it is 'past-modern' not postmodern. New mechanisms, techniques and ways of organizing do exist but they exist on the foundations of modernism. The beliefs in progress, rationality and truth which grew from the Enlightenment still exist. If anything, the modernist project is reaching its ultimate point with the 'end of nature' in sight (Giddens, 1995). Our world is still a modern world with a modern state but it is a different world to that which existed in the post-war era and and as a consequence states operate in new ways through a new set of mechanisms.

# Chapter 6

# Legitimacy, Authority and Bureaucracy

The core mechanisms of power of the modern state are the triad of legitimacy, bureaucracy and force. This chapter focuses on legitimacy and bureaucracy. Why people acquiesce to the state is one of the fundamental questions relating to the power of the state. Obedience to the state pivots around the question of whether there is legitimate authority (the liberal position) or whether it is authority backed by force (the Marxist position). In most developed states people obey state regulations, state officials and state direction without the use of force most of the time. If a traffic light is red we stop, we send our children to school and we don't steal from our neighbours. As Joel Migdal (2001: 252) reminds us:

> No matter how vaunted the bureaucracy, police, and military, officers of the state cannot stand on every corner ensuring that each person stop at the red light, drive on the right side of the road, cross at the crosswalk, refrain from stealing and drug dealing and so on.

States, in order to have stability, need to ensure that subjects obey without the presence or threat of force. Consequently, the issue of legitimacy and force resonates with the fundamental issues of liberal political theory from Hobbes onwards: the problem of order and the issue of how people can have security without continually being subject to force. It also relates to moral and philosophical questions that cut across political philosophy and religion.

The question of why we don't steal from our neighbours (or, as social psychologists phrase the question, why we follow orders to harm others) is answered in a number of ways. It could be that we are moral beings and therefore we see the consequences of stealing and so act in ways that are good. For rational choice theorists we are good because we fear the consequences of bad behaviour, be it prison or hell. For the sociological approach (or what Migdal calls the cultural approach), ranging from Goffman to Foucault, we are socialized into certain

109

patterns of behaviour and the social cost of breaking out of these norms is very high. What is crucial to states is that they have the ability to make laws that are obeyed without the use of force.

All states – whether democratic or non-democratic – make a claim to the legitimacy of their rule. The claim may be that the system is democratic and that there is a contract between the citizen and the state. Alternatively, the state has some access to a higher authority, be it God in the case of the divine right of kings, or the path to complete social harmony in the case of the Communist party. It may even be that the imposition of authoritarian or military government is necessary to sustain order. Legitimacy is central to states because it bestows a core resource of power: authority. A state without legitimacy can usually only have power through force, which is why imperial powers or dictatorships are often so brutal. Illegitimate power does not have authority and is often an ineffective form of power (Hall, 1994: xi). Therefore, as Rousseau noted, no state is strong enough to survive solely through force and hence has to convert the force into obedience (Poggi, 2006: 93). As Migdal (2001: 52) claims:

> The most potent factor determining the strength of the state, legitimacy is more inclusive than either compliance or participation. Legitimacy involves an acceptance of the state's rules of the game, its social control, as true and right. It means the acceptance of the social order associated with the idea of the state as people's own system of meaning.

Modern states provide a unique combination of legitimacy and bureaucracy, allowing them to develop infrastructural power and so control societies without an overt and constant dependence on violence (see Schroeder, 2006: 4). Legitimacy and bureaucracy are intimately connected because through bureaucracy the state can authoritatively distribute resources and order society, which if combined with legitimacy, can be done without constant recourse to force. This makes for more effective governance and in principle reaffirms the legitimacy of the system. However, the process of legitimization is often based on a series of myths such as ideas of nation or sovereignty residing with the people.

This chapter is concerned with how legitimacy and bureaucracy provide the foundation of the power of the modern state. However, the key question is whether consent, or legitimacy, is based on an acceptance of the right of the state to rule or whether it is dependent on the state's ability to exercise force, or to manufacture consent, and to do this through establishing an essentially mythical legitimacy.

## Legitimacy and the liberal state

The power of the state within liberal theory is based on the idea of legitimacy. People obey government because it is legitimate and therefore has the authority to issue orders or laws. This conception of power goes back to Hobbes and Locke and the notion that government is based on a contract with the people (although Hobbes and Locke saw this contract in very different ways). For Hobbes the sovereign has absolute power but that power is legitimate because it comes from an authority based on consent. The people surrender their right of self government to a single authority who then has the legitimacy to rule on their behalf (Held, 1996: 77). Without consent, the state is operating with pure power and not legitimate authority (Riley, 1973). For Locke (2002 [1752]) it is also the case that people can choose to submit to the authority of the state but, more importantly, in terms of maintaining legitimacy, there has to be consent. Legitimacy is then based on consent which results in a need to develop democratic elements within the polity.

Within the liberal definition of legitimacy and authority although consent is central (if only pragmatic: Held, 1996: 249), it is not always necessary. Often politicians talk of the need to make the right decision (for example, to go to war without overwhelming public support) and they then appeal to process and the national interest as mechanisms for legitimizing decisions where consent is absent. Politicians will frequently invoke the need to make unpopular decisions. Consent is not necessary for particular decisions but in order to underpin the system. It is the process of elections and decision making that is given consent and so politicians will appeal to the constitution or the parliamentary process as mechanisms that support decisions that do not have popular support. It is ironic that so often when there are indications of dissent through riots or strikes, states often see this as giving the state legitimacy to reassert authority (Hall, 1994: 30). This was certainly an important argument for the dictatorships of Chile and Argentina. They had the right to suspend the democratic order because the degree of social unrest legitimized the need for firm authority (but which was in fact force) (Pereira, 2005). Much of the liberal appeal to authority depends on the notion that it is consensual and legitimate. Yet in many states authority may be based on other claims, whether they be religious, monarchical or technocratic, or, in communist systems, a claim to a higher knowledge that is not available to the mass of people (this is the Wizard of Oz view of authority, an authority based on supreme knowledge which of course is unveiled as a sham). Such a notion of authority is strong in systems based on the cult of the personality where the leader is presented as having a superior understanding of the world – the legitimacy of the system is based solely on the authority of the leader. This is a form of what Max Weber calls charismatic authority: 'resting on a devotion to the exceptional sanctity, heroism or exemplary character of an individual person' (Weber, 1978: 215).

In liberal systems authority is often not based on consent, or the leader, but on the legitimacy of the procedures for appointing leaders and making legislation. For David Beetham (1991) legitimacy is linked to the existence of clear sets of rules that are related to shared beliefs and some degree of consent. In the British system much is still made of the fact that in order to become Prime Minister a party leader has to go to the Queen and be asked to form her government. A crucial element in liberal and conservative theory is the 'rule of law'. As the Conservative legal theorist Lord Hailsham argued, the rule of law is as real as the table of the House of Commons (Hailsham, 1947). In other words, the law has such authority that it has to be obeyed and the law is legitimate because it is ratified by a set of procedures. Political leaders often appeal to external sources in order to claim legitimacy and this legitimacy confers authority.

The notion of legitimacy is central in both democratic elitist and pluralist theory. For democratic elitists government may be remote and exclusive but elites need approval (through elections) in order to rule legitimately (Held, 1996: 168). Pluralists are much more sceptical about the idea of elite rule and therefore believe that states have to be constrained through the need to satisfy the range of interests within a society. Therefore the state is legitimate in the sense that it reconciles the interests of various groups and, perhaps more importantly, consent is illustrated by the absence of political dissent (see Dahl, 1961).

For Weber it is legitimacy and bureaucracy that are the defining feature of the modern state and the source of its extensive power. Weber in his analysis of the modern state sees government in the modern state based on its ability to assert binding authority. Again, as Beetham (1991) argues, legitimacy makes it possible for the dominant groups to rule and limits their power by binding it through a set of rules. In other words, legitimacy acts in two ways.

Nevertheless, religious, rational choice, institutional and cultural explanations of authority actually rest on the notion that obedience to authority, like the Marxist approach, is actually a legitimacy based on some external constraint or threat. For religious notions it is a fear of God, for rational choice it is because there are incentives for good behaviour, and for institutional/cultural explanations there are rules and norms that have consequence if broken. In this sense, it is unclear what authority is other than legitimate force (which of course, as we will discuss below, it may be).

However, authority as a mechanism for rule is often viewed as more than applying legitimacy to mechanisms of coercion. For Weber (1978: 31), there is something intrinsic to authority:

Action, especially social action which involves a social relationship, may be guided by the belief in the existence of a legitimate order. The problem that the action will be so governed will be called the 'validity' of the order in question.

As Weber (1978: 36) points out, people do not always follow rules because of custom or self-interest but because an order has validity. Weber sees the basis of legitimacy as having four distinct sources:

- tradition – something is valid because it always has been;
- affectual, which is emotional;
- value rational in terms of coming from an absolute belief;
- positive enactment which is legal either through voluntary agreement or imposed by a legitimate authority.

For Weber (1978: 215) the principal form of authority in the modern state is rational 'resting on a belief of the legality of enacted rules and the right of those elevated to authority under such rules to issue commands (legal authority)'. Where there is legal authority obedience is to the established order and to the person who is in a position of authority, not to the person *per se* (which is often the case with traditional authority or charismatic authority). For Weber the purest form of this legal authority exists within a bureaucratic organization where someone has authority as a consequence of position and others in the organization follow legitimate orders. As Migdal (2001) highlights, this presumes a unified state which is separate from society, whereas the reality may be that the process of transmitting authority is replete with conflicts. Weber is creating ideal types and in reality authority often does not translate into people following orders, as the literature on street level bureaucracy demonstrates; people do not simply take on the decision of their superiors. Legitimacy, and therefore power, is partial and continually contested.

Authority and legitimacy are obviously closely related but they are not the same. Authority is often backed by coercion. However, if an authoritative figure has complete legitimacy there is no need for coercion. For example, if a person chooses to join the Catholic church and this decision is made in later life, she is not joining because of the way she was brought up (it is not traditional authority) but because she has read the Bible and accepts the Catholic church as the one true church. Consequently, she submits to the church's rules and the authority of priests because she believes it is legitimate. The legitimacy is, as Weber and Locke suggest, based on consent. There is no coercion backing the authority but agreement and it would be possible to leave the Catholic church and join another if there were threats of coercion. In this sense legitimacy enables authority without force. It is in Beetham's sense power exercised within a set of rules.

The crucial question is: are the mechanisms of legitimacy real or are they just means of justifying authority? For example, the priest's authority comes from being God's representative on earth. If there is no God then that legitimacy is in reality mythical. In the famous Milgram experiments (Milgram, 1974) the subjects were prepared to administer electric shocks to other subjects when asked to by an authority figure, even though there was no coercion. Stanley Milgram illustrates how easily people succumb to authority and are ready to comply even if the authority figure has no legitimacy.

This of course raises the issue that has received considerable attention from social psychologists: why do people obey rules even when these rules may be about committing immoral acts? From a social psychology perspective the response to authority is in many ways automatic and not a reference to a conscious fear of punishment for not obeying. For some it is a consequence of our moral framework, and the existence of alternative moral frameworks explains why some disobey orders and others do not (Tyler, 1990). It is remarkable, for example, how hidden camera television programmes can achieve strange behaviour from members of the public if they are directed to act by someone in a uniform. Charles Helm and Mario Morelli (1979: 321) point out: 'Milgram reasoned, and with some force, that if an experimental scientist, with no coercive threat lurking, could achieve this degree of compliance, just imagine the degree of control it implied for the state'. For Bauman (1989) Milgram demonstrates how ordinary people can be driven to extraordinary acts by authority. Helm and Morelli (1979: 324–5) suggest that Milgram sees 'obedience as the reflection of a psychological mechanism whereby the individual slips into an 'agentic state' viewing himself as the mere instrument of authority and lacking any responsibility for the acts he performs'. The point is that Milgram sees the individual as subject to authority acting almost as an automaton and without moral autonomy. The problem from this perspective is not so much the nature of the authority but the nature of human beings; obedience occurs in the face of hierarchy. This perspective reveals the weakness of the liberal position. People do not obey because contracts create legitimacy, but because authority structures create obedience. Consequently, authority may be founded on fear, force and hierarchy rather than contract, and it becomes a very effective form of power in the modern state when combined with bureaucracy.

## The modern state: bureaucracy, authority and force

Weber, whose analysis of the modern state continues to have considerable relevance, saw the power of the modern state resting on authoritative allocations of resources. The key foundations of the authoritative allocation are bureaucracy and the monopoly of legitimate violence. The issue of force and violence is dealt with in Chapter 7, but as we have seen above, it is difficult to understand authority without some reference to force – or at least some form of sanction. What is interesting and important about bureaucracy is that it is in many ways the key source of power of the modern state. It is bureaucracy that enables the state to intervene in society in ways unavailable to non-bureaucratic organizations. For example, an organization that relies on force can only have power as far as it can extend its force. An organization that depends on charismatic leadership is only successful as far as people accept the charisma and belief in its leader. For all the sanctions and authority and resources of the Catholic church, it has no sanctions over my behaviour if I choose not to believe in its doctrines (although this is not of course the case in countries where the Catholic church has considerable influence over the state). Developing an effective bureaucracy depends on both authority and coercion. Bureaucracy embodies this complex relationship between authority and force because, whilst bureaucracy is based on authoritative and binding rules, the rules are authoritative in that they derive from due process – which may be democratic or may not – and they are binding in the sense that if someone does not obey them, there will be sanctions. Bureaucracy almost never relies completely on authority – it is always authority backed with force. Yet it is difficult to conceive of effective bureaucracy without some conception of authority – the hierarchical chain in bureaucracy functions because subordinates accept the decisions of their superiors and continue to pass a decision down the bureaucratic chain.

Bureaucratic power is directed at two sets of agents. One is the people within the bureaucracy and the other is the subjects outside of the state who are the targets of the authoritative actions. In terms of those within the bureaucracy, Weber pointed out that bureaucracy works on the basis of hierarchy and subordination. However, modern bureaucracies face considerable tensions between the need to have subordination and the need to have people with the professional skills to make autonomous decisions within a particular situation. Moreover, increasingly decision making and policy implementation occurs across various state and often non-state agencies, meaning that the 'subordinates' may be working to different organizational logics or cultures to those who are the decision makers. The new right's critique of bureaucracy recognizes its failure to maintain legitimacy. Consequently, as we will see in Chapter 8, states are increasingly trying to develop mechanisms which enable the policy makers to control those on the ground to deliver policy in more indirect ways. Geddes *et al.* (2007) provide the example of police officers who, when presented with policy initiatives from superiors have considerable discretion in terms of implementing these decisions on the ground. Police officers can be sceptical about the knowledge and authority of those above them and therefore make their own decisions about how to treat particular incidents within their beats.

Whilst acknowledging the problems and limits of bureaucracy there is little doubt that bureaucracy is a central feature of modern states. Much of the current debate on governance suggests that the key features of bureaucratic organizations are being undermined. Rather than decisions being delivered through hierarchical line bureaucracies, we are seeing a fragmentation of the state with policy being made through decentralized and delayered organizations based on networks of partnerships rather than hierarchies. As Rod Rhodes (1997: 54) maintains, reforms in public services have led to 'experiments with new ways of delivering services [that] split up the old departmental bureau-cracies of central and local government'. However, in this claim two different arguments are being run together. One is the notion that the state no longer controls the delivery of all public goods and increas-ingly these goods are being delivered by an array of public, private and voluntary actors; and the second is that bureaucracy is therefore less important. However, the second does not follow from the first.

Whilst it may be true that policy making and delivery in some polit-ical systems is more fragmented, it is not true that bureaucracy is less important in modern societies. We may have a vast array of choice over who supplies our telephones but they are all bureaucratic organiza-tions. It may be that care for the elderly is being delivered through part-nerships of organizations and that they are organized as a network. Nevertheless, all of these organizations are bureaucracies that work together to deliver public services. It is impossible to operate in modern-day life without encountering a myriad of bureaucracies. What seems to have changed is the position of the state as the monop-oly bureaucracy. Today many private companies are massive bureau-cracies delivering a complex variety of services. If we consider companies like Tesco or WalMart they deliver services ranging from loans to insurance, to home delivery, to web-based shopping.

Consequently, despite the changes in the state and the ways goods are delivered, it is impossible to conceive of modern society without bureaucracy, and so bureaucratic power remains a central feature of the state in the twenty-first century. Despite the evidence of Michael Lipsky (1980), bureaucracy limits the bounds of discretion for the delivery and therefore ensures the standardized production of services. Because bureaucracy is based on authority rather than force, it extends the range of state power by building relationships of consent and accommodation.

It is this unique combination of legitimacy and bureaucratic institu-tions that provides modern states with considerable capacity (Jackman, 1993). Force is expensive and often ineffective as the situa-tion in Iraq illustrates; a powerful army has considerable problems if it lacks legitimacy. Bureaucratic organizations that can operate without force enable states to obtain both information and control over a vast array of people. By cooperating with state bureaucratic procedures we enable the state to affect our behaviour.

But for bureaucracy to work there has to be a degree of legitimacy and compliance by citizens. In 1990 the British Conservative government introduced a local taxation system based on a payment for every adult member of society. The tax bore very little relation to ability to pay, with those on high incomes paying the same as those on low incomes, and many people saw a considerable increase in their local tax bill. The consequence was a relatively large-scale non-payment campaign which made the collection of the tax complex and expensive, and eventually it was abandoned (Butler *et al.*, 1994). As a former government minister has admitted, when a number of people had considerable mobility, 'it was almost impossible to trace them and implement the system' (BBC, 2003). Many people simply stopped registering to vote and so could not be traced. Where people could be identified, local authorities had to take people to court to make them pay and *in extremis* they would be imprisoned for non-payment – which of course makes the collection costs greater than the tax.

This example illustrates the point made by Migdal that state and society cannot be easily divided. For the state to work effectively it needs the cooperation of society, highlighting the centrality of legitimacy to modern state power. As Robert Jackman (1993: 40) reminds us: 'A set of political institutions is legitimate to the extent that most citizens have a predisposition to regard compliance with the officers of those institutions as appropriate and reasonable'. Of course this conception of the relationship between legitimacy and bureaucracy is based on a liberal notion of legitimacy and many radical critics would argue that whilst consent is clearly an effective mechanism of elite rule, it is a manufactured consent that is representative of power rather than agreement.

The problem with liberal theory going back to Hobbes is that it equates legitimacy with justice or normatively good rule. The sense is that if a state has legitimacy then it in some ways has the support of the population. There is, as Jeffrey Friedman (1990: 62) points out, an ambiguity in legitimacy:

> To introduce the idea of legitimate power as a way of explaining the fact that X obeys Y sometimes means that X obeys because he regards Y as legitimately in command; but at other times it means that Y gets X to obey by exercising coercive power although the use of coercion is regarded as legitimate.

Liberal theory finds it difficult to separate legitimacy and coercion; a point that has been developed by a number of critics of liberal approaches to power.

## The problem of authority

Authority and legitimacy are difficult concepts in terms of power. They are often used by political theorists and political leaders to justify the use of state power to achieve specific goals. For instance, Tony Blair and George Bush justified the Iraq war on the grounds that the war was legitimate and put considerable effort into justifying its legitimacy by saying that they were establishing democracy in Iraq. Bush claimed in a speech:

> One of the hallmarks of a free society and what makes our country strong is that our political leaders can discuss their differences openly, even in times of war. When I made the decision to remove Saddam Hussein from power, Congress approved it with strong bipartisan support. I also recognize that some of our fellow citizens and elected officials didn't support the liberation of Iraq. And that is their right, and I respect it. As President and Commander-in-Chief, I accept the responsibilities, and the criticisms, and the consequences that come with such a solemn decision. While it's perfectly legitimate to criticize my decision or the conduct of the war, it is deeply irresponsible to rewrite the history of how that war began.

A range of writers including Karl Marx, Antonio Gramsci, C Wright Mills, Steven Lukes and Herbert Marcuse have attempted to demonstrate that consent is not a result of agreement but rather signifies acquiescence, or is manufactured. Authority is not legitimate government but a mechanism for legitimizing force. It is a form of normative power, or an example of the third dimension of power. Liberal theorists in a sense accept the assumption of contract theory: if there is a mechanism for consent then the rulers have legitimacy and so they have a right to exercise authority. However, the key question is not whether the mechanism for consent exists but the effectiveness of that mechanism. It is an empirical rather than normative question whether consent is real (and it cannot be assumed, as it is by pluralists and rational choice theorists). One of the key mechanisms for states and other powerful organizations to exercise power is through co-option (see Saward, 1990). Effectively, states create mechanisms of consent – elections, processes of consultation, formal and informal networks – which means that there is a process of consultation, but the impact of these mechanisms on the final outcome is questionable. It effectively legitimizes the final decisions but it does not mean that those outside the elite have power. What the voluminous literature of policy networks demonstrates is that interests are involved in decision making when they accept the rules of the game (Marsh and Rhodes, 1992a; Smith, 1993). As Michael Saward (1990: 62) points out: 'In turn, in the right circumstances, this can increase the general perception of government legitimacy, since widely salient views are *seen* to be taken into account' (emphasis in original).

Migdal (2001: 16) argues that the state is shaped by image and practice: 'the image of the state is of a dominant, integrated, autonomous entity that controls, in a given territory, all rule making, either directly through its own agencies or indirectly by sanctioning other authorised organisations – business, families, clubs and the like to make certain circumscribed rules'. Central to this image is the notion of legitimacy and the idea that the state in some way above any other organization represents the people (Migdal, 2001: 17) which of course is central to legitimacy. States, however self-interested or kleptocratic, present themselves as representing all the community and the nation (which is why nationalism is such an important element in legitimacy and authority). Because the state does not really exist as a unified and bounded organization it needs myths to enable it to create an impression of unity and separation from society.

The problem is that the sources of legitimacy, for example, the French revolution or the ideology of Marxism, are myths for justifying power rather than sources of normative agreement amongst people. National myths legitimize state power rather than build real consent between people and so these myths are about creating a liberal sense of legitimacy; the absence of any explicit opposition to the political system.

Acquiescence may then be an indication of power (force), not legitimacy. Steven Lukes (1974) and John Gaventa (1980) point out that pluralists assume that the lack of expressed grievances assumes agreement or consensus. The assumption of pluralism is that if people have grievances they can express them and if there is sufficient dissatisfaction people will either form groups to lobby government or vote out the existing parties. However, as many have demonstrated, from Marxist (Miliband, 1969) to rational choice (Olson, 1965) perspectives, there are considerable barriers to the poor and weaker groups in society organizing, and therefore the lack of expression of dissent is not an indication of consensus but of a lack of power. As Gaventa (1980: 19) argues:

Through the invocation of myths or symbols, the use of threat or rumours, or other mechanisms of power, the powerful may be able to ensure that certain beliefs and actions emerge in one context while apparently contradictory grievances may be expressed in others. From this perspective, a consistently expressed consensus is not required for the maintenance of dominant interests, only a consistency that certain potentially key issues remain latent issues and that certain interests remain unrecognized.

Gaventa then illustrates how the miners in the Appalachian region of the US, despite being poor in a relatively wealthy region, have not expressed their dissatisfaction with the system. Gaventa demonstrates the complex ways in which institutions and symbols work 'against the powerless to the benefit of the powerful' (Gaventa, 1980: 254).

The way that myths reinforce legitimacy can be illustrated within political systems, not just communities. If we look at three modern states, Britain, France and the United States, each has a distinctive 'governing myth' which is the mechanism for legitimizing elite rule by essentially presenting it not as elite rule. These are what Richard Merelman (2003: 9) calls, 'a legitimising discourse' which 'is any body of ideas, images, or practices that portrays a political regime to be functioning as its power holders claim it to be functioning, and in doing, provides support to those who exert power in the regime'. In these three countries the myths suggest a democratic political process which in effect legitimizes the rule of an elite. In Britain the myth is the notion of the Westminster model or, more particularly, parliamentary sovereignty. This myth, which has existed since the nineteenth century, explicitly promotes elite rule but legitimizes it through the notion of accountability. The Westminster model is based on the assumption that Parliament is sovereign and therefore decisions should be made within Parliament – with other arenas of power such as local government deriving their authority and legitimacy from Parliament. It is MPs and the Cabinet who make decisions. Democracy is not about participation but about accountability and so exercised *post hoc*. Ministers make decisions but are accountable to MPs and to voters for their decisions. If a minister makes the wrong decision s/he should resign. If government performs poorly then the electorate will vote them out. Ministers in the House of Commons and in the media continually refer to Parliament as the basis of their legitimacy. However, the model is a myth, not a reflection of reality. Ministers rarely resign because of their responsibility for actions, the House of Commons is not an effective

mechanism for holding ministers to account, party discipline undermines the mechanisms for accountability (Judge, 1993) and so what is
supposed to be a system for controlling elite power is in reality a mechanism for sustaining it.

In France the governing myth is the notion of republicanism. French
republicanism is legitimized by the symbolism of the French revolution
which continues to be part of French political life. In France the state
operates through a Rousseauian concept of the general interest with
the role of the state being to guard against individual and group interests and so safeguard the interests of the nation (Saurugger, 2007). As
Sabine Saurugger points out (2007: 389): 'elected representatives stand
for all citizens and not only the interests of a limited territory or specific
group, as it is forbidden for MPs to constitute interest groups or to
become advocates in the assembly'. Government decisions are seen as
being in the general not private interest. As a consequence, the state in
principle rejects legitimate access for interest groups to the state and
emphasizes the secular nature of the Republic and its representation of
all French citizens as identical. Through the legitimation of republicanism the French state identifies its actions as those of the nation as a
whole, and the actions of opponents as illegitimate and as representing
private interests. The mythical element of republicanism is highlighted
in France in relation to the issue of race relations. France uses the myth
of republicanism to suggest it treats all citizens equally and integrates
them into French society. As Jon Henley (2004) highlights, this in fact
hides the failure of integration:

> For the most sacred article in all France's grand republican and secu-
> lar creed is the principle that everyone is equal and indistinguishable
> in the eyes of the state: no matter where they come from, all French
> citizens are identical in their Frenchness. In the much-vaunted
> 'Republican model of integration', all immigrants go through the
> Gallic mill, shedding their ethnic and religious differences and
> emerging as shining new French citizens. In theory. In practice, this
> explains why France cannot say, and does not know, how many citi-
> zens it has who are of north African origin, or who are Muslim, or
> who are Jewish. For the purposes of the Republic, it simply does not
> matter. It explains too why France does not know how many chil-
> dren of its north African immigrants leave school without useful
> qualifications, or fail to get a job.

In the United States the legitimizing myth is the notion of pluralism –

or what is known more colloquially as the 'American Dream'. The political system in the US is built on the notion that it is the most democratic system in the world and that anyone from whatever background can get to be President (something that both Sarah Palin and Barack Obama have claimed). Merelman (2003: 18-19) demonstrates that core features of pluralism – that power is distributed in competing power centres, that political leaders are coalition builders, that policy making is reactive and that the outcome is gradual reform – provide the legitimizing discourse for politicians, just as republicanism in France and the Westminster model in Britain are used to justify the actions of politicians in these countries. Likewise, these features seem to be mythical in that consensus was assumed but the reality was considerable political conflict and the exclusion of key groups – such as blacks – from the political process. In the contested 2000 election between Al Gore and George Bush it has been suggested that some black voters were prevented from voting in Florida by having their names removed from the register as felons (Rakove, 2001). Thomas Frank (2004) has argued that the strength of this myth has enabled the Republican party to maintain a large working class vote despite the fact that Republican policy rarely favours their interests.

John Hall (1994: x) argues that consent can allow societies to coerce more and the Marxist view is that legitimacy is a mechanism to validate the essentially coercive nature of the state. Notions of authority and legitimacy within democratic systems are based on pluralist assumptions that society is based on consent (Migdal, 2001). The point of a range of writers is that the consent is not a natural outcome of agreement with the system but is manufactured (see Marcuse, 1964).

Herbert Marcuse developed perhaps the most comprehensive account of the way in which consent is manufactured in modern society. He (1964: 11) maintains:

> Technical progress, extended to a whole system of domination and coordination, creates forms of life (and of power) which appear to reconcile the forces opposing the system and to defeat or refute all protest in the name of the historical prospects of freedom from toil and domination.

For Marcuse modern capitalism uses material security as a mechanism for undermining people's political consciousness and therefore prevents any systematic challenge to the existing state system:

The distinguishing feature of advanced industrial society is its effective suffocation of those needs which demand liberation – liberation also from that which is tolerable and rewarding and comfortable – while it sustains and absolves the destructive power and repressive function of the affluent society. Here, the social controls exact the overwhelming need for the production and consumption of waste; the need for stupefying work where it is no longer a real necessity; the need for modes of relaxation which soothe and prolong this stupefaction; the need for maintaining such deceptive liberties as free competition at administered prices, a free press which censors itself, free choice between brands and gadgets.

He suggests (1965: 140) that:

Materially as well as ideologically, the very classes which were once the absolute negation of the capitalist system are now more and more integrated into it.

For Marcuse, the market and the media become the mechanisms for creating false needs in humans which means they desire material comfort above liberation (Amidon, 2000).

## Nationalism and legitimacy

From both a liberal and radical perspective, it is clear that legitimacy is an important mechanism for state power. It extends the range of the state and is much more effective and efficient than force. States are engaged in a process of continually reproducing legitimacy. As Jackman (1993: 98) highlights, states need to be involved in a never-ending process of manufacturing and reproducing the symbols of legitimacy. The combination of myths and the manufacturing of consent are illustrated in the greatest of all legitimizing mythologies for the state – nationalism. Nationalism is based on the idea that a state has a people who can or cannot grant legitimacy to the rulers but who can be ruled by the state (for example, much modern politics is about a clash of nationalities – can the British nation rule over the Scottish nation, or the Spanish state rule over the Catalan nation?). As Migdal (2001: 250) states: 'National ideologies create master narratives that may well be dealing with issues such as the consolidation of power or the collective expression of identity.' Nationalism legitimizes many aspects of the modern state: the idea that people belong to a territory; that the state has sovereignty within the territory; that the state is the representative of the people; and that there are borders to the state. Nationalism is a core symbol in tying people into the state by creating a relationship between an individual and a state – a person is French and it is the French state – the state is legitimate because it represents French people. Nationalism enables states to express authority over a particular region and then, with sovereignty, nationalism effectively justifies why the state has control over a particular part of the earth. All those people within that part, whether or not they have been bound by a Hobbesian contract, have little choice but to submit to its authority.

## Fear, trust and authority

The Milgram experiment, and much of the debate on authority, locates authority in trust. We obey because we trust the people making the decision. In the Milgram experiments the volunteers were faced with an experimenter in a white coat which signified authority. We are often prepared to obey people because we trust what they are saying. If a doctor says we need an operation we do it on the basis of trust. If a police officer says we can't go down a road we trust the grounds on which that decision has been made. This form of trust is important in modern states because many decisions are presented as technocratic and we are expected to follow the advice of experts. However, there is now a long acknowledged decline in deference, and significant evidence of a decline in trust which could undermine claims to authority.

Marc Hetherington (1998), for instance, argues that in the United States there has been a steady decline in trust in politicians and this decline in trust makes it difficult for political leaders to achieve their desired outcomes. Moreover, it is not just politicians who have suffered from a decline in trust but scientists as well. Issues such as genetically modified food, nuclear power and a range of food scares have led to increased scepticism about science and scientists (see Slovic, Flynn and Layman, 1991; Lee, Scheufele, and Lewenstein, 2005). The absence or existence of trust is seen as important in terms of the debate on social capital. For those working within a framework of rational choice, trust is an important mechanism for ensuring collective action. Trust is a mechanism for overcoming the prisoner's dilemma. If there is trust between the actors then they can cooperate knowing that others in the game will not defect. Moreover, there seems to be evidence that trust between people in a community (social capital) leads to higher levels of participation and more trust in politicians (Newton, 2001; 2006). Consequently, a decline in trust would seem to have important consequences for political authority.

This then leads to an argument (which is discussed more fully in Chapter 7) which suggests that states are increasingly using fear as a mechanism for re-establishing authority. For instance, Adam Curtis has argued that the idea of an international terror network has been created in order to develop a climate of fear, and he argues 'that no-one questions the illusion is because this nightmare enemy gives so many groups new power and influence in a cynical age – and not just politicians' (BBC, 2005). Again this illustrates the complexity of a notion of authority based on legitimacy when the roots of authority are complex. Authority could in a sense be a means of ensuring illegitimate rule. Fear and trust are ways of ensuring obedience. People have fears and trust authority to deal with them. Little attention is paid to the role of states in developing fear. For example, fear of immigrants (and particular immigrants) is used by governments to legitimize restrictions on immigration.

## Conclusion

The basis of power of modern states is bureaucracy and legitimacy. In many ways it is these elements that distinguish modern states from pre-modern states. Pre-modern states may have traditional authority based on God or inheritance, or both, but they usually lack bureaucracy. The combination of legitimacy and bureaucracy creates a significant expansion in state capability because power becomes intensive and is based on a considerable resource base. States with bureaucracy can obtain both information and resources. With legitimacy they are able to use this information and resources to order societies which are delimited through an appeal to nationalism. Legitimacy and bureaucracy create a direct control over outcomes. People, in principle, obey bureaucratic rules because they are legitimate.

There is little doubt that consent or legitimacy is an extremely effective mechanism for enabling states to act. Legitimacy blurs the line between state and society so that the population – as Foucault suggests – become implicated in ruling themselves. We tend to obey laws and respond to state requests for information, pay our taxes and obey police officers. If we do not, state rule breaks down. States without legitimacy either have a tremendous security apparatus or they fail. Thus the debate between liberals and radicals is not over the importance of legitimacy but whether it is based on consent or is manufactured.

Of course, in many ways this is a false divide. Legitimacy, whatever its nature, has to be won. States have to make concessions, co-opt and have structures for participation if they are to gain legitimacy. Winning consent and manufacturing consent are effectively equivalent. States may win legitimacy by meeting demands, suppressing dissent, or by having mechanisms for participation. If these fail then states have to have recourse to violence and so in all political systems legitimacy is always backed by force and it is the role of force in modern states which we examine in the next chapter. Legitimacy also highlights the partiality of state power. Legitimacy is a central resource for state power but legitimacy has to be gained or manufactured, hence illustrating the interdependence between state actors and civil society. Legitimacy requires state actors to operate within certain rules and to persuade citizens to support the state. As a consequence, states pay considerable attention to how they exercise power. For example, the decision to go to war in Iraq without the support of large sections of the population had considerable impact on the legitimacy of both Tony Blair and George Bush. Because they lost legitimacy, there were strong constraints on their options in the final years of both administrations. Legitimacy consequently provides states with a considerable mechanism for influencing citizens but it is always constrained by its tenuous nature. Similarly, bureaucracy has to be supported by either legitimacy or force so that people obey the rules that are transmitted by the bureaucratic machinery. Both bureaucracy and legitimacy present the state as a collective institution – they support the myth of the unified state exercising power on society as a whole; the basis of bureaucracy in democratic society is that rules apply equally. However, legitimacy and bureaucracy are easy to subvert. In neither case do they provide the state with direct control over citizens and therefore whilst states may legitimately pass laws and use bureaucracies to implement them, the outcomes are often not what state actors intended. Many of the forms of power that we discuss later in the book are intended to prevent these subversions of state intentions.

# Chapter 7

# Force and Terror

In traditional discussions of state power, power is based on legitimacy and coercion. Coercion is exercised in a way that is intended to be legitimate but undoubtedly states have considerable recourse to forms of violence. To oversimplify, there are two broad approaches to the role of force in states. What may be called the liberal view, developed from the work of Hobbes and Locke, sees the state as based on an implicit contract between citizen and state and in this case force is used to protect the citizen from those who do not maintain the terms of the contract. From a Hobbesian perspective a strong state is a mechanism for protecting citizens from each other. In the liberal perspective, people have the right to property, life and liberty and the state is justified in using force against those who threaten those rights. The liberal democratic view sees the state as restrained by democratic procedures and force is used as a mechanism for controlling deviants and not 'law abiding citizens'.

Alternatively, the critical perspective, which covers a range of different empirical and theoretical positions, sees the state as a concentration of power which may use democracy or hegemony to legitimize its power but, if the surface of the legitimacy is scratched, the full force of the state is revealed. Whilst the state may appear to be a democratic mechanism in Western liberal democracies, it is one backed by significant force – as Weber recognized, the state has a monopoly of legitimate violence. For liberals there is an important difference between totalitarian, or authoritarian, regimes and democratic regimes. In authoritarian regimes force is central to the capabilities of the state but in democratic regimes it is used as a last resort in order to protect citizens and the democratic process (and within the legitimate rules). For critical thinkers, all states will resort to violence but democratic regimes, in order to maintain legitimacy, attempt to restrict the use of violence to particular circumstances.

Peter Baldwin (2003: 106) argues that modern states no longer rely on force because, 'The modern state no longer instructs, commands and punishes. It eructates, informs, persuades and discourages' (a theme returned to in later chapters). Anthony Giddens (1985: 295) argues that 'Totalitarianism ... is a tendential property of the modern state' and moreover no modern state is immune from the potential of totalitarianism. Like Zygmunt Bauman, Giddens sees totalitarianism as being bound up in the nature of state power within modernity. This chapter will examine how force and terror is used by states and suggests that whilst force and terror are central to authoritarian regimes, liberal states, despite the emphasis on persuasion, continue to use force as a mechanism of power. It will examine the case of the shoot-to-kill policies in Northern Ireland and Spain to illustrate how the sorts of terror tactics used in authoritarian regimes can be drawn on in particular cases in liberal democracies.

## Force and terror in authoritarian regimes

Authoritarian (and what are sometimes called totalitarian regimes) are defined by the fact that force and terror is essential to their being. Often these regimes have limited legitimacy, but there are authoritarian governments which have had considerable popular support as Hitler did at the end of the 1930s and Stalin did following the Second World War. Alan Bullock (1991: 998–9) demonstrates:

> Victory in the greatest of all Russia's wars marked the critical point in the relationship between Stalin and the Russian people ... As the Russian Armies freed their country of the German invaders, all the powerful emotions of traditional Russian patriotism, magnified by the losses and the suffering, were focused on the heroic figure of Stalin.

Yet this legitimacy can often be short-lived, as Bullock argues was the case for Stalin. Richard Overy (2004: 98), on the other hand, maintains that Stalin had a high level of support until his death, and it was only Khrushchev's secret speech in 1956 that started to undermine Stalin's mythical authority. Nevertheless, by their very nature authoritarian regimes are not based on consensus (although some, such as Mexico until 2000, do have a complex process of co-option) and so they do not have the support of a significant part of the nation. Consequently, authoritarian regimes are dependent on force for the delivery of public goods. The authority of the state is not based on widespread legitimacy but on pure physical power. At certain times force, which can be fairly regularised and bureaucratized, descends into terror when it is used beyond any formal, or legitimate, mechanisms and in many cases without any real control.

The role of force and terror in authoritarian regimes is justified through an ontological distinction between liberal and authoritarian conceptions of the self. The modern liberal state to some degree was built on the establishment of the individual. Much liberal thought is thus concerned with the relationship between the state and the individual. In authoritarian regimes the individual only exists in relation to a wider organizational structure, whether it is state, nation or class. There is no sovereign self. For Marxists, the use of revolutionary state force against the individual was legitimate on the grounds that it was focussed on achieving the class interests of the working classes. For Trotksy (1938), the means are subordinated to the end, and if the end is moral then activities to achieve that end are moral. The dismissal of the individual is illustrated by Orwell's *1984* where a department exists to re-write individuals in and out of history according to how they are viewed by the leadership. Such a view is not fanciful. It was common for Stalin to have liquidated comrades removed from photographs. The subjugation of the individual is starkly illustrated by the most brutal of authoritarian regimes: Cambodia under Pol Pot. According to a Deputy Secretary of the Cambodia Communist party: 'The leadership apparatus must be defended at any price. If we lose members but retain the leadership, we can continue to win victories ... There can be no comparison between losing two or three leading cadres and 200 or 300 members. Rather the latter than the former' (quoted in Chandler, 1999: 16). Moreover, authoritarian regimes are often about rebuilding the individual in the image of the state. In the Soviet Union the ultimate goal was to develop 'Soviet Man' who was the complete and committed communist.

Nevertheless, whilst force and coercion are a key element in authoritarian regimes, many of these states were modernist, explicitly aimed at achieving the transformation of society. Therefore, their power could not rely solely on force, which is a limited mechanism for achieving complex social goals. Consequently, authoritarian states created state capability through three mechanisms: force/coercion, charismatic leadership and bureaucracy.

## Force/coercion

Authoritarian regimes are underpinned by a large security apparatus. This is often based on a secret police but sometimes on the use of the army and, especially in Latin America, through the use of quasi- or para-statal military organizations. For instance, the East German state undoubtedly developed a comprehensive and extensive security regime which essentially involved almost the whole population in the process of surveillance (either watching or being watched) (Funder, 2003; see Chapter 10). James Scott, and others, demonstrate how the Soviet leadership was able to force Soviet peasants into collectivization, in an exercise based almost solely on force. Regimes such as Pol Pot's in Cambodia, although obviously a long way from a modern state, were based on high levels of violence. Overy (2004: 210) suggests that in Nazi Germany and the Soviet Union the security apparatus was never large enough to ensure permanent surveillance of the population. Whilst in these cases surveillance may have been partial, in smaller states like Cambodia and well-established authoritarian regimes such as East Germany there is little doubt the control of the security forces was extreme.

However, there are two important points to consider. First, authoritarian states vary considerably. Some, such as Argentina 1976–83 and Brazil 1964–83, were much more focussed in their use of force, concentrating on particular groups, whilst Chile had a much more embracing approach to the issue of security. As Anthony Pereira (2005: 2–3) demonstrates, in Brazil political repression tended to be formally administered through a legal process, whereas in Chile there was a legal process but it was conducted by the military and in secret. On the other hand, in Argentina the Dirty War resulted in people being 'disappeared' by the military without reference to any legal process. As Pereira points out:

> The regimes varied in the degree to which their authoritarian legality broke with preauthoritarian legal forms, as well as in the extent to which the treatment of political prisoners was regulated by law (what I call the judicialization of repression). (Pereira 2005: 5)

Second, it is not necessarily the size of the security apparatus that is important but the perception of its reach amongst the population. As we will see below much of the impact of authoritarian regimes is based on the state achieving goals through fear.

## Charismatic leadership

Authoritarian regimes do not rely on force alone. They often have considerable authority and legitimacy; however this legitimacy is not based on democratic processes but commonly on a cult of the personality/charismatic leadership. Many authoritarian regimes are based on a personality cult revolving around personalist dictatorships; this has clearly been the case in China, the Soviet Union and Nazi Germany, but is also important in small authoritarian regimes such as Communist Romania and North Korea, and many post-communist regimes face problems with breaking with the notion of a strong and charismatic leader.

The authoritarian system is usually based on the notion of a single leader whose power is unquestioned. Legitimacy exists within the strong or charismatic leader. Even in systems where power is in principle shared, such as Communist systems where there is a *politburo*, or military dictatorships where there is usually a committee of senior military figures, a single leader usually emerges. Power is, therefore, conducted almost solely through the leader. As Bullock (1991: 483) maintains, Hitler 'thought of power purely in personal terms' and was opposed to 'any form of bureaucracy'. Ian Kershaw (1998) emphasizes the way in which Hitler based his power on charismatic authority. Consequently, in many authoritarian regimes the power of the state is synonymous with the leader.

## Bureaucracy

Nevertheless, many authoritarian regimes are modernist states and therefore much of their power derives from bureaucratic capability (again this is particularly true in relation to Nazi Germany (Kershaw, 1998). As we saw earlier, Bauman demonstrates the importance of bureaucracy to the scale of the Holocaust in Germany. Authoritarian states would be highly limited in their ends if they worked purely through force. As Bullock (1991: 479) points out: 'The Führer state consisted of two different types of authority in parallel: the traditional state bureaucracy, and an alternative executive, extra-constitutional and extra-legal...' The bureaucratic side lacked coercive power and the extra-legal side lacked a separate finance office. It is common for authoritarian regimes to have a dual structure, which is usually focused around the party and the state. The Leninist party-state was based on a state bureaucracy that is effectively shadowed by the party structure, allowing the party to control the bureaucratic machinery. This Leninist party-state structure has been followed in non-Marxist regimes, most notably in Taiwan and Mexico. This structure is relatively effective because it is based on party functionaries taking orders directly from the party leadership and then supervising the state in ensuring that the orders are implemented. The party becomes an important mechanism for both infrastructural and despotic powers and in Nazi Germany and the Soviet Union the party was a central instrument (Overy, 2004: 132). Often within these systems there is considerable patronage. Party functionaries are in a position to offer jobs within the state and in systems like Mexico it is the patronage element which ensures that bureaucrats follow the demands of party bosses. The fact that positions are often dependent on the party, or the goodwill of party officials, gives the party a tremendous resource in terms of achieving goals in a way that is not completely dependent on force. The Leninist model is based on the idea that party members become state office holders (Overy, 2004: 161).

Authoritarian states have power through bureaucratic mechanisms but these mechanisms are often backed by force rather than legal norms and legitimacy. If we see states as having a range of mechanisms for achieving their goals, authoritarian regimes will frequently use mechanisms of force. Even bureaucratic processes are facilitated by their close association with force and violence. Perhaps more importantly, there are periods when force clearly breaks the bounds of legality and creates terror.

## From force to terror

Often authoritarian regimes, as we have suggested, attempt to use repression through a legal process. This was certainly the case in Brazil and to an extent for a large period of time in the Soviet Union. However, authoritarian regimes often descend into periods of terror, whereby any pretence of legality is dropped and often people are arrested for reasons that are unclear and then summarily imprisoned or executed (a condition described well by Franz Kafka in his novel *The Trial*). It is rare, as in the case of Cambodia, that authoritarian regimes are based on a permanent terror. In others they can occur for particular periods, as in China's cultural revolution or the Stalinist purges of 1930s. So whilst authoritarian regimes have periods of terror where force is used in an arbitrary manner, with little attempt to legalize the process, the extent and nature of the terror varies greatly. Moreover, the impact of terror varies from the Cambodian example, which includes the whole society, to others like Brazil, where illegitimate force was directed at a small group of 'subversives' (Pereira, 2005). For example, even in what have often been referred to as totalitarian societies, Overy (2004: 210) argues that most ordinary Russians and Germans would have had little sense of the terror that existed in their societies:

> No one in either system could be unaware that State Security was out there, but for the ordinary citizen, uninterested in politics, lucky enough not to belong to one of the groups stigmatised as enemies, the attitude was likely to be prudent respect, even approval, rather than a permanent state of fear.

This view has a logic because the capacities of states are limited but it is disputed by a number of historians who accept that while, in certain regions of the Soviet Union, the impact of the secret police may have been focussed, for many the fear of the terror was common (see Brower, 1987) and the impact of the terror extensive (Conquest, 1987).

Terror is a mechanism of power within authoritarian regimes that varies in how and when it is used. Often it occurs in the turmoil of the establishment of a new regime, as illustrated by the original modern terror in the early stages of the republican government following the French revolution. In Spain the Franco regime executed at least 200,000 people in the years immediately following the civil war (Beevor, 2006: 405). In Chile and Brazil the highest number of extra-judicial killings occurred shortly after military coups. In the Soviet Union the peak horror of the Stalinist purges occurred in 1937 and 1938 when nearly 700,000 people were executed (although strangely the death penalty was abolished in 1947 and when it was reintroduced in 1950 there were no executions [Overy, 2004: 195]).

There are also differences in the degree to which terror maintains a legal framework. As Pereira (2005: 52) points out, in Argentina 'The military regime 1976–1983 largely dispensed with any kind of legal strategy, and it engaged in total and merciless war on the alleged agents of subversion.' In other regimes the maintenance of a legal form can be important and even the Stalinist purges maintained a façade of legalism. People were formally arrested, interrogated and tried (see Applebaum, 2003).

The fundamental feature of terror is that it extends the power of the state through fear. In terms of power, at one level it seems like pure force and often many people are brutally and directly killed – millions in the case of the Holocaust and Pol Pot's Cambodia, and hundreds of thousands in countries like Guatemala. However the main impact of terror is not through force but more in 'anticipated reaction'. If the state is powerful and arbitrary then people fear the state and behave in the way state actors want without the state having to act directly. It is a form of Lukes' second face of power. Overy and others may be correct in arguing that even in Nazi Germany and the Soviet Union the respective terror was relatively focussed, but its power is through the generation of fear and uncertainty. In Argentina, those who disappeared appeared fairly random; often they had not even been involved in political activity, and the majority were abducted in their homes without any formal arrest (Pereira, 2005: 136; Pion-Berlin and Lopez, 1991: 64). Although those who disappeared were many, they were only a small part of the population. Nevertheless, the fear was generalized throughout society. For Stalin, control was exercised by the fear that at any moment a party cadre could lose his position, be arrested or killed (Lewin, 1991). The terror did not have to touch everyone directly to be effective – it is a mode of governance. As Alec Nove (1987: 415) says:

> I agree strongly with Stephen Cohen that the Terror deeply affected the lives and behaviour also of those *not* arrested. Everyone knew the consequence of an incautious remark, or even of not reporting such a remark if made in one's presence to another. (Emphasis added)

Terror is often about establishing control over party, state and society. Stalin's terror was focussed initially on the peasantry in order to force collectivization and to transfer resources to the city in order to finance the industrialization process (Davies and Wheatcroft, 2004). Subsequently, Stalin's attention turned to the party leadership, eliminating his rivals such as Bukharin through show trials. Finally, terror spread to the whole party and wider society. As Bullock (1991: 543) demonstrates, Stalin's purges

> deliberately aimed at destabilizing the party by removing the security of tenure which might allow a future growth of opposition to take place. Nor was terror any longer to be restricted to the party. The purges of the NKVD and of the officer corps of the armed forces which now followed show that he was concerned to destroy potential opposition.

As Moshe Lewin (1985) has pointed out, this destabilization occurred throughout society and was a mechanism for establishing a new order, and new sets of power relations within the Soviet Union. Lewin (1985) sees the revolution as creating a 'quicksand society' with considerable social mobility, and the terror both capitalized on this social change and attempted to impose a different order which effectively secured Stalin in power. Through creating what Lewin sees as disequilibrium, Stalin perhaps believed that he would be the only person to control Soviet society. However, it is important not to see this terror as part of a coherent plan controlled from the centre, but made up of a whole set of party officials at different levels undertaking often conflicting decisions and producing unintended outcomes (Reichman, 1988).

The terrors in the Soviet Union and China were generalized and indeed shook their respective societies, creating Lewin's quicksand society or the Kafkaesque sense that everyone was on the point of being caught up in the processes that were unleashed (and indeed processes that were beyond the control of the leaders who unleashed them; this was particularly true in the Chinese cultural revolution which developed its own momentum). Other terrors have been more focussed. The Nazi Holocaust, whilst of course extensive, was focussed on clearly identifiable groups: Jews, gays, Slavs and communists. The terrors in Latin America and Spain also had a specific target, the left-wing opposition, even though it was often loosely defined. It is interesting to contrast the Soviet and Latin American terrors. In Latin America there was always a distinct class – the rich – who were separate from the terror and the terror existed to protect them. It was clear that a plutocrat was not going to be 'disappeared' in Argentina. The terror was focussed on the perceived enemies of the state. The Argentine military dictatorship saw a left-wing subversion that was attempting to destabilize the state and they set out to defeat it (Pion-Berlin and Lopez, 1991). Stalin, on the other hand, created a generalized terror that could have included anyone. An enemy was identified (Trotskyites, fascists, saboteurs) but who was one and who was not was random. In Argentina the aim was to ensure the dominance of the upper class through the defeat of left-wing opposition. In the Soviet Union it was to ensure Stalin's control through his ability to remove any opponent, real or not. Nevertheless, both types of terror were limited by the centre's dependence on local agents to carry out the acts of murder and arrest. As Pion-Berlin and Lopez (1991: 80) demonstrate, in Argentina:

> [t]he Dirty War had an unpredictable edge to it. The security forces abducted many unsuspecting citizens because false leads often led to

the sudden and arbitrary apprehension of individuals who were guilty of nothing other than indirect association with someone else.

However, it is important to point out that even with the tools of fear and terror authoritarian regimes are not always effective. Despite their apparent powers they do not have total control of society. Indeed, force and terror often exist in the absence of effective infrastructural power.

## The problem of totalitarianism

The assumption certainly in much of the Cold War literature on authoritarian states is that they had mechanisms to ensure total control of their societies – the *1984* model of Big Brother symbolized these types of states (for a discussion see Reichman, 1988). However, we need to recognize that states are complex organizations even in so-called totalitarian regimes. In a way the totalitarian regimes are the hard cases – the ultimate modernist states – and if they are unable to control all aspects of their societies it emphasizes the partiality of states in general.

It is important to recognize that there is a tremendous range of types in authoritarian regimes – some have more despotic and infrastructural power than others. Some, such as the government in Singapore, have high levels of legitimacy. Other countries in the Eastern Bloc such as Poland, Hungary and Yugoslavia retained more spaces that were separate from the state, even if this was only within the confines of family and close friends (Frentzel-Zagorska, 1990). For instance, the Catholic church in Poland maintained a distinctive and autonomous position in Polish life and indeed, 77 per cent of Polish agricultural land remained in private hands, although strictly controlled by the state (Lipton *et al.*, 1990). As Janina Frentzel-Zagorska highlights, Poland and Hungary retained embryos of civil society which could quickly develop once the Soviet Union's control on Eastern Europe collapsed, and Michael Bernhard (1993: 310) illustrates how in Poland the opposition was able to carve out some degree of public space which could develop into civil society during the 1980s, before the collapse of the Soviet Union. Revisionist historians of Stalinism have argued that even in the 1930s the Soviet state was often chaotic and contradictory and continually restrained by social forces (see Fitzpatrick, 1982, 1986). Lewin (1991: 262) notes that Stalinism was infected by the contradiction that binds all authoritarian states – and indeed perhaps is a fundamental problem for all states:

Personal despotism is, of course, an 'over centralized' system by definition. And from this point of view, the growing complex business of ruling an enormous country in the throes of hectic transformation renders such a despotism 'impossible' by definition. Personal control is an absolute must for the despot, but in order to rule effectively he must delegate. Nevertheless, he cannot do both at once. Many institutions are needed to accomplish complex tasks, and for this they need autonomy. But autonomy is precisely what an autocrat or despot of the Stalinist type cannot allow.

The universal contradiction that Lewin (1991: 261) points to is that the more power that Stalin amassed in his hands, the less he was able to control, so highlighting the tension between autonomy and control that exists for all states. With terror it is extremely difficult for the central state to retain control. Once illegitimate violence is released then it is used by the perpetrators for a whole set of personal ends. Whilst political leaders have one set of goals, those on the ground have another – personal vendetta, aggrandisement, love of killing – and this of course brings into question the notion of the bureaucratization of terror proposed by Bauman because in the end killing and torturing is not a process. In many ways the collapse into terror is a response to the lack of control. Because authoritarian leaders do not control their parties (in China), states (in the Soviet Union) or societies (in Argentina) they use extreme force to try to impose control. Terror is a sign of weakness, more than strength. It is a mechanism that states use when they do not have infrastructural power or lack hegemony, but without these mechanisms even terror is hard to control.

The second feature that creates a problem for authoritarian states is that whilst they are based on the notion of a unified and all-powerful state, there are often significant divisions with authoritarian states with conflicting interests. Overy (2004: 73) and Kershaw (1998) highlight how in Nazi Germany there were conflicting power centres developing policies and fighting for resources, and Hitler's attention.

Third, authoritarian regimes are faced with spaces they cannot control. It may be that they aim to control the whole of a society, and indeed to turn society into a political space, but this is not a situation that can be completely achieved. Authoritarian states often do not have direct access to society because their position is based on opposition to certain social groups, and so they rely on bureaucrats or military forces to deliver. Consequently, the bureaucrats or security personnel continue to have some degree of autonomy on the ground. Even within a repressive apparatus, such as the *gulag* system, there were tremendous differences in regimes between camps, depending on the camp governor and then depending on how individual guards treated individual prisoners (Applebaum, 2003). With states always being limited in their capabilities, there are groups and activities that are ignored or not captured by the state. Overy (2004: 76) illustrates that both the Soviet Union and Nazi Germany depended on large and multi-layered administration:

> Though much of what they did depended on policy decisions ... generated from the centre, the intermediate and peripheral rings of administration had to interpret these instructions and translate them into legal or social or economic reality. There existed through the system ample opportunity for subjective interpretation, limited local improvisation, jurisdictional wrangling, even conscious disloyalty.

The Soviet state, for instance, paid little attention to nomadic groups in the tundra and it never focussed on criminal activity in the way it searched out political activities (Applebaum, 2003). Nove (1987: 413) points out that, even during the terror in the Soviet Union, 'Many orders are misunderstood or distorted by their executants, or are vague, ambiguous, contradictory'.

States in authoritarian regimes are like other states – power is a capability. How it is used depends on patterns of dependence and the ability to use resources. In authoritarian regimes the relationship between legitimacy and force is different from liberal democratic regimes. In democratic societies force has to be legitimized whereas often in authoritarian regimes it is an alternative to legitimacy (although there are frequently attempts to legitimize it). Authoritarian states use the first dimension of power; we can observe them making people do things that they would not otherwise do. In Tiananmen Square in 1989 or Czechoslovakia in 1968, force is used directly on the people but at other times the threat of force is close to the surface. This is the point of the Soviet terror; people followed orders because they were too aware of the consequences of not acting in the ways that were expected. What is interesting in the case of the Soviet Union and Eastern Europe is that despite tremendous attempts by the regimes to 'educate' the population, neither the third dimension of power or Foucault's 'socialisation' processes worked. That the Soviet regime was unable to manipulate wants seems to create a theoretical problem for

Lukes and Foucault because it suggests that in liberal democracy there is some degree of consent that did not exist in the East. Overy (2004: 73) makes the point explicitly: 'the paradigm of completely unrestricted power, exercised in coherent centralized polity by men of exceptional ruthlessness who brooked no limitations or dissent was, and remains, a political-science fantasy'. Authoritarian regimes are often ineffectual states because they do not have the capability to deliver public goods through cooperation and as a consequence their goals are subverted throughout the process of implementation. In the Soviet Union a highly centralized economic planning system was unable to deliver its goals because it was easy for plant managers to evade the targets set by the planning ministry and indeed the targets created perverse incentives in terms of outputs and so contributed to the collapse of the system (Gregory, 1990).

Authoritarian regimes base their power on force but with force their power is both limited and crude. (More particularly authoritarian regimes survive by building a network of supporters around them who receive considerable benefits, and force is applied to those who are excluded from state patronage and so have nothing invested in the regime). The mechanisms of dependence that exist in democratic regimes exist in authoritarian regimes. Authoritarian leaders are in complex relationships with the range of actors that they need to implement decisions and therefore rely on legitimacy and bureaucracy. However, the key point is that authoritarian regimes highlight the limits of modern states and their ability to have total power. It illustrates the ways in which states are continually looking for new mechanisms for achieving goals. It is also the case that coercion is not limited to authoritarian regimes.

## Using force and terror in 'democratic' regimes

Force and terror are crude and inefficient mechanisms of raw state power. Indeed, they are often used to impose modernist forms on premodern peoples and states use force when they lack legitimacy or other bureaucratic mechanisms for controlling their territory. However, the cases of Chile, Argentina and Brazil demonstrate that relatively developed societies with democratic institutions can turn to dictatorship and force at times of crisis (Pereira, 2005). In these cases we see states shift regime and hence develop force and terror as central mechanisms of the state. Yet another interesting facet of the question of force is the way in which democratic regimes use force and terror as part of their array of powers. There is a strong assumption that force in authoritarian regimes is extra-legal. Despite attempts, as we have seen, in some cases to use force through legal processes, the view of authoritarian regimes is that legal processes do not protect the accused and often the use of force is disproportionate. Within democratic regimes when the state uses force, it is legitimate and subject to due process. For instance, if a police officer kills someone in Britain, the killing will be subject to police investigation. There are cases in Britain and the United States of soldiers being tried for murder when they have been involved in killings as part of military activity. Force is very much part of the mechanism of democratic regimes, but this force is seen as being used when it is justifiable (and within the rule of law) (see Ron, 1997). Indeed it is the argument of some international relations scholars that not only do democracies not fight wars with each other, but they are much less likely to use force internally (Rummel, 1994).

Nevertheless, it cannot be disputed that democratic states exercise violence both externally and internally. Considerable attention has been paid to the issue of the external use of violence by democratic states, when for instance they have been involved in wars. There can be no doubt that the United States has used tremendous force in wars in Vietnam and the Middle East. What is also striking is that considerable efforts are made to legitimize the use of force. There is a presumption (or an argument) that there is either a just war defence, that the war is legitimized by the UN, or a broad international coalition, or that at the least war is in the national interest and in that sense protecting the interests of the people.

Whilst democratic states will always ensure justification for external force, it is also the case that there are a number of states that have been highly democratic at home with government bound by the rule of law, but which abroad have exercised force in highly authoritarian ways. The British Empire for instance effectively operated a dual system of government. Within Britain, at least from 1928, there was universal suffrage, and other elements of a liberal democratic system, such as the rule of law and a free press, had existed longer. Yet throughout the British Empire the government operated in a way that was anti-democratic and based on force. Even as late as 1957 when liberal democracy was apparently firmly established in Britain, the government was prepared to use considerable force in an attempt to crush the Mau Mau rebellion in Kenya. At least 12,000 people were killed in an attempt to repress the rebellion and many were executed for crimes other than murder. In addition, high levels of brutality were used in camps for Mau Mau prisoners with widespread torture and beatings, and the unsanitary conditions allowed typhus and other diseases to spread (McGreal, 2006; for a discussion of how disease in the Third World reflects power, see Farmer, 2005). There were, and continue to be, attempts to legitimize Empire as the White Man's burden, or a process of bringing democracy, but the truth is that Empire was based on the use of high levels of political, and illegitimate, force (Gopal, 2006). The British state, although it was democratic, was prepared to use illegitimate force externally.

The use of external force is not confined to the past. In the case of the United States, Guantánamo Bay has been used to detain prisoners and hold them without trial and allegedly subject them to torture and ill-treatment. The issue is that with Guantánamo the usual rule of law of the United States did not apply and prisoners were held without any charge and without the means to mount a legal defence. For example, many detainees were not given a date for a trial. The position of the Guantánamo Bay detainees was certainly extra-legal and they were not held on domestic territory, specifically so that they were not covered by domestic law.

The United States has also been accused of using 'extraordinary rendition' flights whereby CIA agents arrest terrorist suspects in one country and take them to another county where they are tortured (Grey, 2006). Many of these suspects have been kept in 'ghost' prisons without any legal recourse. A number of terrorist suspects seem to have 'disappeared'. At some point they have been arrested by the CIA but their whereabouts is unclear. It is also apparent that there are prisons in Eastern Europe and North Africa where suspects have been detained. According to the Legal Affairs Committee of the Council of Europe, the US authorities have been careful to try to keep these prisons secret (Committee on Legal Affairs and Human Rights, 2006: 5):

> It is interesting to recall that this ABC report, confirming the use of secret detention camps in Poland and Romania by the CIA, was available on the Internet for only a very short time before being withdrawn following the intervention of lawyers on behalf of the network's owners. The Washington Post subsequently admitted that it had been in possession of the names of the countries, but had refrained from naming them further to an agreement entered into with the authorities. It is thus established that considerable pressure was brought to bear to ensure that these countries were not named.

It is unclear what arguments prevailed on the media outlets in question to convince them to comply. What is certain is that these are troubling developments that throw into question the principles of freedom and independence of the press. In this light, it is worth noting that just before the publication of the original revelations by the reporter Dana Priest in early November 2005, the Executive Editor of the Washington Post was invited for an audience at the White House with President Bush.

As the European Council (2006: 9) report makes clear, the United States has developed a web of rendition, imprisonment, and possibly torture since before the events of 11 September 2001:

> The chief architect of the web, the United States of America, has long possessed the capacity to capture individual targets abroad and carry them to different parts of the world. Through its Central Intelligence Agency (CIA), the United States designed a programme known as 'rendition' for this purpose in the mid-1990s. The CIA aimed to take terrorist suspects in foreign countries 'off the streets' by transporting them back to other countries, usually their home countries, where they were wanted for trial, or for detention without any form of due process.

The other point to note is that the European Council report makes clear that other countries within Europe have either cooperated or at the least turned a blind eye to the activities of the CIA and the United States. Many of the cases discussed by the European Council report demonstrate arbitrary arrests, the complete absence of due process and, in many cases, brutal treatment. The EC report (2006: 46) states that in one case after considerable ill-treatment:

> Eventually Binyam began to co-operate in his interrogation sessions in an effort to prevent being tortured: 'They said if you say this story as we read it, you will just go to court as a witness and all this torture will stop. I could not take any more ... and I eventually repeated what they read out to me. They told me to say I was with bin Laden five or six times. Of course that was false. They continued with two or three interrogations a month. They weren't really interrogations – more like trainings, training me what to say.'

What is significant in this example is how similar the process described here is to the processes conducted by the NKVD during the Stalinist purges where suspects would be pressurized into making false, and often unbelievable, confessions.

The use of irregular and/or illegal force in the treatment of terrorism is not unusual for democratic states; it is not something confined to the United States. Russia has used similar methods in dealing with Chechen rebels. In the early 1970s in Northern Ireland, the British government used both internment, where suspects were arrested and imprisoned without trial, and techniques of interrogation which included (1) hooding, (2) wall-standing, (3) subjection to noise, (4) relative deprivation of food and water and (5) sleep deprivation. The British government faced considerable criticism for using these methods, which were developed in colonial administrations, and was forced to abandon them when it lost a case at the European Convention on Human Rights brought by the Irish government (Kennedy-Pipe and Mumford, 2007). What is of significance here is that legal institutions prevented the British government from continuing with this method (although there have been continual allegations that the British government used torture in dealing with terrorists in Northern Ireland). The relationship between states and issues of terror is highly complex. Similarly, James Ron (1997) demonstrates how in Israel torture was systematically carried out on Palestinian suspects between 1988 and 1990. However, the evidence suggests that following international pressure the interrogation techniques became more subtle; often there were attempts to avoid bruising and broken bones, and there was greater institutionalization of the interrogation process (Ron, 1997: 276). In an interview published on the White House official web site, the Vice President of the United States, Dick Cheney, appeared to condone the use of forms of torture.

## Democratic states and internal repression

There is an assumption that goes back to Hobbes and which is strongly held within Conservative ideology but also acknowledged in other democratic parties, that state force, when subject to legal norms, is legitimate. In this sense violence is not repression but is about protecting citizens from disorder. If a criminal is locked up in prison that is a use of force but it is force that is legitimized by the fact that the criminal is a threat to innocent people, needs to be reformed or punished and has been dealt with through due process. There is a social contract in the sense that a criminal knows that if he/she breaks the law a prison sentence may follow. This is different to the authoritarian regimes outlined above where often those arrested and killed were not aware that they had transgressed.

Nevertheless, there are two points to consider here. The first, reflecting Gramsci's view of hegemony, is that force is ever-present in democratic states. Considerable amounts of money are spent on what Marxists call the repressive state apparatus of police, military and secret services. Moreover, in many cases it is not clear whether people obey laws because they agree with them or because they fear the consequences of breaking them, which is legitimate violence by the state. Hence modern states exist on the basis of the integration of force into the process of legitimation. This force is inherent partly because of two conceits of modern states. One is the notion that modernity is fragile; unless we maintain order the Hobbesian war of all against all is just around the corner. We only have to be aware how often the media and politicians highlight the threats to society, whether they be from violence, crime, or poor behaviour. Second is the idea of modernist states as a 'muscle bound version of the self-confidence about scientific and technical progress' (Scott, 1998: 4). This means that the modern state, unlike the liberal state, is not concerned only with order but is intentional in the sense of attempting to achieve specific goals and these intentions, even if well meant, can be based on forcing people to do things they do not want to do.

Whilst violence and force in democratic states are seen as legitimate and used against law breakers, not innocent citizens, the notion of legitimate and innocent is often contested. Again, the problem is endemic within the idea of a democratic state. Democratic states are based on the notion that people can oppose the state and can demonstrate against government policy, but often there is conflict over the extent to which the demonstration or opposition is legal.

There are a number of democratic states that outlaw certain political parties (Bale, 2007). In Spain, Herri Batasuna has been banned and Germany has banned Communist and Nazi parties in the past. In Britain, Sinn Féin was prevented from making statements on television for a number of years. These types of repression are rare and justified on the grounds that the parties being repressed are either violent or anti-democratic – or both. Nevertheless, bans do exist and the United States illustrates how liberal and democratic states can use violence in cases of domestic politics. Three examples in the United States demonstrate the way violence can operate: the repression of blacks until the 1960s, McCarthyism, and the repression of socialist movements.

For much of the early twentieth century US local government and civil society effectively used force to exclude blacks from political activity, until the central state used greater force to ensure that blacks were granted the rights that existed in the constitution. There is also evidence that the central state used highly repressive measures to control the civil rights movement and effectively destroy the Black Panther movement (Davenport, 2005). However, as Schultz and Schultz (1989: 3) point out:

> Political repression in America has been consequential; it has had major, long-term effects. The brutality used to subjugate Black people in the South, for example, not only caused them to live for generations in poverty and misery, but it also affected the balance of political power in that region, allowing southern ultraconservatives to become entrenched in pivotal positions within the national government, affecting its policies on issues from civil rights to foreign relations.

The second example is the McCarthy campaign against communists. At the height of the Cold War, there was organized repression both of communists and of people suspected as having communist sympathies:

> A host of actions against Communists was taken by the states, including disqualifying them from public employment (including from teaching positions in public schools); denying them access to the ballot as candidates, and prohibiting them from serving in public office even if legally elected ... and outright bans on the Party. Forced registration was a means toward achieving these ends. (Gibson 1988: 513)

As Gibson (1988: 514) suggests, the repression effectively destroyed the Communist party in the United States and affected the employment of millions, many of whom were not members of the Communist party. Moreover, McCarthy's Senate Committee of Un-American Activities, strongly supported by the FBI under Edgar Hoover, forced Americans in front of Senate to admit or deny Communist party membership, and many people were blacklisted as a consequence of the committee's activities. McCarthyism, with its paranoid fear of the spread of communism in the United States, has an echo of the Stalinist concerns over Trotskyites and saboteurs in the Soviet Union in the 1930s. McCarthy, like Stalin, used fear as a mechanism for strengthening his political power and for attacking political opponents. Of course, McCarthy was unable to sustain his position and was forced to end his activities by Congress.

The third example is the repression used against the American socialist movement. Socialists and trade unions in the late nineteenth and early twentieth century suffered considerable harassment and repression from various levels of government and business. This was particularly true during the First World War, when the war was used as an opportunity to crush the Industrial Workers of the World (IWW). Before and during the war members of the IWW faced arrest and censorship and 166 members were tried under the 1917 Espionage Act (Fried, 1991: 38).

Forms of repression are normal parts of the polity in all political regimes. Either systematically, as in the case of blacks and socialists in the United States, or more as one-off campaigns in terms of the French Riot Police in 1968 or the violence committed against the British miners in the strike of 1984. The argument of the state is usually that in these acts of repression they are upholding the rule of law in the face of violent protest. However, there are cases when democratic states appear to move beyond the legal face of the law and seem from some perspectives to be adopting the mechanisms of authoritarian regimes.

## Terror, fear and death squads in democratic regimes

Fear of an external threat is consistently used as a mechanism for developing and justifying particular activities abroad. Again, Stalin's purges were very much legitimized in terms of the external threat to the Soviet Union. A similar mechanism has been used in the West. The whole war on terror has been used to justify an extension in state powers in terms of arrest. For example, in Britain the 2005 Prevention of Terrorism Act provides:

> the power to lock someone up in their own house; the power to stop other people visiting that person; the power to remove any item of property from that person's house; the power to tag that person; the power to ask that person to surrender his or her passport, to report to a police station and to produce any information demanded of him; in other words, the power to incarcerate that person. These powers are to be exercised against anyone whom the Home Secretary deems to be involved in a terrorism-related activity. Such a

person is defined in the broadest possible terms as, for instance, someone engaged in conduct that gives support or assistance to individuals who are known or believed to be engaged in terrorism-related activities. It is the intention to detain such people without trial for an unlimited period, contrary to the most basic principles of English law. (House of Commons, *Hansard Debate* 23 February 2005: Col. 386)

The Act gives the state much greater powers of arrest and imprisonment than have ever existed in the past. For the Home Secretary these measures are justifiable because:

Al-Qaeda and its network are qualitatively different in five ways that I shall set out to the House. First, their ideology is entirely destructive in nature. They wish to destroy religious toleration and tolerance; they wish to destroy freely elected democratic government; they wish to destroy the rule of law in our society; they wish to destroy free discussion and freedom of opinion in the media and elsewhere; they wish to destroy equality for women; they wish to destroy our market economy. The destruction of those things and values for which we and our predecessors in the House have fought for centuries is qualitatively different from terrorism of different types in the past when individuals fought for particular freedoms, as they saw it, in certain circumstances. Al-Qaeda and its colleagues seek to impose on us a nihilist regime. (House of Commons, *Hansard Debate*, 23 February 2005: Col. 333)

Specifically, the existence of weapons of mass destruction and the danger they posed was central to the case for the war in Iraq both in Britain and the United States. In one specific case the British government authorized tanks to surround Heathrow airport on the day before a crucial vote in the House of Commons. The government said that it had strong intelligence of a potential attack but others were more sceptical. What this highlights is how the use of fear is a useful resource for government because governments say that they are the only ones that can assess the extent of the danger. They have information from the security sources that, by its very nature, cannot be revealed and we have to trust that the information is true. Of course, what the weapons of mass destruction case highlighted was that the information from the security services was incorrect and the threat that was said to exist was not really there. Fear then plays an important role. This is not some strange conspiracy theory. Peter Lilley is a Conservative MP and a former Cabinet Minster. He revealed in a debate in the House of Commons that he was temporarily Home Secretary and found himself signing papers for a whole range of secret activities. He revealed in his speech:

> However, one felt that other processes were being kept secret simply to retain the mystique of the organizations, because they like having secrets and being able to say, 'We can tell you, Minister, but you mustn't tell anyone else'. Departments have an interest in emphasizing the importance of what they do, so the secret services and the police likewise have no incentive to understate the threats and risks – both general and specific – that the country faces. That is not to deny that we might face an enormous risk, as I said earlier, but we should want to assess and deliberate on each individual case with scepticism and put it to an independent legal test. (House of Commons, *Hansard Debate*, 2 February 2005: Col. 382)

The point being made by these examples is that use of fear as a tool of the state is not solely a mechanism that exists within authoritarian regimes but one that democratic governments also use.

One of the most controversial and difficult to demonstrate elements of state force is the way that security forces operate within the context of internal terrorism, such as the IRA in Northern Ireland, ETA in Spain and the Red Brigades in Italy. Terrorism creates a number of difficult dilemmas for democratic regimes. The central dilemma is that terrorist organizations use violent means and are undemocratic in their goals. Unlike external enemies they are difficult to identify. They often exist within a framework of strong local support and as such cannot be easily singled out from 'law-abiding' citizens. The problem for democratic states is how to defeat terrorists without compromising the key features of democratic society such as the rule of law, the right to a fair trial, and the right to life. Governments involved in dealing with terrorists have often found it difficult to maintain the line between legal and dubious activity and often there are complex, and compromising, relationships between security forces and terrorist organizations. This is particularly the case in Northern Ireland and Italy where there were competing terrorist groups, which has led to suggestions that the security forces colluded with particular groups in order to defeat other groups of terrorists. In this sense certain terrorist groups have acted in a similar way to death squads in Latin America, having a loose and deniable link to state security forces and then being used to kill state enemies. There have also been suggestions in the case of Spain and Britain that the state has developed shoot-to-kill tactics where, rather than trying to arrest terrorists, security forces have chosen to kill them (Sluka, 2000, Aretxaga, 2000).

In the case of Britain and the IRA it often happened that suspects were followed or ambushed and then shot, most famously when three IRA members were shot dead in Gibraltar whilst planning a bomb attack. John Stalker, a former Chief Constable charged with investigating shoot-to-kill, claimed in his autobiography that there was no direct evidence of shoot-to-kill but considerable indications that such a policy occurred. According to Bradley Bamford (2005: 595):

It has been argued that a 'shoot-to-kill' policy was sanctioned at the highest levels of the British Government. Although never officially admitted, the large number of terrorists killed during this period, in circumstances where many believe that an arrest could have been made, is seen as evidence that such a policy existed. For seemingly inexplicable reasons it appears as though the security forces, having known in advance about an attack, waited until the last possible moment to apprehend or kill the terrorists. That method of operating went against the British Government's entire counter-terrorism policy that emphasized prevention and police intervention at the preparatory stages of a terrorist plot.

In the British case there was always some ambiguity around shoot-to-kill in the sense that the security forces could argue that they were working in difficult and dangerous circumstances where it was not possible to arrest the suspects. Consequently, it could be claimed that the death of the terrorist was a result of the situation and not a policy.

Nevertheless, the human rights group British Irish Rights Watch concluded after extensive investigation that:

The materials on which the report is based strongly suggest that agents of the state have been involved, directly and indirectly, in the murder of its citizens, in contravention of domestic law and all international human rights standards.

In greater detail than the official Stevens Enquiry report (2003), they detail the strong evidence of a systematic link between members of the security forces and paramilitary groups who would then kill suspected republican terrorists. In particular, they suggest that a secret army unit the Forces Research Unit infiltrated Brian Nelson into the Protestant Ulster Defence Association and used him to carry out murders of republicans. This relationship is substantiated by a number of sources (Urban, 1992).

The Stevens Enquiry set up by the government and undertaken by a senior police officer found (Stevens, J., 2003: 3):

> Collusion, the wilful failure to keep records, the absence of records, the withholding of intelligence and evidence, and, at the extreme, of agents being involved in murder.

The questions that arise concerning the nature of power in democratic states are fundamental. Some have claimed that there was high-level knowledge of the relationship between the security forces and paramilitaries through the Joint Intelligence Committee. It would be difficult and worrying to say that Ministers had direct knowledge of these activities, and finding the truth in these sorts of situations is notoriously difficult. Nevertheless, as Bamford (2005: 603) points out:

> [I]f the security forces were essentially operating on their own, as Mark Urban and the Stevens Inquiry have suggested, then the situation was even worse because it showed a complete lack of control on behalf of the government for its security forces. Some have suggested that those practices subtly transform the nature of a liberal democratic state. According to Ronald D. Crelinsten and Alex P. Schmid, 'when agents of the state begin consistently to shoot suspects without bothering to arrest them, or to mistreat them during interrogation in order to force confessions, then the state has moved far along the road to a regime of terror.

In the case of Spain there is little ambiguity that elements within the state supported the creation of the 'Grupos Antiterroristas de Liberación' (GAL) groups, which conducted a dirty war against the Basque paramilitary group ETA between 1983 and 1987. The group

was funded by secret funds within the interior ministry and was operated by members of the Guardia Civil who recruited the freelance
assassins (Aretxaga, 2000; Woodworth, 2001). A former Interior
Minister, José Barrionuevo, was sentenced to 10 years in prison for his
role in the creation and support of GAL (*BBC News*, 29 July 1998).
GAL assassinated a number of ETA members and sympathizers and a
number of people with no connection to ETA or terrorism, and under-
took at least 40 attacks, many of them inside France. As in the case of
Northern Ireland, there is considerable evidence of the rule of law
being flouted and the police and security forces obstructing the search
for evidence (Woodworth, 2001). There are indications that the organization of GAL went deep inside the Spanish state and some suggest
that the Spanish Prime Minister at the time knew of the existence of
GAL (Woodworth, 2001: 275). Indeed, investigation into GAL
revealed a paper written by the Spanish security service setting out the
*modus operandi* of such an organization (Wordsworth, 2001: 316). As
the Spanish philosopher Fernando Savater argued, it could not be
denied that there had been 'criminal terrorism organized and carried
out by state functionaries, with an outcome of at least 30 deaths'
(quoted in Woodworth, 2001: 320).

What the cases of the British FRU (Force Research Unit) and GAL
demonstrate is that democratic states have been prepared to use terror,
in the sense of illegitimate use of violence (Woodworth, 2001: 10), to
achieve political ends. There are continual arguments about the degree
to which these types of arrangement are separate from the state, but it
is also the case that at times the democratic state did not use its power
to bring these units or individuals within the law. The examples of
terror in democratic regimes highlight the tensions that exist within
modern states. They are subject to different pressures. As we saw in
Chapter 5, their legitimacy is based on the tension between the idea of
democracy and the notion that the state is sovereign. It is a clash
between a Lockean and Rousseauian notion of sovereignty. Is sovereignty located in the individual or in the collective? If it is in the collective and the state determines the public interest, can the state act in
ways that are above the law? In Spain this tension was more acute
because at the time of the GAL it was a relatively new democracy and
many of those who operated through GAL had worked as police officers and security service officials during a dictatorship. It could be
argued that they carried the methods of the dictatorship into the
democracy. The investigations into GAL were part of the process of
consolidation of democracy. In Northern Ireland the situation was not

helped by the fact that the army was involved in an ambiguous situation. In a normal war situation, the role of the army is to kill the enemy. When they become involved in internal security they are subject to a different set of rules, for which they are not prepared or trained. However, what both cases demonstrate is how there was, for a considerable time, an inability, or unwillingness, for those in authority to impose the rule of law. It also demonstrates the fragility of democratic procedures even in established democracies. When governments have to deal with internal terrorism, the normal processes of policing are not very effective. Often the police are excluded from the process or, at the very least, they are treated with considerable suspicion. Consequently, the authorities rely on 'intelligence', the secret service, and special forces such as the SAS. The very secrecy of these organizations makes it extremely difficult to maintain the normal lines of accountability and it becomes relatively easy for certain institutions or individuals to transgress the boundaries of legality. In addition, the importance of deniability means that proving such transgressions can be difficult.

## Conclusion

Is there any comparison between force in authoritarian regimes and democratic states? On one level there is a similarity in that both types of state use physical force and fear to achieve a specific end. However, there are considerable differences in how these mechanisms sit within the frameworks of state apparatus. As we have seen, there are times within authoritarian regimes when force becomes central to the governing code of the state; it is the chief mechanism through which the state operates. Not everyone may be directly affected by force but the eternal presence of force in the society is a mechanism for ensuring that people obey the state. In some cases force fills a vacuum left as a consequence of a lack of legitimacy, but sometimes the violence is part of the legitimacy – the state is making a claim to be a strong state that is protecting the people from some internal or external threat. Violence is also used frequently as a mechanism for ensuring particular political and social changes. In democratic regimes overt violence is not endemic but is used to deal with particular events, and usually the use of violence has to be carefully legitimized. Even in cases of external violence such as Kenya and Guantánamo, democratic states face considerable and long-term pressure to justify, legitimize or apologize for the violence. The violence is seen as an aberration, not as normality. It is usually presented either as a system failure (someone used violence when they shouldn't have) or to deal with exceptional circumstances (such as the IRA in Northern Ireland and ETA in Spain).

Two, in a sense contradictory, points need to be considered. First, democratic and authoritarian regimes are not necessarily distinct categories. The line between democracy and authoritarianism is not an either/or where a state moves from one to another, but a continuum. As can be seen in the complex process of transition, states contain both aspects (Grugel, 2001) and certainly countries such as Russia have considerable problems in breaking with their authoritarian past. Second, whilst Spain, the US or Britain can be accused of using extralegal powers, this does not mean that they are similar to the regimes of Hitler's Germany or Stalin's Russia. There is not a systematic and arbitrary resort to violence in democratic regimes in the way there was in Nazi Germany and the Soviet Union. Moreover, considerable investigation has followed the misuse of power in democratic regimes in ways that do not occur in authoritarian regimes. The point is that force and terror are tools that are available to states. All states use force both internally and externally as mechanisms for providing the public good. There are times when all states use their coercive resources to attempt to modify the behaviour of citizens. In democratic regimes there are constraints on terror but, as we have seen, there are occasions when techniques of terror are used in a particular context. This does not make democratic states authoritarian.

The point of examining force and terror within modern states is firstly to demonstrate that they are important tools for both authoritarian and democratic regimes but also that their impact is both dependent on other elements of power and it is partial. There have never been authoritarian, or non-authoritarian, regimes that have had such a clear monopoly of legitimate violence that it has enabled them to completely control their society. Force is a very limited resource of power and it can only be used for short periods of time and on limited groups of people. Most authoritarian regimes combine force with developing considerable networks of support amongst key elites. Like other resources, force offers states only a limited means of control, but it is a central element in the modern and *past*modern state.

# Chapter 8

# Rationality and Regulation

Chapters 6 and 7 of this book examined the traditional mechanisms that states have used to exercise power and the partial and limited impact that they have in terms of outcomes. In the chapters that follow the focus is on the alternative mechanisms that the state has developed in the late twentieth and early twenty-first century such as rationality, regulation, risk, and surveillance. However, none of these mechanisms are new. Modern states, as we have seen with the development of bureaucracy, have used rationality, regulation and surveillance. Christopher Dandeker (1990: 194) reminds us how rationality is implicit within bureaucracy and surveillance is a central aspect of the modern state. So this is not a claim that the modern state is operating in a completely different way, but that there has been a change in the emphasis and the nature of the mechanisms; and these different mechanisms affect the nature of the relationship between the state and the citizen and the ways in which policymakers construct policies. As we have seen, state power has always been limited and partial but in the *past*modern state new, more complex mechanisms of power are increasingly being used, and these are mechanisms of power that focus on individual, rather than collective, behaviours. The development of a rational choice assumption concerning power and bureaucracy has led to the development of new mechanisms of state power.

Rationality is a core element of the modern state. Rationality is based on the idea that there is some knowable and discoverable absolute truth which presumes causality; in this case policy intentions will result in specific outcomes. This assumption of science and truth means that states can be mechanisms for progress. Social problems can be identified, analyzed and corrected. Bent Flyvbjerg (1998: 36–37) suggests that power defines rationality and so with changing power relations a different conception of rationality is developed. What has occurred in recent years has been a new conception of rationality. Ironically, new right, conservative and liberal thinkers such as Friedrich Hayek (1944) and Michael Oakeshott (1962) did not accept the Enlightenment conception of rationality as applied to states. They rejected the idea that the state could gain sufficient knowledge to plan rationally. However, new right theory has substituted a notion of individual rationality; arguing that it is individuals who act on their own rational self-interest. The presumption developed from classical economics but increasingly incorporated into conceptions of public policy is the notion that individuals are utility maximizers, and therefore the mechanism for modifying behaviour is the process of changing incentive structures. This belief in market mechanisms and utility maximizers introduces a further element in state power. Rationality and regulation are explicitly control mechanisms but they are unlike bureaucracy or force, which depend on direct control of the next link in the chain; rather, they are hands-off mechanisms (Carter, 1989); they are not about direct control over individuals or groups. Hence the rational choice conception of power, in theory, introduces a new tool for government.

For critics of bureaucracy there are two problems with the traditional mechanisms. First, there is a substantial distance between the top and the bottom of the chain and so like Chinese whispers there are continual adjustments to the decisions as they pass through the bureaucratic chain. As a considerable body of literature demonstrates, the decision makers cannot control the implementers of policy (see Hill and Hupe, 2003, for a review). Second, people are able to subvert decisions; for example many programmes such as subsidies for olive trees in the EU are vulnerable to considerable fraud. Rationality and regulation recognize the failure of bureaucracy and try to establish more effective indirect controls that operate through market-like mechanisms (which in reality create different problems). Once market relations can be used as a mechanism for conceptualizing state–citizen relations, the principal–agent model can be introduced into the delivery of public goods. Yet without real free markets there is a need for regulation. Thus this chapter is concerned with how market conceptions of the state have led to incentives and regulation becoming important mechanisms for state power.

## Rational choice ontology and incentives

Within state policies there are ontological assumptions. What this means is that state policies often make assumptions about how people act and the nature of social reality. These assumptions are usually implicit and the state officials making the policies are usually unaware of them; they are such a part of the fabric of the social world that they are unquestioned and assumed to be true. However, we can see in political ideologies such as Conservativism, Communism and Christian Democracy explicit assumptions about the nature of being and the nature of human agency (for instance, much of the intellectual argument within Marxism in the 1960s was about whether people were free agents open to emancipation of the human spirit or bearers of structure). So in constructing policies, officials and politicians make assumptions about how people will react to the policies and in doing so they are making assumptions about the nature of human beings. Modernism often sees people as passive and reactive (pawns in Le Grand's [2003] term), but open to improvement of their social conditions (which in turn will make them behave in more socially responsible ways – this is the way in which modernist rationality is connected to state building; if people are provided with welfare and protection they will develop attachments to the nation state [see for example J. S. Mill [1974]). From this perspective, they are defined as passive recipients of state policy (Scott, 1998). Of course, it is often the case that the assumptions of policy makers are not consistent. Policies in some areas see the public as passive, and in others as reflexive, some in behavioural terms and some in terms of citizens with rights. The ontological assumptions of modern welfare states were partly based on modernism. Within modernism, because of its Enlightenment roots, the fundamental value is knowledge. Knowledge is the key to reason and social improvement. Of course, knowledge is not democratic but is concentrated within the hands of experts – scientists and professionals. The democratic, modern welfare state is built on a notion that experts make decisions, not the people, and so democracy is limited to accountability rather than participation. The social democratic state is statist and its ontological assumptions resonate with a range of different traditions from Plato's philosopher king to J. S. Mill's worries about the tyranny of the majority (and Ivor Jennings' warnings about 'trucking with the multitude', Lenin's faith in the state as a source of social change and, more broadly, the Enlightenment/ modernist belief in social progress). This often led to social democratic regimes taking measures to improve the social conditions of the poor without consulting with the poor about what they wanted, and hence the social housing projects of the 1950s and 1960s which led to the disruption of communities (Willmott and Young, 1960) and a growing despondency with the state as a mechanism for solving problems. From this modernist position the degree of democratic engagement is limited because those within the state have greater knowledge both in terms of information and also about possibilities and what is the public good. From this perspective politicians and bureaucrats are trustworthy because the professionals and decision makers are acting in the public interest and not their own private interest; it is a Rousseauian conception of a general will. Julian Le Grand (2003: 5) clearly sets out the assumptions concerning human motivation and agency in relation to the social democratic state:

> The democratic socialists assumed that the state and its agents were both competent and benevolent ... those who operated the welfare state could be trusted to work in the public interest. Professionals, such as doctors and teachers, were assumed to be motivated primarily by their professional ethic and hence to be concerned only with the interests of the people they were serving. Similarly politicians, civil servants, state bureaucrats, and managers were supposed accurately to divine social and individual needs in the areas concerned, to be motivated to meet those needs and hence to operate services that did the best possible job from the resources that were available.

The point that Le Grand makes about the social democratic state is that the collectivist notion of the state that developed during and after the Second World War saw officials and professionals acting collectively – as knights in Le Grand's terms. The collectivist state was built very much on power being shared between three elite groups – politicians, officials and professionals (and indeed, the policy network literature in the US and Europe highlights how many technical issues of policy were delegated to sub-governments made up of this triad; see Marsh and Rhodes, 1992a; Jordan, 1990) – and with the notion of citizens being in receipt of their beneficent policies.

Policy makers often develop policies on the basis of contradictory ontologies. One is the citizen as a reflexive actor; this is the notion that individuals 'are self-aware and typically monitor their own actions and are able to adjust these actions if, for example, they are not producing the desired effect' (Stones, 1996: 43). The notion of reflexivity leads to an assumption that power and decision making is better located within citizens than the state. In other words, policy can be made through deliberative mechanisms and decisions can be devolved downwards to those with the knowledge to make decisions at a local level (Fischer, 2003) and, as we will see in Chapter 10, people are in a position to make calculations in relation to risk.

Whilst governments around the world are experimenting with deliberation and devolution, increasingly states are developing policies based on citizens as rational actors and a rational choice ontology has begun to imbue a wide range of policies – especially those concerned with modifying human behaviour. The development of this ontology in public policy can be linked to the increasing influence of neo-liberalism and public management amongst government. As Colin Hay (2004b: 502) argues:

> [P]olitical parties vying for office now couch their political rhetoric to a considerable extent in terms of: (1) the non-negotiable character of external (principally economic) imperatives; (2) the powerlessness of domestic political actors in the face of such (ostensibly self-evident) constraints and (3) the need, in such a context, to displace responsibility to quasi-independent and supra-democratic authorities such as independent central banks.

The point that Hay is making is that states in the West have imbibed the neo-liberal conception of the state which sees the role of the state in economic policy as at best limited, possibly ineffective and often positively damaging, and this conception is to be found in the rhetoric of political leaders. It can be seen as a mechanism of legitimizing certain economic policies, in particular tight controls on borrowing, inflation and labour market reform. Hay (2004b: 514) suggests that in the British case the economic crisis of the 1970s was narrated in terms of a public choice conception of the relationship between states and markets. David Harvey (2005: 5) suggests that neo-liberal ideas of the free market and limited state have become the 'dominant conceptual apparatus' which is so 'embedded in common sense as to be take for granted and not open to question'. As we saw in Chapter 1, these sets of ideas are legitimized through the process of being established as the consensus. From the perspective of Lukes and poststructuralists, the neo-liberal agenda is presented as the limit of the possible and therefore is not questioned (and of course is presented as a legitimate way to behave rather than a power relation). For example, states legitimize labour market or welfare spending policies by reference to the limits of the market or globalization when in fact they are using it to legitimize their policy choices (see Watson and Hay, 2003). For some authors neo-liberalism takes on quite considerable powers in shaping not only how we think about economics but all aspects of social life. For Penny Griffin (2007: 222):

Neo-liberal discourse ... monopolises contemporary economic 'common sense'. Intrinsically (re)productive, historically conditioned, institutionalised and power-laden, neoliberalism regulates the identities of the objects it governs according to certain specific, gendered standards of normalisation ... [N]eo-liberal discourse constructs realities that necessarily restrict options, suitable behaviours and life identities of those it acts upon.

Harvey (2005) and Griffin make a strong claim (which is reflected in the perspectives of many analysts of both national and international politics: see Harris, 2007; Shore and Wright, 1999; Mitchell, 2001). However, we need to be careful not to reify neo-liberalism, something that happens in much of the literature where it is treated as an independent causal mechanism in explaining a range of outcomes. Griffin appears unintentionally to ascribe agency to what are a set of incoherent, inconsistent and differently interpreted and implemented ideas. We have to recognize that neo-liberalism is a highly contested concept and the imposition of neo-liberal economic experiments in the Soviet Union and Iraq, and public opposition to the consequence of neo-liberal policies, has made many states resistant to the full-scale adoption of neo-liberalism (a point Harvey [2005: 70] partially acknowledges). Whilst the Washington consensus may exist in the minds of international institutions, how its policy prescriptions are applied in particular countries varies greatly and is often the subject of rhetorical acceptance but actual resistance (see Grugel and Riggirozzi, 2007).

Neo-liberalism has not been adopted wholesale even in countries like Britain and the United States, because states have retained considerable capacity, often in areas of welfare and economic policy. What has occurred is that state policies in some areas have incorporated elements of neo-liberal thought as mechanisms for increasing rather than reducing state power. Neo-liberalism opposes state intervention as distorting market choices. Nevertheless, the economic conception of rationality, and its development through the principal–agent model, has been adopted in a range of policies and used as a way of making people change the way they behave. Interestingly, Bruno Frey (1993: 96) could suggest fifteen years ago that there had been little application of public choice in public policy; and even then it seemed to be in the rarefied area of electoral systems. Now, however, rational choice assumptions are being used in a range of policy areas, not as part of a widespread adoption of neo-liberalism but as providing states with a new mechanism for shaping outcomes. As Le Grand (2003: 23) maintains, a number of countries have shifted to market-based mechanisms for delivering public services because they 'were viewed as better placed to harness the forces of self-interest to serve the (newly discovered) consumers of public services'.

Both new right and public choice theories are critical of the idea of the citizen as passive recipient and of states as working in the collective interest. They introduced through rational choice utility maximization a new ontology into public policy. This view of human nature is derived from the notion of *homo economis* which, as Amartya Sen (1977) illustrates, can be directly linked to the work of Francis Edgeworth in the late nineteenth century, but has its roots in the work of Adam Smith and Thomas Hobbes. What is interesting about rational choice ontology is that it provides the state with a new mechanism of power. Force and authority assume that people can either be pushed or intimidated into certain patterns of behaviour. Authority assumes there is some sort of, at least implicit, contract where decisions are based on consent. With rational choice people are seen as economic actors who will respond to particular incentives. Rational choice sees individual choice as the basis of political action (John, 1998: 116) and therefore it opens up a new tool for state actors in attempting to modify behaviour. Many governments throughout the world have been influenced by the so-called new public management (NPM). NPM is based on introducing a market rationale into the public sector. The main impact of NPM has been on public sector reform which has led to a considerable injection of market rationale into processes of governance. There are three ways that rational choice assumptions have been used to affect outcomes. One is the direct use of incentives to change behaviour, the second is the creation of quasi-market relations through creating choice in the public sector, and the third is through regulation of the market. A core underpinning of this approach is the principal–agent model because it replaces bureaucratic relations with market relations.

## Principal–agent theory

As we saw in Chapter 6, power within bureaucracy is based on authority relationships; someone in the hierarchy acts in a certain way because the superior has authority. For new right critics this is problematic in many ways, not least in the sense that bureaucrats would only be working for their own interest and not those of their superiors or the public (Niskanen, 1973). As Patrick Dunleavy (1991: 151) summarizes:

> Any individual has a necessarily limited span of control in supervising the behaviour of others ... But at each stage in the upward flow of communication officials filter the information they pass upwards in order to defend their self-interest, suggesting some key limits on the effectiveness of the top-down systems.

Because subordinates control information, it is difficult for superordinates to be in control. The principal–agent model aims to create incentive structures to ensure that those delivering the service (the agent) provide what the superordinate (the principal) wants without direct control. It is intended to increase the ability of superordinates to control by replacing authority with a market mechanism (the mechanism could be price, another incentive or choice – in the sense that the principal can choose another agent to supply). Principal–agent theory originated in economics and business but is now widely used, especially in terms of the issues of control in terms of government agencies (see Pollack, 2001; Thatcher and Stone Sweet, 2002). It is based on the idea that the principal P (which could be a government department) wants the agent A to provide a particular service and the key issue is how to devise an appropriate incentive structure to ensure that A delivers what P wants. It assumes that both principals and agents are utility maximizers (Shavell, 1979). The problem for the principal is that he/she does not have sufficient information about the service that is being delivered and so has to create the correct incentives to ensure that the policy or service is delivered in the way intended without paying too much (which is why the issue of government contracts is often so controversial) (Hart and Holmstrom, 1987). Mark Thatcher and Alec Stone Sweet (2002) extend the principal–agency model to government control of quasi-independent agencies such as regulatory bodies (which are discussed below). They see the principals as 'political officials who use their authority to establish non-majoritarian institutions through a public act of delegation' and agents exercise the delegated power (Thatcher and Stone Sweet, 2001: 4–5; and see Flinders, 2008). The benefits in this relationship are that the agent has discretion in how services are delivered but the principal has to set sufficient control to ensure that the agent delivers what the principal desires.

Through rationality and regulation we see state actors attempting to create new levers of control over actors both within and outside the state. With policy implementation increasingly moving outside of line bureaucracy with agencification and privatization, governments are using both incentives and regulation as ways of trying to control bureaucrats who are at arm's length. In a sense, the consequence of the principal–agent model is that the government has to introduce another layer of control through regulation to ensure that the agent is delivering what is desired at an appropriate standard. For example, if the provision of foster care shifts to the private sector, how do state actors ensure that standards of care are maintained if a private organization is not subject directly to the rules of state bureaucracy? The answer is a process of regulation.

Regulation is a complex process. Regulation is about setting a broader framework of control than the strict rules of Weber's bureaucracy; it allows the state to steer without directly controlling through setting the boundaries of behaviour, which are often enforced by an external agency (see King, 2007; Moran, 2003). The nature of regulation varies greatly. It can be based on audit (reviewing what has been done), through creating targets whereby the agent has to achieve certain goals, or by processes of marketization where league tables are combined with choice of services in order to allow consumers of public goods to leave a poorly performing service. Regulation can be undertaken by government or by external and semi-independent organizations, and it often differs for the public and private sectors. Regulatory forms of control are based on ever-improving information systems. Processes of audit, targets and developing league tables depend on the ability to collect vast amounts of information. Through this process dual bureaucratic structures develop, separating those delivering the service from those collecting and assessing the data. Moreover, unlike incentives, regulatory processes face the same problems of traditional bureaucracy; the difficulty of obtaining robust data. As is well documented (Boyne and Law, 2005), data are often manipulated, behaviour is changed and sometimes completely false information is provided. Moreover, regulation has long been recognized as being subject to capture, with those being regulated able to adapt the rules to their interests (Wilson, 1980; Moran, 2003). The 2008 financial crisis highlighted how a highly developed structure of financial regulation was actually ineffective at regulating the banks and ensuring that they operated within sound banking practices. All bureaucratic organizations have great difficulty connecting the organizational goals with the actions of those who deliver the service on the ground. And incentives and regulation have developed as mechanisms for improving central control.

## Incentives and public policy

Incentives have been used as a way of changing behaviour in a growing number of policy areas such as welfare, the environment and education. In certain areas the incentives can be relatively simple – for example increasing the price of fuel in order to tackle global warming; in others the nature and impact of incentives is much more complex. They are all, however, based on an assumption of utility maximization. One area where incentives have been used widely is in health policy and this has three explanations. First, doctors have considerable professional power; there are few policy makers or managers who can challenge their medical decisions and hence despite attempts to control their behaviour both through policies from central government and increased managerialism, doctors have retained considerable autonomy. Because neither an official nor a manager can be in the consulting room, it is difficult to modify doctors' behaviour, and indeed it is relatively easy for doctors to appeal to outside sources if faced with what is seen as undue political pressure. Consequently, if doctors are to change their behaviour they have to choose to do so and the belief (or experience) of policy makers is that they will not respond to authority but to a changed incentive structure which punishes deviant behaviour. Second, the cost of health care is extremely high, and tends to rise exponentially, so officials have considerable incentives to attempt to control expenditure. Traditional bureaucratic politics are poor at limiting health care costs and so there is faith that the market mechanism can improve efficiency and control costs. Third, there is a considerable amount of expenditure on health research and whilst much is clinical, a large amount of research is by health economists who evaluate policies and propose reforms. Health economists tend to bring with them a utility maximizing model of human behaviour and design reforms based on the assumption of utility maximization (to which politicians and officials have been increasingly open). Economists have shaped the direction and nature of health reform and we have seen an inculcation of rational choice ontology into health policy.

In terms of public choice, health causes a problem because there is a tendency of increasing demand and costly supply. This situation applies in public systems in Britain, where supply is limited, and in private systems in the US, where there is often oversupply at very high costs. Consequently, a core feature of health service reform has been to change the incentive structure of patients and doctors to overcome the demand and supply problems. Dan Hausman and Julian Le Grand

(1999: 3) argue that prior to the introduction of a quasi-market in health care in Britain, doctors (GPs) – had a 'material incentive to refer patients to others for treatment rather than providing treatment themselves', thus also contributing to waiting lists. As a consequence, the government consciously and explicitly changed the incentive structure of GPs. GPs were given a limited fund to spend on services for patients and therefore had to make a choice about who was referred to consultants. Moreover, any surplus was to be retained by the practice and so GPs had an incentive to use funds efficiently. With the election of Labour in 1997, incentive structures were rearranged with the creation of primary care groups.

The incentive mechanism was extended when the government established new contracts with GPs. The new contracts provided extra funds for treating patients and improving services. The intention was that the money would provide incentives for extra treatment. The aim was that GPs had to meet particular targets for health care. According to the BBC (BBC, 17 January 2007):

> Meeting a particular target equates to a certain number of points – which this year will be worth £124 each. There is a total of around 1,000 points available. When the contract was being negotiated, the government estimated GPs would meet about 70% of the target. Instead – and the BMA says it warned of this – GPs hit around 90%.

The incentives produced more of the desired behaviour than the government expected and in addition, GPs decided to keep more of the extra income for their own salaries rather than investment in the practice. The key point is that it is very difficult for states to deliver health care when it is based on semi-autonomous professionals. Command rarely works and legitimacy has limited purchase because professionals have an alternative legitimizing code in their professional ethic. Consequently, governments have increasingly used incentives.

Health care is one area where incentives are well-established mechanisms for modifying behaviour. It is an indication of how the utility maximization model is being widely used both in designing social policy and for changing behaviour. Probably the best established policy is the concept of welfare-to-work policies which originated in the United States but are now used widely across the world. These policies – which have developed most significantly in Britain and the United States – are based on very complex and contradictory sets of ontological assumptions. People are assumed to be moral agents who could act differently in terms of looking for work or childcare but who are also rational agents who respond to particular incentive structures (suggesting that they are morally neutral) (see Chapter 11). What is undoubtedly the case is that economic 'salvation' is seen through policies that focus on individual behaviour and not social or collective policy solutions. As Karen Clarke (2006) suggests, social inclusion is seen to work through individual opportunity.

This view contrasts strongly with the assumptions of postwar social democratic welfare policy. With the initial creation of welfare states welfare provision was seen as a right and, as Hugh (2008) points out, it was based on intrinsic motivations. Within T.H. Marshall's (1950) concept of citizenship access to welfare was a core element of citizenship within a social democratic model. However, the new right saw welfare regimes as creating dependency relationships, with people unable to break out of welfare support because the benefits were often greater than low-paid work; they focussed on the individual moral consequences and not the collective social impact (the moral elements of these types of policies are discussed in Chapter 11). In the United States where welfare was never seen as a right, but as a safety net for the 'deserving' poor, there was growing pressure to create a system to 'disincentivize' welfare claims. The Personal Responsibility and Work Opportunity Reconciliation Act of 1996 replaced Aid to Families with Dependent Children with Temporary Assistance for Needy Families (TANF) (see Smith, 2007). According to Danziger *et al.* (2002: 2):

> TANF reduces the likelihood that a single mother can 'choose' to remain a welfare recipient, because even if she finds that economic benefits of work do not exceed its cost, cash assistance is conditional on the performance of work-related or community service activities.

With a 60-month total limit on benefits, the incentives to return to work are high.

Similar incentive-based policies have been used in education, waste collection and teenage pregnancy. In education it is increasingly the case that teachers and head teachers are rewarded for performance and are set targets for standards which have to be met in order to receive specific rewards. For Le Grand (2003: 117) the success of the policies 'lies in the robust motivational structure of the key actors. In a school, the relevant decision-makers are head teachers. In the quasi-market, the actors are motivated in large part by a desire to preserve or improve the financial health of the institution.'

Increasingly, countries within Europe are using a range of economic incentives intended to increase the amount of recycling (Ventosa, 2002). These can be collective benefits such as rewards to communities for increasing the amount of recycling or individual benefits such as announced in Britain, which allows councils to give tax reductions to those who recycle more. Or they can be disincentives, as exist in the United States, where you have to pay for what you throw away (Ventosa, 2002). As Ventosa highlights, the problems with pay-as-you-throw schemes is that there is a strong incentive for fraud and fly-tipping, which highlights the difficulties of developing the most appropriate incentive structures. Of course, the recycling case provides a good example of the dilemmas illustrated by behavioural economics. If we assume that recycling is a moral good, then rather than focussing on changing norms, governments are using financial incentives to influence behaviour. Consequently, recycling is about an economic transaction and this of course creates the problem that as incentive structures change, then the success of recycling declines because people are taught to be economic actors who may want to off-load externalities, rather than moral citizens who recycle because it is a collective good. Moreover, as Richard Titmuss (1970) demonstrated, shifting moral responsibilities into economic exchanges can have adverse effects (see New Economic Foundation, 2005: 6). One study of a number of incentive schemes in Sussex (UK) demonstrated that certain types of schemes, with relatively low cost incentives, did appear to raise the amount of material recycled (WERG, 2006). However, it is not clear whether the publicity associated with the incentives led to a greater awareness of recycling.

Perhaps more surprisingly, a utility maximization framework has also been applied to the issue of teenage pregnancy (see also Chapter 11). From this perspective, potential mothers are seen as making a rational decision about pregnancy. For girls from poor backgrounds with limited employment opportunities it is argued that pregnancy provides status, a role and through the welfare system a secure level of income that is significantly higher than welfare provision for a single adult. Consequently, for some teenagers it is rational to become pregnant. For example, according to a UK Department of Education and Science (DES) report (2006: 8):

> Teenage pregnancy is strongly associated with the most deprived and socially excluded young people. Difficulties in young people's lives such as poor family relationships, low self-esteem and unhappiness at

school also put them at greater risk. From the perspective of young people in such circumstances, *early parenthood can appear a rational choice*, providing a means for marking their transition to adulthood or having somebody to love in their lives. There are also some communities in which early parenthood is seen as normal and not a cause for concern. (Emphasis added)

But the best predictor of teenage pregnancy is being the child of a teenage mother, suggesting a strong social as well as a utility maximizing influence (DES, 2006: 14). Interestingly, a study by an economist argued that policy in Britain had increased sexual activity and sexual disease by making contraception more available. According to *The Guardian* (5 April 2004):

> The author of the report, Professor David Paton of Nottingham University Business School, said: 'In this case it appears measures aimed at reducing teenage pregnancy rates induced changes in teenage behaviour that were large enough not only to negate the intended impact on conceptions, but to have an adverse impact on another important area of sexual health – sexually transmitted infections.' He said the government assumed that adolescent sexual activity was the outcome of random decisions but his research suggested that teenagers thought rationally about the decision to become sexually active, so when the cost of birth control went down, its use went up.

In the US rationality has been used at the federal level to try and change the behaviour of states in relation to policy on teenage pregnancy. Through TANF states were given incentives in terms of extra grants if they reduced the levels of teenage pregnancy, and a number of states have expanded their programmes as a consequence (Costello and Henry, 2003). The point is that in both the United States and Britain policy on teenage pregnancy has been to present teenagers with a more realistic sense of the cost and benefits so that the decision is no longer rational (one popular policy is to leave young girls with a realistic doll for a night so they find out the time and effort involved in looking after a baby) and to change the structure of benefits so that they are less favourable for teenage mothers and, through welfare-to-work, so that babies do not provide an opt-out from the labour market.

Incentives, although now a central element of the capabilities of states, are problematic and limited levers. They assume rationality in a narrow sense of utility maximization. Much behavioural economics, for example, highlights how other forms of rationality operate. The example that is often given is taxi drivers, who work untill they have earned a certain sum of money regardless of the amount of business. So on a quiet day they will work more hours and on a busy day fewer. A utility maximization model would predict that taxi drivers would work when it was busy and not when it was quiet (Camerer *et al.*, 1997). For behavioural economists changing behaviour could be about changing social norms. For example, it is very difficult to police domestic violence and therefore a better form of control is to make it socially unacceptable (New Economics Foundation, 2005).

Incentives also create pathological behaviour – people try to bend the rules in order to achieve rewards. Jacob and Levitt (2003: 843) inform us that

> High powered incentive schemes are designed to align the behaviour of agents with the interests of the principal implementing the system. A shortcoming of such schemes, however, is that they are likely to induce behaviour distortions along other dimensions as agents seek to game the rules.

They found in their work looking at incentives for improving school results that about 5 per cent of teachers cheated as a consequence of the incentive scheme (although presumably 95 per cent did not cheat). Likewise in Britain when hospitals had to meet targets to reduce waiting time in hospitals, in order to meet the four-hour deadline many patients were treated after 3 hours and 55 minutes. There can be little doubt that incentives affect outcome and what is more important is that governments are increasingly using incentives, rather than threats or coercion, to achieve outcomes.

There are often mixed and contradictory incentive structures. In adopting these types of policy governments are often combining two different and conflicting ontologies: the utility maximizer, what Le Grand calls the knave, and the public sector ethos, Le Grand's knights. In the public sector actors are increasingly given incentives and expected to respond to market signals, and then rewarded for performance. Yet at the same time the government wants them to work for the public good. It may be difficult to sustain these two demands in tandem because when people expect incentives and rewards the public service ethos will be driven out.

Whilst it would be possible to run higher education purely on market grounds this may cause problems. One way to improve the education system could be to reward universities according to demand or exam success. Yet to do this would undermine the system. It is expected that admissions and examinations are based on some notion of quality. If I was paid for the number of students I taught, I would have an incentive to teach as many as possible and therefore make my courses popular rather than intellectually rigorous. If I was to be paid for exam performance I would no longer be able to grade my own students. The trust element of higher education would disappear and, consequently, there would be a much higher cost with the need to increase the level of external validation. Incentives create difficulties because humans are reflexive. This means that incentives do not have the same appeal to each person and people game play or ensure they maximize rewards with minimal changes to their behaviour. If policy makers are going to modify behaviour, they have to continue to adapt the incentives as human ingenuity subverts them. Incentives also concentrate on the cost structure and not the social situation of the agent, and as social situations are infinite, then the impact of incentives is never predictable. Incentives have been introduced as a new mechanism for states to achieve their goals but, like other mechanisms within the modern state, they have limited purchase and considerable flaws. However, incentives are only one mechanism within the rational choice canon – regulation and choice are also being developed on similar assumptions in order to produce desired social outcomes.

## Regulation and choice

The most direct application of utility maximization is through changing incentives. However, the principal–agent model opens up other possibilities which are related to rational choice assumptions about behaviour. One is choice. Choice becomes an important tool in policy with a rational choice framework because the assumption is that providers of services will provide a better service if they believe that customers are able to exit; thus replicating market relations. The other route is regulation.

### Regulation

Regulation is important in principal–agent relations as a mechanism for trying to ensure that the discretion of the agent is limited – because with public goods (and indeed many private goods) it is not possible just to specify a particular outcome because regard has to be paid to issues of equity and quality. As a result, states have to put in place regulatory regimes to ensure that the agent provides a reasonable standard of service. In doing this the state is trying to redress the information asymmetries that exist between the principal and the agent. Regulation also has a second function within a utility maximization framework, and that is to create 'market-type contexts' in the absence of real competition (as in the case of the privatization of utilities) (Lodge, 2002: 52); it has a role in underpinning the market where there is market failure (Jayasuriya, 2001). For Michael Moran (2003: 88–90), regulation is about colonizing traditionally non-market relationships with market criteria, whilst at the same time increasing the influence of the state. With regulation we see an important and complex shift within state power. The state retreats from an area either by delegation to an agency or privatization. Nevertheless, states are dependent both on ensuring that services are delivered, and on public support, and therefore state actors are rarely prepared to leave public services to actors they do not control. Consequently, the process of privatization and 'agencification' is followed by a process of regulation. The state relinquishes one mechanism of power – bureaucracy based on legitimacy – and replaces it with another – regulation based on principal–agent arrangements (although some such as Mitchell [2001] suggest that the retrenchment of the state allows the voluntary sector to fill the gap and so relieves the state from responsibility for providing goods).

There has undoubtedly been a significant expansion in regulatory regimes over the last twenty years. David Levi-Faur (2005: 13) argues:

> Regulatory expansion has acquired a life and dynamics of its own. Regulatory solutions that were shaped in North America and Europe are increasingly internationalised and projected globally.

For Levi-Faur new forms of governance emerging from new public management, neo-liberalism and globalization have led to little de-regulation, and regulation is necessary for the efficiency and organization of markets. Indeed, he demonstrates that in the areas of electricity and telecommunications, regulatory agencies have spread to over 60 and over 100 countries respectively (Levi-Faur, 2005: 18). Another important point is that changing conceptions of risk (Moran, 2003), which are discussed in Chapter 10, have led to increased regulatory policies. Governments are concerned both with externalities of private sector activity and their own liabilities and so have licensed a growing number of bodies to limit potential dangers to people (for example the UK Criminal Records Bureau to undertake checks on those working with children). Hood *et al.* (2001) suggest that there are more than 'two regulators for every doer and more than ten regulatory organizations for every major government department' (Levi-Faur, 2005: 20). For Levi-Faur the regulatory state is a qualitatively different way of organizing capitalism and therefore a new mode of state intervention. However, as he recognizes, regulation has long existed and it is better to understand it as an extra tool in terms of state power rather than indicative of a new form of state organization. Regulation exists for particular problems where utility maximization ontologies can be applied, but states are not consistent and will use regulation alongside contradictory mechanisms. Indeed, the whole issue of regulation is caught within the dilemma of autonomy and control (see Per and Christianson, 2006). The principal–agent model and regulatory mechanisms imply a light role for the state, relying on a Hayekian notion of local knowledge being the most important element in the delivery of policies. However, states are more concerned with outputs and hence attempting to develop regulatory regimes that achieve particular goals.

The process of regulation is complex and multifaceted. For Moran (2003: 13) regulation 'is a form of cybernetic control: the regulator is a governor receiving information about the state of a system and its interaction with the environment'. Regulation occurs through a range of mechanisms: setting prices, ensuring that there is competition in the awarding of contracts, enforcing contracts, setting targets, requiring information or auditing performance. Indeed, there is little agreement within the existing literature on what is included in regulation as opposed to legislation. The aim of regulation is always to affect outcomes either directly or indirectly. A regulator may say to a police force: you need to meet a certain target for preventing street crimes, or to a teacher: you must teach these skills. The discretion in achieving those outcomes varies. Cris Shore and Susan Wright (1999) highlight the complexity of regulation in relation to higher education and see it as a set of power relations that are legitimized in terms of accountability:

> Over the past two decades higher education in Britain and in other industrialized states has undergone a process of radical reform or structural readjustment. A key element of these reforms has been the

introduction of mechanisms for measuring 'teaching performance', judging 'research quality' and assessing 'institutional effectiveness'. These mechanisms are intended to ensure 'accountability', a principle justified on the rational and democratic grounds that those who spend taxpayers' money should be accountable to the public. Measuring performance is characteristically framed in terms of 'improving quality' and 'empowerment', as though these mechanisms were emancipatory and enabling.

Moran (2003: 133–4) highlights how in its education system Britain has seen a complete transformation of the regulatory regime from one which was based on cooperation between professional groups, and conducted largely below the view of government, to one in which a range of regulatory bodies are involved in the detailed monitoring of schools in a much more adversarial manner:

> [I]n the space of less than a decade, a cooperative, enclosed, oligarchic world has been broken open. Micro-management of the school system from the centre was now so great that Ministers were forming views on such detail as particular methods of teaching. In the course of the 1990s, the country acquired one of the most ambitious schemes of school inspection in the world.

In addition to incentives, inspection by regulatory agencies, targets and league tables have been used to closely control the activities of schools and to limit the autonomy of professionals. Regulation is an exceptional tool for states. On one hand it ties in to a rhetoric of smaller government and 'hands-off' government, but what it actually does is to provide what can be a forceful lever for state policy. States cannot live with the logic of neo-liberalism. Whilst many states have accepted a reduced role for states in markets, regulation has ensured that they continue to provide a strong framework for the way policies are implemented. Traditional bureaucracy is based on the sense that state directives have legitimacy and so will be implemented. Regulation based on a rational choice ontology is distrustful of other actors and therefore creates mechanisms for ensuring that outputs are met either through contract, audit or targets; the assumption being that self-interested utility maximizers are morally weak. Regulation is often combined with incentive schemes because an important element in the regulatory process is the rewarding of those who meet targets or pass inspections, again introducing the same sorts of pathologies that develop with the incentive-based policies described above. There is also an important way in which regulation reconceptualizes the nature of state power. The point that Kanishaka Jayasuriya (2001) makes is that it involves a shift from positive to negative coordination; this is coordination more concerned with procedural guidelines (for example setting the target inflation rate for a central government) rather than designing specific policy interventions. Jim Buller and Matt Flinders (2005) highlight how this is also part of a process of depoliticization whereby the decisions are now presented as technical decisions outside the realm of politics. Again this is the case with central bank independence but can also be seen in examples such as biotechnology, where regulation is placed in a 'scientific domain' and so is isolated from political and social pressure (Salter and Jones, 2002: 337). These changes have important implications for the relationship between citizens and decision making, but also, as we will see in Chapter 11, this is increasingly leading state actors to more and more convoluted relations with particular policy issues.

## Choice

Choice is not easily conceived of as a form of power but it relates to the discussion of power and rationality in two ways. First, in classical economics choice in markets gives consumers power and forces firms to become efficient or to go bankrupt. In following the rational economic actor model, states are changing citizens into consumers who have the power of exit and therefore are able to force producers of public goods to improve services (Needham, 2007). The ability to choose is a reflection of having power. This leads to the second facet of power within choice. Choice is intended to change power relations between producers and consumers of public goods. Through choice there is a combination of two different notions of agency. On the one side the rational choice perspective sees agents responding to incentives, but on the other the choice ontology sees actors as reflexive, making choices in relation to the best services.

Choice, however, is seen as a mechanism for changing power relations between citizens and providers. Le Grand (2003) sees the traditional welfare state as placing considerable resources and authority in the hands of producers, and those who receive public goods are essentially passive. In traditional public good production this led to highly standardized behaviour, and at least a cursory similarity between Communist and Social Democratic regimes, in that both provided citizens with very limited choice in public goods. So in both East Germany and Britain citizens received universal health care where the standard of care provided was similar to all recipients. In the case of public housing in Britain, for instance, the role of citizens was extremely passive. Often people were moved from particular communities to new public estates from, say, around the Liverpool Docks to the North Liverpool suburbs or from the East End of London to Essex. People had little or no choice over what house they received, they could not repaint their houses and they were given rent books with codes of conduct which were intended to govern how people behaved in public housing. Power then lay completely with the provider, and choice was intended to realign the relationship, as the UK Prime Minister Tony Blair said in a speech in 2003:

> Choice mechanisms enhance equity by exerting pressure on low quality or incompetent providers. Competitive pressure and incentive drives up quality, efficiency and responsiveness in the public sector. Choice leads to higher standards … The over-riding principle is clear. (Quoted in Public Administration Select Committee, 2004/5)

The rational choice ontology is deeply integrated into the way choice operates to change the behaviour of public service actors. The choice agenda is about applying economic theory to public services.

Choice has been used increasingly in the United States and Britain, Sweden and other countries as a tool for improving public services in areas such as health, education and housing. For example, in the United States the problem with health care has been the way in which insurance systems have pushed up costs. As a consequence, payers of health care – both government and insurance companies – have looked at ways to reduce costs. Initially payers used 'prospective payment schemes' whereby they paid average costs and so the providers had an incentive to reduce costs and to avoid high cost patients. In the second scheme payers created 'preferred payer organizations'. The payers choose a provider, forcing competition between providers and reducing costs (Burgess, Propper and Wilson, 2005: 25). Choice mechanisms have been used more extensively in education on a number of occasions. In the UK, Sweden and some states in the US, parents have in principle been given choice and money follows students, and there is some suggestion that this has resulted in improved services (Hoxby, 2002). However there are still considerable questions related to whether consumers want choice and how real the choices they have are.

## Conclusion

One of the key mechanisms of power for modern states has traditionally been command. States would direct either through force or authority. The new right rhetoric about the state has led to a debate about reducing the role of the state; the shift from steering to rowing and the failure of principals to control the agents through traditional bureaucracy. The new right saw rational actors undermining processes of implementation. States in a number of countries took on board the rational choice critique and in a range of state activities state actors have inculcated the language of economic theory and adopted a rational choice ontology. Consequently, rather than changing behaviour through command there has been an increased emphasis on incentives, regulation and market mechanisms, all of which assume that humans act as rational utility maximizers and will respond to economic (or quasi-economic) signals in particular ways. There is a view that there is a degree of predictability in incentive models that does not exist in command models. Command depends on people obeying; in a sense they have to do what an external actor directs but command is a blunt instrument. With rational choice models it is the actor him/herself who makes the choice to act in a certain way on the basis of the incentive structure and in that sense, in principle, resolving the problem of non-compliance. Incentives, whether positive or negative, are seen as much more efficient mechanisms for achieving desired outcomes. Incentives are therefore seen as resolving the pathologies of bureaucracy but they do so in a way that focuses on the behaviour of individual agents or at least people in particular situations, such as teenage mothers or benefit claimants. In addition, these strategies assume that problems are resolved through the actions of individuals rather than wider socio-economic change. For example, the problem of teenage pregnancy is not resolved through reducing inequality but through getting teenagers to make different choices within their existing social situation.

The problem is, if we assume people are rational, then it is difficult to design the correct incentives. Often incentives are contradictory and the way they are perceived by the designer is often not how they are perceived by those who are subject to them. Moreover, policy makers are not consistent. Policy makers operate with a range of implicit and contradictory ontologies and therefore design policies with different expectations of human behaviour. There are few public services where only market signals are used to control outputs. Even in the private medical system in the United States doctors continue to have a professional ethos. State actors expect those delivering services to operate both to market and public sector criteria. In the British public sector it is now common for public sector workers to have performance-related pay, but at the same time not to be concerned solely with monetary gain. Targets and incentives also produce pathologies. Rather than providing the required service, agents – if they are rational – act to fulfill the targets and so behaviour can be changed in perverse ways. Perhaps the greatest problem, however, is the assumption that people are rational in the utility-maximizing sense. It is apparent in the case of choice that it is difficult for people to act as utility maximizers because they do not have complete information. Moreover, they may want to choose values like community over the best option. There is considerable evidence that people act in ways that are counter to rational utility maximization and consequently incentives do not produce expected outcomes.

# Chapter 9

# Surveillance

In Spike Lee's film, *Inside Man*, a team of bank robbers manages to escape from a bank surrounded by police by putting all the hostages in masks and boiler suits. The bank robbers, dressing in the same suits, mix themselves with the hostages and so when they burst out of the bank the police do not know who is a hostage and who is a bank robber. It is impossible to identify the innocent and the guilty. As a consequence everyone is handcuffed and taken to the police station for interrogation. This is a metaphor for security since the attacks of 11 September 2001 (9/11). The state finds it difficult to identify who is innocent and who is guilty. Those who seem to be innocent have the potential to be guilty and it would seem that many who appear to be guilty are innocent. Indeed, one of the factors that is striking about the investigation of the London bombing on 7 July 2005 is that the report demonstrates the unremarkable nature of the backgrounds of the suicide bombers and the surprise that they came from inner-city Leeds and not from abroad. They demonstrated no signs of being potential terrorists but appeared like many other British Asians.

This new post-9/11 situation both reflects and reinforces a remarkable shift in the nature of state surveillance. As we saw in Chapter 2, Foucault saw surveillance as a mechanism for inculcating values into people and as a way of defining the good; the process of social surveillance established good and bad norms of behaviour. The presumption of post-9/11 surveillance is that the bad are hidden. The potential for illegal behaviour is widespread and so the state needs continual vigilance to ensure it catches the bad amongst the innocent. However, this shift is not a consequence of 9/11; rather, 9/11 has exacerbated a process that had already started and which has been enhanced by technology and by the inherent modernizing nature of states (Lyon, 2003). States have always attempted to watch and control populations. Technology now makes this more effective but it also changes the processes of social control. This chapter illustrates the ways in which surveillance is developing as a new form of state power and the impact that surveillance has on the way state actors understand deviant behaviour. As we will see, surveillance is a core power of modern states, but

increasingly the processes of surveillance have become more individualized and are having an impact on how deviancy is observed. Moreover,
in many ways surveillance is extending the gaze of the state beyond those
who break the law to the whole citizenry, and especially those who are
deemed *likely* to break the law. What increased surveillance does is to
increase the capacity of the state, and it changes the balance of resources
between citizens and the state. Citizens have always had a great ability to
subvert state goals because the gaze of the state could not observe citizens' actions in real time. The new forms of surveillance allow the state
to gather data on what people are actually doing and therefore enforcement becomes simpler. Digital information sources have substantially
increased the ability of the state to store data and observe the actions of
citizens. It is a significant development of state power.

## Developing surveillance

States, especially modern states, could not exist without some form of
surveillance. As Anthony Giddens (1985: 17) claims, 'All states involve
the reflexive monitoring of aspects of the reproduction of the social
systems subject to their rule'. In other words, the maintenance of a state
system depends on some monitoring of the population in order to
ensure that the system is maintained. States (not in the way that the
modern state is conceived) cannot exist without boundaries and these
borders require the surveillance of goods and people. Similarly, modern
states, and most pre-modern states, need taxation to sustain their activities and in order to tax the population there is a need for surveillance.
The best example of this process of surveillance is the Domesday Book
of William the Conqueror, which was compiled in England in 1085–6
in order to estimate the economic resources of the country for the
purpose of tax. James Scott (1998) illustrates how, because states relied
on land for taxation revenue, this led to the development of standardized measures in order for tax collectors to be able easily to assess the
tax due. Scott also highlights how the development of the modern state
is predicated on the creation of permanent surnames. As he points out
(1998: 65), in almost every case the creation of names 'was a state
project, designed to allow officials to identify, unambiguously, the
majority of its citizens. When successful, it went far to create legible
people'. The processes of surveillance that developed subsequently
such as property rolls, censuses and conscription lists depend on the
existence of names (Scott 1998: 65).

It is only with names that the whole process of surveillance in a modern sense can occur. As Scott points out, names and photographs allow for the existence of identity cards and passports, enabling states to watch the movements of individuals across borders or even within countries. Nevertheless, as Edward Higgs (2001: 176–8) demonstrates, most of the surveillance in the pre-modern state (in the case of Britain), whilst more than face-to-face, was carried out at the local level. Even in the case of taxation, this was recorded and organized at the local level and the existence of lists of taxpayers nationally was not to check payment but to audit the work of local tax offices.

Of course, one of the most important developments in terms of surveillance has been the creation of the census, which can be traced back to Roman times but became increasingly established as routine and systematic in the nineteenth century. (Although as Higgs [2001: 180] points out, the census had limited uses in terms of surveillance.) At the same time the development of cities and the breakdown of community forms of social control led to the establishment of the police who were responsible for surveillance of particular sections of the population (Innes, 2003; Lyon, 2003). A whole set of factors came together partly resulting from an increasingly mobile society with the loss of face-to-face contact. The development of motor cars and registration plates and the preparation of war all contributed to the development of increasing methods of surveillance (Lyon, 2003).

One of the most important developments has been a shift from the census, which was the first national form of data collection, but which produced largely aggregate data, to more institutional level data, which allows state actors to observe and control the individual. One of the early developments, which allows quite specific control and dates from the nineteenth century and the establishment of nation states, is the introduction of identity cards. These were introduced in Britain in war time for a limited period (Elliot, 2006) but they have been much more widely used in continental Europe. France and Germany have had an identity card system since the war. In Russia and the Soviet Union internal passports have long been important mechanisms for controlling the population (Matthews, 1993). In Spain identity cards have existed since the Franco regime and since 1976 all people over 14 have had to have an identity card with a centrally provided Número de Indentificación Fiscal (NIF) which is used in a range of transactions.

The second element in the individualizing of data was the introduction of welfare systems. When the United States Congress passed the 1935 Social Security Act it became necessary for every worker to have a social security number so that earnings could be recorded centrally (Garfinkel, 2000: 18). With the existence of both unique identity numbers and identity cards it was relatively easy for states to track individuals. The notion of individual records became even more endemic as a part of government with the development of the taxation system (Higgs, 2001: 190).

The ultimate development of this system occurred within the East European bloc where in a number of states complex systems of surveillance of individuals developed. The Communist regimes built highly complex and vast systems of internal security. The foundation of the system was the secret police, which often subjected individuals to detailed and direct observation. Yet the more insidious element of the system was the way in which ordinary people were incorporated into the system in order to provide evidence on friends and neighbours. Files released since the collapse of the Berlin Wall demonstrate how, especially in East Germany, the process of surveillance involved approximately 300,000 people who were providing information to the security services (Funder, 2003).

What Eastern Europe and the development of welfare systems demonstrate is that bureaucracy can be an effective mechanism for watching populations and controlling their activities. Surveillance is not a new development. What is new is the impact that technology has had on the processes, uses and implications of surveillance. As Stephen Graham and David Wood (2003: 228) remind us, 'Digitization facilitates a step change in the power, intensity and scope of surveillance. Surveillance is everywhere. Computers are everywhere'. Digital technology and, increasingly, biometric technology have had the same impact on the process of surveillance that naming had; it has allowed the state to develop more and deeper forms of watching citizens. More importantly, the development of digital technology changes the nature of power:

> Today's circuits of communication and the databases they generate constitute a Superpanopticon, a system of surveillance without walls, windows, towers or guards. The quantitative advances in the technologies of surveillance result in a qualitative change in the microphysics of power. (Poster, 1990, quoted in Graham and Wood, 2003: 230)

The process of digitization has opened up a whole new range of mechanisms of surveillance. CCTV is becoming widely used in American and particularly British cities and this is increasingly developed into automated systems and face recognition systems whereby the cameras are able to pick out particular people (Garfinkel, 2000; Whitaker 1999). Developments such as global positioning systems and mobile phones mean that it is possible to track the movements of individuals. As Reg Whitaker (1999: 95) points out, 'in Britain, cell phone-tracking data are being retained for a two year period and have been made available to law enforcement agencies'. Of course, tracking use of the internet is now relatively easy and well established. In Britain automatic number plate recognition technology is used by police forces to record and store data on millions of car journeys a day and this data is now being stored for five years (partly because digital storage makes it very easy to collect and store vast amounts of data) (*The Guardian*, 15 September 2008).

The extent of surveillance in Britain, which is probably the country where digitized surveillance is most developed, is illustrated by an official report by the Information Commissioner. The report begins by saying:

> We live in a surveillance society. It is pointless to talk about surveillance society in the future tense. In all the rich countries of the world everyday life is suffused with surveillance encounters, not merely from dawn to dusk but 24/7. Some encounters obtrude into the routine, like when we get a ticket for running a red light when no one was around but the camera. But the majority are now just part of the fabric of daily life. (Information Commissioner, 2006: 5)

The report demonstrates the way in which the modernist project of a bureaucratic state that can order and tax society has made a qualitative change with the integration of computers and digitization into the process of social surveillance. Technological changes in telecommunications like the development of mobile phones and the ability to track the movements of users, the introduction of CCTV, and digitization, which allows their automated use, mean that the levels and intensity of surveillance have increased rapidly. In 2004 over two million people were fined in Britain for speeding as a consequence of being caught on camera. As the report reminds us:

> The intensification of surveillance of the motorist is set to expand rapidly. In March 2005, the Association of Chief Police Officers demanded a national network of Automatic Number Plate

Recognition (ANPR) 'utilizing police, local authority, Highways Agency, other partner and commercial sector cameras' including the integration of the existing town centres and high street cameras, with a National ANPR Data Centre, with an operational capacity to process 35 million ANPR reads every day increasing to 50 million by 2008, stored for two years. (Information Commissioner, 2006 18–19)

Also important is the development of databases which not only hold vast amounts of data, but pull together data from different sources making it possible to track the movements and contacts of individuals. As the report states, every transaction creates a data trail that can be linked to an individual. Databases are being combined with biometric data – identification of individuals through iris, facial features and fingerprints – to provide powerful surveillance mechanisms for the police and security forces. In addition:

Surveillance practices are increasingly referenced, organized and located through Geographical Information Systems (GISs). Many actually track the geographical movements of people, vehicles or commodities using RFID chips, Global Positioning Systems (GPS), smart ID cards, transponders or the radio signals given off by mobile phones or portable computers. (Information Commissioner, 2006: 24)

Surveillance is a central element of the modern state and it was the development of surveillance and bureaucratic structures which allowed states to organize vast amounts of data that allowed the modern state to function. New technology has led to an exponential growth in the forms of surveillance, who is surveyed, how much data can be collected and ways of using and sharing power. These new forms of surveillance have had a qualitative effect on what the state can do and how it operates. This chapter will examine the implications of new forms of surveillance for the state.

## The implications of surveillance

In liberal theory the role of the state should be limited to ensuring that the behaviour of individuals does not harm the interests of others. Whilst the state does attempt to restrain people, coercion and control are often applied retrospectively. However, modern states create considerable tensions for liberalism because they are based on ordering and registering information about individuals. Rarely now is intervention limited to occasions when there is a danger of 'harm' to others. As Higgs (2001: 175) reminds us:

> If one were asked to create a list of features of the modern Western state which set it apart from previous political formations, the central collection and analysis of information, especially that on individuals, would be a strong contender for inclusion.

Within the work of Foucault and others on governmentality is the notion that the power of the state lies in the techniques it has for intervention in human behaviour, or even the creation of the subject; in other words, defining what is a good citizen, a criminal, or a terrorist. In the past the crucial techniques of power were plans, reports, the census, and bureaucracy (Inda, 2006: 7). However, the new technologies of surveillance create a qualitative change in how data are collected, organized and used. Consequently, they change the way in which the state intervenes with the subject and change the capabilities and mechanisms through which the state intervenes in society. This new technology provides the state with vast amounts of information but also different types of information. Computers allow governments to connect up many sources of information, but this is not just the information that government used to collect through bureaucratic methods; it is records of contacts through phones and computers, and information on movements through cameras. The approach of Foucault and his followers sensitizes us to the idea that new technologies do not just give the state new resources but change the relationship between the state and the citizen, and with both domestic and international organizations. Like approaches based on incentives, surveillance allows detailed intervention in social policy. Increasingly states are developing policies where problematic families are placed under intense and continual supervision in order to 'correct' their behaviours. For instance, under one programme run by the British Home Office families which are seen as the worst offenders in terms of anti-social behaviour are offered incentives to change their behaviour and also provided with considerable surveillance within the home. At its greatest extent this may involve '24 hour support and supervision from staff in accommodation provided by the project' (Department of Communities and Local Government, 2006). These may be successful and innovative programmes, but the point about them is the extent of state intervention and how that intervention is focussed on individual patterns of behaviour. Moreover, it creates the sense that social problems are resolved through individual, and not social, interventions. Like the use of incentives, the resolution of social problems is seen to lie with individual action and not collective solutions and those under the full gaze of the state have very little room for manoeuvre in terms of subverting state power. Indeed, as Pete Fussey (2008) points out, many surveillance processes accept rational choice assumptions.

The collection and location of information about individuals continues to be within states; it is not challenged by international organizations but it is being increasingly challenged by private companies. States have an important resource in terms of their control of this information. However, there are threats to the state monopoly of information. The European Union is developing a proposal that states develop a database of bank accounts (Félez, 2005). 'The European Parliament has approved proposals on data retention that would compel telecom firms to keep customer email logs, details of internet usage and phone call records for between six months to two years.' The intention is that this material is used in the fight against serious crime and terrorism. Consequently, data-sharing between states is becoming more common. For example, the British Prime Minister, Gordon Brown, has said:

> I am delighted that the UK and Irish governments will now approach the EU for better systems of data sharing so that we can deal with potential threats – whether it is criminal conspiracies or terrorist conspiracies – and work together by sharing data with our other European colleagues in a way that we have not done before. (ZD Net, 2007)

It seems that the British Home Office is part of a programme to ensure that all EU data is 'interoperable' in order to create a European Identity Network within the next three years (*The Daily Telegraph*, 27 November 2007).

It is also the case that the United States is putting increasing pressure both on countries and airline companies to provide data on travellers from other countries. Airlines currently travelling to the US have to provide 19 pieces of information on passengers including names, addresses and credit card numbers. There are proposals to extend this further with EU countries having to provide information on people overflying the US and on the families of passengers (*The Guardian*, 11

February 2008). The EU is resistant to the new demands but the case illustrates the importance of information to states and the extent to which the sharing of data is developing outside national borders.

Of course a considerable amount of data is collected outside the framework of the state. The private sector collects and stores tremendous amounts of information. As Félez (2005: 7) illustrates: 'There are more personal data than ever before in history in the hands of private companies'. Private companies collect data through credit cards, ISPs, loyalty cards, the use of mobile phones, bank accounts and more. However, there are restrictions on sharing this data, although clearly much information is sold on from the original source. It is regulated by government and to a large degree it is available to governments for their use. Moreover, it is only governments that are able to take away liberty as a consequence (Stanley and Steinhardt, 2003).

The vast array of digital information provides the state with power because it creates 'transformative capacity' which for Giddens (1985: 7) 'is the capacity to intervene in a given set of events as in some way to alter them'. States exist within complex networks of power (Mann, 1986: 1) but because of its ability to abstract and act on information, the state is 'the pre-eminent' power container (Giddens, 1985: 14). In many ways the process of surveillance is at the core of state power. States have a capability of surveillance that is beyond the capability of any other organization and they can use their position legitimately to use and combine power. Whilst states may have lost their monopoly of legitimate violence, they do have a monopoly on using the combination of data sources for surveillance.

There are a number of important aspects of surveillance that we have to take account of in terms of understanding power. First, surveillance is a core aspect of modernity. Modern states are based on surveillance. Bureaucracy is essentially a process for surveillance and, as we saw in Chapter 5, audit and information gathering form an essential party of the traditional powers of government. Second, there has been a qualitative and quantitative change in the nature of surveillance. In the modern state surveillance was largely aggregate except perhaps in the case of the delivery of welfare where the individual identification of people was necessary for the delivery of welfare services. The sheer quantity of data that exists, and the developing mechanisms for processing it, means that increasingly surveillance is focussing on individuals. A mechanism is developing whereby the behaviour of everyone is potentially being watched all the time, and this is a mechanism of control of growing importance. We anticipate that we are being watched, and so behave differently, or data about us can be used to constrain our behaviour. Interestingly, this is a shift away from Foucault's view of surveillance. For Foucault, power that has been developed since the nineteenth century has become increasingly depersonalized: 'One doesn't have here a power which is wholly in the hands of one person who can exercise it alone and totally over the others. It's a machine in which everyone is caught'. For Foucault, 'power is a machine that no one owns' (Foucault, 2002b: 99). However, what Foucault does recognize, despite his opposition to notions of historical development, is the way the process of surveillance has changed in relation to social control. The modernist answer to the problem of social control was to place the supervisees in particular buildings, factories, schools, prisons. The 'past-modern' solution is for surveillance to occur in everyday life. One of the purposes of the social worker or the probation officer is to supervise deviants within the community. With the shift away from prisons to the use of community sentences and tagging, the process of surveillance is moving from institutions to society.

However, with the development of new technologies, and the fears engendered by the war on terror, the process of surveillance has extended beyond the deviant. It is based on the notion that we do not know who the criminals are and so we have to watch everyone, and the surveillance acts as a deterrent. CCTV cameras are placed in areas where there are high levels of violence or street crime, speed cameras are placed in known speeding black spots. The issue of speed cameras provides a good example of how surveillance technology has changed the relationship between the state and the individual. Until recently police officers used to catch those people who were speeding, often by following fast cars over a set distance, or with a hand-held radar, and it was a relatively random affair. With speed cameras all motorists – speeders and non-speeders – are under surveillance and the process of catching speeders is systematic and automatic. As a consequence many more drivers are finding themselves with fines than in the past.

The changing relationship between the police and speeders has implications for how criminal behaviour is perceived in general. This is illustrated in the way that notions of zero tolerance and anti-social behaviour are extending the remit of the behaviour that should be controlled, and so expanding the remit of the state by expanding what it is that needs to be regulated. Again, Foucault pointed out how the juridical process is based on reconstructing events in order to establish a person's guilt when a crime has been committed. With modern surveillance large parts of the population are being observed in order to watch if they commit a crime. The aim is not to observe criminal behaviour on its own but to observe all people in particular situations (in the city centre, on particular roads, when they fly to the United States). There are even attempts to develop technology so that it can use information to predict that crime is likely to occur by, for instance, looking at changes in movements of crowds (*BBC News*, 1 May 2002). As Louise Amoore (2007: 221) emphasizes, these new forms of surveillance change the nature of what is seen:

> Here, calculative practices are deployed, in effect, *before* a crime takes place, in order to see or to envisage the individual as criminal. The act of seeing thus becomes an act of foreseeing, pre-empting or anticipating.

Félez (2005:4) neatly summarizes the consequences of these changes:

> Traditionally, a police officer gathered data on people who, in some way, were or may be connected with a specific crime or may be suspected of committing another one. In the case of preventive actions carried out by specialised units or secret services, investigations focused on a small number of individuals whose activities, relations, interests or ideas may indicate they may be committing crimes or actions against the security or welfare of the state. In some way it could be affirmed that the 'enemy' was known and no need for extensive accumulation of data on huge populations was needed. But today this has absolutely changed. The spread of international terrorism and the type of people involved in terrorist attacks – people with no apparent connections with any criminal group or having been living for a long time just as any other ordinary citizen with no suspicious activities – paves the way to the systematic and routine gathering and keeping of data of non-suspects 'just in case' among all of them a terrorist or serious criminal is hiding.

The fact that the surveillance brings more people into the orbit of the state raises interesting questions about trust and relationships in modern societies. Surveillance is not new, as we have seen, and indeed without modern technology certain modern states were built on very highly comprehensive mechanisms of surveillance. Governments in democratic countries have encouraged people to inform where they suspect tax evasion, benefit fraud or child abuse. One of the important aspects of the war on terror has been an attempt to encourage people to provide information on suspicious behaviour. In the United States there has been a conscious policy to develop the surveillance skills of citizens and to get them to report suspicious behaviour (Amoore, 2007). According to Henry Giroux (2004: 212) 'Citizens are recruited as foot soldiers in the war on terrorism, urged to spy on their neighbours' behaviour, watch for suspicious-looking people, and supply data to government sources in the war on terrorism'. Innes (2003: 117) argues that within increased social mobility, 'Surveillance proved a surrogate mechanism for generating a sense of trust between people.' David Lyon (2003: 27) suggests that with the disappearing body, the fact we do not know the people we have contact with means that we need PINs, barcodes and IDs as mechanisms for establishing trust. However, this form of surveillance is based on a sense of distrust. We inform on behaviour we do not like, or on people who are new to the area. The continual need to increase security around credit cards and passports reflects our inability to trust those who are presenting us with their identity cards; they may be forgeries. In this sense social capital may be stronger in areas where there is an *omertà*. In closed communities governed by a strong boss or godfather, those who are distrusted are the outsiders and so people do not inform on their neighbours. The use of CCTV is a reflection of not trusting our own communities, and so needing an external mechanism to regulate behaviour. It is possible that the surveillance mechanisms are doing what neighbours did in traditional communities – watch out for strangers and restrain deviant behaviour through knowing and watching the behaviour of those around them. However, Giroux (2004) has a much less benign view of this process, seeing it as the militarization of public spaces as a response to the war on terror. What is apparent is that surveillance is now present in many countries. Norris, Cahill and Wood (2004: 113) claim: 'Across Europe, 29% of such publicly accessible institutions used some form of video surveillance although ... the proliferation is uneven.' London, for example, has more surveillance than Vienna.

The crucial question is: what does this mean in terms of state power? It could be argued that much of the data that is being collected has little impact on the capability of states. It may be useful for private companies in terms of designing individualized marketing strategies, but its impact on the state is limited. Indeed, it is possible to argue that all that is happening is that the state is likely to suffer from data overload. However, there are a number of ways in which the process of increasing surveillance increases state power.

## Data on individual-level activity and data sharing

The development of new technologies has led to the use of data in different ways. First, it makes it much easier to share information between organizations in government departments but also between the public and private sector. This is partly the case because it is easier to store data, and partly because the data increasingly exist digitally rather than in paper form. One of the problems of the traditional state was that whilst there were efficient horizontal connections, vertical connections were often very weak. For a whole set of reasons, some practical and some political (in the sense of competition between agencies), traditional agencies have been very poor at sharing data. For example, it emerged following the murder of two girls in Soham in Britain in 2002 that one of the reasons why the murderer was allowed to work near children was due to agencies failing to share data (Bellamy and Raab, 2005). New technology makes sharing easier but as Bellamy and Raab point out, it raises considerable problems of privacy. Moreover, because so much data can be stored on laptop computers or data sticks, it can be, and has been, easily lost, raising important questions about the security of data.

## Indirect policing

The way that technology and surveillance have changed the nature of how society is policed – or will be policed in the future – is probably one of the most important changes that is occurring in the role of the modern state. It also illustrates the changing relationship between space and time, which theorists such as David Harvey (1990) and Anthony Giddens see as a crucial aspect of postmodernity. Throughout the twentieth century policing has been focussed around the existence of the body (the police officer to impose order) and so much debate is often about the presence – or absence – of the police officer, as in the discussion of no-go areas or the use of motorized patrols. On the other side, policing has been about the reconstruction of events through investigations (in some systems this is conducted by judges). Traditionally policing is about a physical presence and the reconstruction of events. Surveillance changes both of these processes. First, a considerable part of policing is now done at a distance through, for example, speed cameras. Particularly in city centres, it is the cameras that are watching behaviour rather than police officers. And even when cameras are operator controlled, it is rare that it is the police who are undertaking this role. The other important point is the way in which surveillance changes the sphere of deviancy. Criminologists writing in the 1970s often focused on the intimate relationship between the police and criminals and how the separation between the 'guilty' and the 'innocent' led to an exaggerated notion of the nature and level of crime amongst those who were innocent (Downes and Rock, 1971). With surveillance everyone is drawn into the purview of the potential criminal. It is the development of what is called in legal terms prospective surveillance, which acts as a dragnet capturing all information before filtering out what is relevant in terms of the criminal activity (Kerr, 2003: 15). The mentality that has developed with the war on terror, that we don't know who the terrorists are, has been extended to criminal behaviour. Now everyone is watched.

No longer is monitoring focused on deviants but on everyday behaviour. Technology exists now through satellites to track every car journey and so monitor continually the speed at which motorists travel. If this is introduced, speeders will not be caught but monitored. Of course, this notion of monitoring individual behaviour goes beyond technological surveillances and is developing in the moral ordering of politics where parents are monitored, weight and exercise is watched and children, for instance, are continually observed (see Chapter 11). Technology allows for surveillance to shift from the aggregate level to the individual level. For instance, schools are introducing pupil tracking so that they will have a database that monitors the performance of pupils on a whole range of activities. It is not necessarily the case that these mechanisms are malign; the important point is that they highlight the way the state is changing as a consequence of new technologies. The Marxist theorist of the state, Nicos Poulantzas (1978), wrote of the way that liberalism 'individuates'. He saw it as undermining class relations by creating people as individuals rather than as political actors within the context of classes. The mechanisms of surveillance, and the technology that goes with them, mean that state actors are able to deal with citizens on an individual level and track their attainments in a way that was never possible under traditional types of bureaucracy. Rose (1992) sees this as part of the neo-liberal project with governments increasingly intervening to encourage a new set of personal attributes related to an enterprise culture.

## Recentralization of state power.

As we saw in Chapter 1, much of the current debate about the state concerns the shift from government to governance and the ways in which states are attempting to re-impose control. The development of new technology and processes of surveillance have created the opportunity for the state to recentralize power against the processes of governance. The concept of governance sensitizes us to the fact that changes in society, technology and organizations allow the process of regulation and delivery of public goods to be dealt with in complex ways rather than simply through state provision. This too is a consequence, in part, of technological change. There are now a whole range of organizations, both public and private, that store easily retrievable data on citizens. However, normally the use of this data is organizationally and legally limited. For example, if we provide medical information to our doctor we would not expect, and it would not be legal, for the medical practice to pass this on to an insurance company. Yet these organizational, and to some degrees legal, restrictions do not apply to government. Government has the resources, ability and authority to collect and analyse this data and, of course, to force private companies to share their data with government agencies. The clearest example of this process is in the United States with the PATRIOT act and the development of what is called total information awareness.

The PATRIOT Act (The Uniting and Strengthening America by Providing Appropriate Tools Required to Intercept and Obstruct Terrorism Act) was passed as a direct response to 9/11 and it creates, 'A more expansive approach to security than the United States has previously taken' (Jaeger *et al.*, 2003: 296). What the act does is to relax the constraints of surveillance that previously existed and as a consequence it :

- Expands the circumstance of surveillance
- Increases the definition of records that can be searched
- Introduces a secrecy clause which prohibits disclosure of investigations
- Permits surveillance on electronic and voice mail
- Increases the use of 'roving wiretaps'
- Allows greater use of trap and trace devices
- Allows greater data sharing between agencies. (Jaeger *et al.*, 2003: 299–300)

Peter Gill (2006: 43) highlights how:

> The USA PATRIOT Act dismantled the so-called 'firewall' that was built in the 1970s between information gathered for law enforcement as opposed to intelligence purposes. Non-citizens certified as presenting a threat of terrorism can be detained indefinitely, police and security agencies can gain easier access to electronic communications data and the US Treasury is empowered further to obtain financial information from banks.

It has resulted in increased investigations (Jaeger *et al.*, 2003: 300) and has clearly increased the amount of information available to government.

Total Information Awareness (TIA) was a project set up by the Pentagon following the events of 11 September 2001. It is intended to provide a system that would pull together all available sources of data in order to predict acts of terrorism with an initial budget of $63 million (Lyon, 2003: 91) and it is a logical consequence of the PATRIOT Act. The politics behind this programme are fascinating. It was set up as a direct consequence of 9/11 and John Poindexter, Ronald Reagan's Security Advisor (and someone who had been involved in the Iran–Contra affair), became the head of the Information Awareness Office with its motto of 'knowledge is power' and its logo which was a pyramid with an eye watching the world. The threats revealed by 9/11 made policy makers in the Pentagon believe that they need not be subtle in their presentation of a surveillance system. However, Congress believed that this proposed system was too reminiscent of Big Brother and so stopped funding in 2003.

The aim of TIA was to develop 'predictive technology to better anticipate and act against terrorism' by collecting a much wider array of information about people and then build a model that would enable the intelligence community to predict the behaviour of terrorists. The data would include biometric information gathered from face, fingerprints, gait, and iris and then link this to transactional data on all aspects of people's lives including financial, education, travel, transport, communication and even veterinary information. It would have placed a considerable amount of information in the hands of government about the behaviour of people all over the world in order to run a predictive model. The model was called Wargaming the Asymmetric Environment and according to Tom Armour, an official working in DARPA, the research section of the Pentagon:

WAE hypothesizes that we can identify and model the behavioral range and triggers with a sufficient level of predictive accuracy to be used by the Operational Community... WAE will develop technologies for emulating the behavior of multiple entities, with different goals, and their respective interactions in a single wargaming environment. And WAE will empirically access the concurrent and predictive validity of this environment. (http://www.darpa.mil/DARPATech2000/ Speeches/ISOSpeeches/Armour.pdf)

The aim of TIA is to link different data sources together and to build models which will then enable predictions of terrorist behaviour:

DARPA aspires to create the tools that would permit analysts to data-mine an indefinitely expandable universe of databases ... to analyze, detect, classify and identify foreign terrorists – and decipher their plans – and thereby enable the U.S. to take timely action to successfully preempt and defeat terrorist acts. (Stevens, 2003: 2)

Interestingly, these models are based around game theory and therefore incorporate rational choice assumptions (Whitaker, 2000). They also highlight the way in which the process of surveillance is developing so that state control is increasingly about attempting to anticipate deviant behaviour. It is the continuation of the Enlightenment project, the idea that the process of dealing with terrorists is a scientific process. Given enough information and the correct model then we can know who the terrorists are and when they will attack. Of course, similar Enlightenment notions are built into the growing focus on the relationship between genes and criminal behaviour (Carey and Gottesman, 1996; for a critique see Wasserman and Wachbroit, 2001), which presumes that criminal behaviour can be predicted from genes.

With the loss of Congressional funding TIA has, in principle, come to an end. Nevertheless, Paul Harris (2006) demonstrates that there is considerable, if difficult to gather, evidence that many of the TIA programmes are continuing within different departments and under new names. As Harris points out:

Two of the most important components of the TIA program were moved to the Advanced Research and Development Activity, housed at NSA headquarters in Fort Meade, Md., documents and sources confirm. One piece was the Information Awareness Prototype System, the core architecture that tied together numerous information extraction, analysis, and dissemination tools developed under TIA. The prototype system included privacy-protection technologies that may have been discontinued or scaled back following the move to ARDA.

It is clear that the US government is continuing to have considerable interest in mobile phone and email records and there are attempts to improve both surveillance and data sharing and then to use this information for preempting terrorism.

It is important not to exaggerate the strength of the state in this area. There are considerable difficulties with managing and verifying the vast quantity of information that is available. As Hans de Brujin (2006: 270) points out, the Commission on 9/11 highlighted the difficulties that the intelligence community had in sharing information. Problems of data sharing are endemic in government organizations because they are functionally and vertically organized and therefore bureaucratic organizations, and professional jealousy often limits the extent and manner in which data is shared (6 *et al.*, 2002).

Brujin (2006) also cautions against thinking that by resolving the issues of data sharing all problems will be resolved. As he illustrates, information still has to be selected to be shared and in sharing information, the organization that collected the information loses control over it,which may diminish its impact. Moreover, if information control is centralized there is a danger that the centre dominates the process of information collection and thus ends up receiving the information that is deemed to be important to the centre. Moreover, central control will not resolve problems of information gathering within the lower-level organizations actually responsible for obtaining the data (Brujin, 2006: 279).

As we have seen, states extended their capabilities by developing bureaucracies and networks that enable states to intervene into the far reaches of society. New technologies have added a further aspect to that power, enabling government to intervene in ways that have not been possible in the past. For instance, policies like road charging were very difficult until the technology developed to impose charges on all cars entering a particular area. Government will also be able to charge for road use in general with differential charges for different types of roads and times. The fact that highly complex data can be collected allows government to indulge in social sorting and allows states to identify where particular social policies may be targeted. In the US a company is developing a radio frequency identification chip which can be implanted in people and these could be used to identify 'immigrants, military personnel, casino workers and patients who suffer various degenerative diseases such as Alzheimer's' (Porter, 2006).

Modern surveillance is important because it increases exponentially the amount of retrievable data that is available to government. Moreover, as we have seen, this is individual-level data so that specific individuals can be identified either for punishment or prevention, or for further surveillance. This information is crucial to understanding state power because it changes the balance of the relationship between the state and citizens. As we saw in Chapter 7, even what were called totalitarian states often faced considerable difficulty keeping track of all their citizens. With the new levels of surveillance and new technologies it is theoretically possible, certainly in the case of suspected terrorists, that governments can track the behaviour of individuals. It is technology that places us all in the position of constant surveillance; by using credit cards, mobile phones, emails, computers and cars we subject ourselves to being watched. The poor of the Third World avoid this level and type of surveillance.

It is also the case that people are developing mechanisms for resistance to surveillance. In Britain there have been campaigns to destroy speed cameras and increasingly people who want to evade surveillance are developing new technologies. These can be relatively sophisticated methods such as materials that prevent the reading of car number plates, the use of encrypted emails, and using software that deletes traces of your web history from the internet, to methods of evasion such as wearing a hood, buying a pay-as-you-go phone through a third party, and cycling to avoid road cameras (Rosen, 2007). As we will see in Chapter 12, there are still people who manage to evade the gaze of the state.

## Conclusion

Surveillance has always been a central aspect of the modern state. However, surveillance has in the past been limited to the collection of rather general levels of data which has been highly dispersed through state organizations. Moreover, being paper-based it was easy to mislay and difficult to connect various sets of data. With paper-based forms of surveillance, the state was often overwhelmed by the information it had and it was difficult to use. New technology has greatly changed the nature and scale of surveillance undertaken by states. States and private organizations now collect a whole range of information that was not previously available and the development of digital technology means that information can be easily stored, accessed and networked. Moreover, it allows the state to focus on individuals in ways that previously were limited to intensive surveillance carried out on a small number of people. This has important implications for the resources available to the state and also how the state acts. Indeed, there are two significant changes. The first is that whereas in the past the presumption was that social order focused on the few who could be identified as criminal, surveillance now covers nearly all people in all aspects of their lives. When we shop, drive, walk, make a phone call, send an email or use the internet, data about our activities is being stored. Second, states are looking out for crimes to be committed. The information is being mined in order to predict who may commit crimes, or to prevent crimes. Surveillance is a different form of power from the rationality and regulation discussed in the previous chapter; it is much more hands-on and direct. However, like rationality it is a focus on the individual and on ensuring that people act within certain bounds and, as we will see in Chapter 11, the combination of rationality and surveillance allows states to focus their influence on changing individual behaviour.

# Chapter 10

# Risk

Risk is not normally associated with a form of power. However, what this chapter will demonstrate is that risk is used by states to manipulate outcomes and to make decisions about policy. Risk fits closely with rational choice and surveillance mechanisms in terms of individualizing policy intentions and therefore it is a crucial tool in the development of new mechanisms of power. The concept of risk is becoming ubiquitous in the social and natural sciences. Initially a scientific term, risk is increasingly being used to assess a range of social, medical, scientific, economic and individual decisions in an expanding range of areas. In addition, a number of sociologists have adopted risk as a way of understanding modern society (Beck, 1992; Giddens, 1991; Taylor-Gooby, 2000). Even in political science risk is being used to model decisions in a number of scenarios (Kahneman and Tversky, 1984; McDermott, 1998; Heimann, 1997). Risk has a strong intrinsic appeal because it is inexorably linked to the human condition (a Hobbesian desire for security and an existential desire for ontological certainty) (see Langford, 2002) and because it means that scientific predictions can be expressed in terms of probabilities rather than definitive outcomes (it is safer for the weather report to say there is a 50 per cent chance of rain than to say it will or will not rain tomorrow). The focus of this chapter is how risk is being used as a form of power by state actors. The way risk affects state power is twofold: it apparently makes uncertainty scientific and therefore provides states with knowledge from which to make decisions and it means that governments have to make decisions about risky activity rather than social change; again individualizing the relationship between state and citizen. Risk assessment has become a crucial aspect of public policy. In policy areas such as health and crime, probability is being used as a mechanism for making decisions. Probability is seen as a scientific approach to policy problems, but of course humans are reflexive and therefore uncertainty exists in the ways that people react when new information is made available.

The work of Ulrich Beck and Anthony Giddens has suggested that the rise of perceptions of risk is a consequence of changing social relations in late modernity. This literature has been highly influential but in its grand narrative it underestimates the complexities and ambiguities that exist within the term risk. There is a vehement ontological debate between (and among) scientists and social scientists over the nature of risk. For scientists, both natural and social, risk is measurable and therefore can be used for the construction of predictive models concerning the likelihood of specific events to occur (see Paté-Cornell, 2002: 633). For the critics, risk is subjective – and intersubjective – and consequently the notion of objective risk assessment is flawed. John Adams (1995) highlights both the difficulty of measuring risk (for instance, what is the riskier activity: the one that produces the occasional death and many injuries or the one that produces frequent deaths and few injuries?) and the way in which people modify behaviour in the face of their perceptions of risk (for a summary of the debate see Douglas, 1994 and Thompson and Rayner, 1998). These ontological disputes are further complicated by the politicization of the risk debate. Frequently political debate is framed within the context of competing conceptions of risk (see Perrow, 1999; Margolis, 1996).

Despite these apparent problems, risk assessments are becoming a widely accepted practice in decision making in firms, the public sector and government (Perrow, 1999). The reason that risk is an issue in the context of a book on the state and power is that risk, as Michael Power (2007: 2) points out, 'has become a source of principles for organizing and managing in general'. Risk is a mechanism for justifying intervention or lack of intervention by government, and it essentially places considerable resources in the hands of experts who can measure risk. However, the point is that risk is often presented as an objective mechanism for assessing the likelihood of a set of events. Yet risk is not objective but contingent, and depends on decisions that are often related to issues of power. As Kunreuther and Slovic (1996: 116) clarify: 'Although ... dangers are real, there is no such thing as "real risk" or "objective risk".' Consequently both governments and analysts are caught between matching subjective and political notions of risk with objective risk assessment. Of course, it may be the ambiguities within the term that make it so attractive. Hence, risk is being used by government (and other organizations) as a mechanism for controlling outcomes and assessing knowledge. In this sense it is a new form of power. It is also a form of power in that it is concerned with 'the reflexive monitoring of action' (Giddens, 1984: 5) and how we as individuals or organizations reflect upon the events and situations around us. For instance, in the Middle Ages, and much later, floods were acts of

God or the weather. Now we reflect on the chance (risk) of a flood in a particular area and have the opportunity to take action. This illustrates the power element of risk. If you feel vulnerable to a flood, whether the government will pay for flood defences depends on the risk assessment. It then becomes an important political tool. Whatever the extent of parents' protest for a school crossing, the politicians increasingly do not respond to pressure but the risk assessment; and the risk assessment becomes a mechanism for ignoring or diminishing political demands. Risk becomes another aspect of the way in which political issues are shifted into technical issues and depoliticized (Buller and Flinders, 2005; Burnham, 2007). In these cases power is not about influencing political leaders but about shaping the perception of risk. Hence, some schools ban wireless internet connections because there is a belief that they are a risk to children's health. The irony of risk is that whilst it is seen by writers such as Giddens and Beck as a product of late modernity, it is a highly modernist concept. It is based on a notion that we can in some way measure, in a highly rationalist way, uncertainty and hence prepare for what might happen. If we make the correct risk assessments then we will avoid problems. Like some surveillance measures it attempts to predict future events.

The case study in this chapter demonstrates the difficulties of the use of risk, both in terms of analysing the events and as a policy tool for managing the problems. The study highlights the complex way in which risk is constructed and how the concern of government is risk *management* rather than risk *assessment*. In addition, risk changes the patterns of dependence because it allows governments to determine the level of risk, which it is hard for citizens to challenge. The chapter begins by examining different interpretations of risk.

## Understanding the dimensions of risk

Understanding risk as a form of power is not helped by the very different academic definitions of risk. There are three main approaches to defining and measuring risk. The first sees risk as a measurable and predictable phenomenon (the scientific). The second sees risk largely as a matter of perception related to specific incidents or issues (the cultural). The third sees risk as a way of understanding the nature of late modern society and the reactions of individuals to that society (the sociological). It is important to review these approaches if we are to understand how risk is used as a mechanism of power.

## Risk as science

The first type of risk analysis is essentially positivist. It is a view held in a range of disciplines that risk is knowable and measurable. According to Paté-Cornell (2002: 633):

> If done consistently and accurately, the quantification of risk (probability and consequences of different outcome scenarios associated with hazard) allows ranking risk mitigation solutions and setting priorities among safety procedures.

This is the approach to risk that is now used in cost-benefit analysis, measuring insurance risks, and in a whole range of decisions, ranging from medical to road safety to understanding financial markets and to lending money or investing overseas. Risk, from this perspective, is identifiable and measurable. This approach has been adopted by Claudio Cioffi-Revilla (1998) who suggests that politics is uncertain because it is made up of many unknowable individual decisions. However, for Cioffi-Revilla the problem is not the uncertainty *per se* but that political scientists have taken uncertainty to mean haphazard and therefore unknowable:

> I believe the conclusion to be drawn from these developments is not that a science of politics is impossible simply because uncertainty is ubiquitous, consequential, and ineradicable; but that our choice is between a rigorous understanding of politics, which must include uncertainty, or no understanding at all. God *does* play dice with politics, but the outcomes are patterned not haphazard.

For Cioffi-Revilla it is possible to model uncertainty and therefore predict the occurrence of risk. This modelling of risk behaviour in individuals has been developed further through psychometric approaches such as prospect theory (Weyland, 1998, 2000; Kahneman and Tversky, 1990).

## Risk as perception

The notion of risks as objective and knowable is deeply held within the scientific community. As Michael Thompson and Steve Rayner (1998) recount, scientists have attempted to make a clear distinction between real and perceived risk with the underlying paternalistic view that once people have information, they will then know the true extent of the risk (for a detailed discussion of risk management see Powell and Leiss, 1997). However, the work of Douglas (1985, 1992, 1994), Douglas and Wildavsky (1983) and Adams (1995) has highlighted the falsity of this dichotomy. Adams (1995) illustrates that, even within a scientific framework, any accurate measure of risk is impossible. People react to risk by 'seeking to manage it'. Therefore any attempt to quantify risk will fail because, '[researchers] aggregate measures of past risk taking by large and disparate populations of risk takers, and they are part of the evidence that shapes the perception of risk which influences future risk taking' (Adams, 1995: 14). In other words, if people know that there is a probability of something happening, they will change their behaviour which changes the probability and so 'there is not the remotest possibility of ever devising a model that could predict reliably all the consequences of these interventions' (Adams, 1995: 23). For Adams, these problems are exacerbated because so much of the data used for risk assessment is unreliable.

Mary Douglas highlighted the ways in which risk cannot be isolated from culture; 'ways of seeing' influence how risk is perceived. For Douglas (1994) risk cannot be divorced from politics. This perspective is taken further by poststructuralist views that reveal the impossibility of decoupling risk from power. For Sheila Jasanoff (1999: 139):

> Studies of scientific controversies about risk have revealed the complex processes by which reliable knowledge about the environment is constructed. Consensus on such 'facts' as the risk of formaldehyde or DDT arises not from demonstrated deaths, disability or environmental damage, but from repeated confrontations amongst disparate scientific observations, their interpretation by experts and stakeholders, and the ingrained and social commitments of decision making institutions.

Risk from this perspective is not about real uncertainty or harm. It is, in Foucault's term, a 'power/knowledge' construct (see Jasanoff, 1999: 137). For Foucault, power and knowledge 'imply one another'. They cannot be separated. Consequently, risk becomes a form of knowledge that has important implications for power. Those who assess risk and who determine the decisions based on risk have power. The question becomes not what is the risk but who determines the risk.

## Risk and late modernity: the sociological approach

Developing the politicization of risk into a broader social theory, Giddens and Beck see risk as a way of understanding society in late modernity. From this perspective risk is not just about assessing dangers; the way we 'interpret risk, negotiate risk, and live with the unforeseen consequences of modernity will structure our culture, society and politics' (Franklin, 1998: 1). For Giddens (1998: 25), 'A risk society is where we increasingly live on a high technological frontier which absolutely no one completely understands and which generates a diversity of possible futures'. In Giddens' view industrialization manufactures risk through producing high-risk processes and increasingly reflexive individuals.

Beck suggests that the consequence of modernity is a shift to a new modernity as the modernizing process has created a range of forms of risk. Consequently, the key stratifying principle of society is not the distribution of wealth, but the distribution of risk. In attempting to produce wealth and reduce uncertainties a new set of uncertainties has been created. As modernity is the producer of these new risks they are ubiquitous: 'Hunger can be sated, needs can be satisfied, but *civilization* risks are a *bottomless barrel of demands*, unsatisfiable, infinite, self producible' (Beck, 1992: 23, emphasis in original). Moreover, for Beck, the scientific monopoly in determining risk is undermined by social groups that have different criteria for assessing risk. For the consequences of modernization are so apparent that the legitimacy of scientists is called into question. Increasingly politics, as Foucault would suggest, is a struggle over 'rationality claims' (Beck, 1992: 59).

Whilst (as we will see below) many elements of Beck's argument are analytically useful for understanding the centrality that risk has attained in contemporary political discourse, there are a number of problems with his approach. Beck switches from questioning the science to questioning the scientists or their particular method because he appears to see the environmental risks as indisputable facts. So, on one side, Beck sees risks as contestable and part of a power/knowledge construct, but, on the other, his conception of a risk society is based on a presumption that there is indisputably a set of risks that arises inexorably at a certain state of modernity: 'it is also and especially in denial and non-perception that the *objective community* of global risk comes into being. Behind the variety of interests, the reality of risk threatens and grows, knowing no social or national difference anymore' (Beck,

1992: 46, emphasis in original). Indeed, as Byron Marshall (1999: 267) illustrates, there is more than a hint of teleology in Beck:

> The generalisability of the risk society is contingent on specific structural conditions of an advanced social welfare system that Beck assumes will emerge in other nation-states and will be sustained in (West) Germany and Scandinavia. In other words, following modernisation theory in development studies, presumably an end-state of causal change obtains, an advanced stage of modernity which is reached via flexible modernization. Every nation state presumably follows this trajectory.

Under the guise of a critique of rationality Beck produces a questionable historicist and scientific view of modernity and risk. For Beck (1994: 5–6):

> The transition from the industrial to the risk period of modernity occurs undesired, unseen and compulsively in the wake of the autonomized dynamism of modernization, following the pattern of latent side effects. One can virtually say that the constellations of risk society are produced because the certitudes of industrial society dominate the thought and action of people and institutions in industrial society. Risk society is not an option that one can choose or reject in the course of political disputes. *It arises in the continuity of autonomized modernization processes which are blind and deaf to their own effects and threats.* (Emphasis added)

Beck sees an increase in risk and risk perception as an inevitable consequence of late modernity, but this leads to an assumption that there are now more risks, rather than issues being packaged differently or risk being used as a way of either highlighting or tackling political problems. The issue is one of how risks are presented rather than one of risks being greater than before. Whilst certain risks are rapidly amplified by the media, there is no evidence that people feel risk more deeply than a hundred years ago or that people are more conscious of the fears of new technological frontiers. There were numerous generalized risks that affected all classes in pre-industrial and early industrial societies (Elliot, 2002: 300). The presence of death was much more real in the nineteenth century; in most modern societies the discussion of death is almost taboo. The relative absence of death from common discourse may have changed the value we place on life, which has increased perceptions of risk. Beck does acknowledge that the rise in risk is linked to the nature of decision making rather than necessarily new risk (see Elliot, 2002), but the main motor behind the risk society is the changing nature of industrial society and the growing reflexivity of individuals. Like positivists, Beck and Giddens actually see risk as uncontested, whereas the discussion below illustrates its multiple meanings and the non-linear development of perceived risks.

Whilst risk is a 'fuzzy' concept, it is being used both to analyse developments in society and more prosaically to make, or, more often, justify policy; and this is why it is used as power – it becomes part of a process of legitimation. However, the practice of states taking risk assessment as part of the policy process is problematic. At the same time, analysing governments in terms of dealing with the risk society is also full of problems because it assumes that risk is the latest stage in the development of modernity. These problems arise because risk is contingent. As people like Adams, Douglas and Jasanoff have demonstrated, risk cannot be separated from power. Whilst risk is set up as a rational mechanism for policy making, in practice it is used politically (see Perrow, 1999). The epistemological arguments are overlain by political battles so that even if we could measure risk, the meanings of the risk cannot be divorced from power and political decisions. The problem for the Labour government in Britain, for instance, is that problems are exacerbated by their use of risk in the three ways outlined above. In terms of policy making it is used in the objective sense. In terms of policy implementation the government is clearly concerned with perceptions of risk and how policies are perceived. Consequently, it is concerned with risk management. In terms of the broader ideological commitments of the government, there is an explicit recognition of the need to take account of greater feelings of insecurity in terms of dealing with policy ranging from food to welfare to immigration. It is highly problematic to use risk as an objective policy tool and the contingent nature of risk means that notions of the risk society overemphasize the lineal developments of risk. The next section will examine how risk has become increasingly important in policy making.

## Risk and government

Whilst risk has become an academic boom area, it has also become central to policy making, especially in Anglo-Saxon countries (there is an interesting study to be done on the cultural understandings of risk and how they differ across cultures; intuitively – and there is statistical evidence to support this – it seems that attitudes to risks and driving are very different in Southern Europe compared to Northern Europe for instance). In both Britain and the United States risk has become a central tool within government partly as a response to scientific development, both in terms of new scientific discoveries around chemicals and radiation and the development of risk assessment techniques.

In recent years, and especially since the events of 11 September 2001, risk assessment and management has become a core government activity. Hennessy (2000) points out how, during the Blair government, risk became central to the policy process. In the United States risk has also been developed as a mechanism for organizing policies across a range of different areas. As the National Infrastructure Advisory Council recommended, the government there should

> Establish a risk management oversight function in all federal agencies. Risk management is most effective in the private sector when corporate governance structures oversee risk management to ensure accountability, promote standards, and prioritize resources against threats and vulnerabilities. Government would benefit from establishment of similar risk management accountability and oversight structures. (http://www.dhs.gov/xlibrary/assets/niac/NIAC_RMWG_transltr.pdf)

In the UK in March 2000 the Centre for Management and Policy Studies (CMPS) ran a seminar for senior officials and ministers on risk and policy development. The summary of the seminar resolved that, 'Risk management should be an integral element in both long-term policy development and normal project development procedures' and Permanent Secretaries were identified as the risk managers of departments (CMPS 2000).

However, risk is not a new concept but has developed, particularly in the United States, in line with scientific development. In the United States risk assessment developed in the context of the growth of regulatory agencies in areas such as food and the environment which were established to protect consumers from potential harm (National Research Council, 1983). Indeed, these agencies

> have attempted to coordinate risk assessment activities ... most notably through the Interagency Regulatory Liaison Group (IRLG), which formed a work group on risk assessment to develop a guide-

line for assessing carcinogenic risks. … It examined the various approaches used by the four agencies to evaluate the evidence of carcinogenicity and to assess risk. The IRLG then incorporated these evaluative procedures into a document. (National Research Council, 1983: 42)

The groundwork for risk analysis in the US started in the 1950s with atomic testing and the need to assess the dangers of radiation where 'risk characterisations' were used to assess atomic dangers (National Research Council, 1983: 54–5), and the first major risk analysis was provided by the Nuclear Regulatory Commission in 1975 (Von Winterfeldt, 2006). At this time engineers were making crude risk assessments concerning the ability of the levees in New Orleans to withstand a category 3 hurricane; even though as Detlof von Winterfeldt (2006: 29) points out, 'one of the previous hurricanes had risen above category 3'. What is crucial is that the notion of risk assessment and risk management became integrated into a range of policy processes where policy makers needed to assess the potential dangers from an activity. For David Vogel (2001) risk regulation was established within the policy process much earlier in the United States than in Europe. This is particularly apparent in the case of the Food and Drug Administration (FDA), where risk assessment became a core element of its judgements over the suitability of additives, pesticides and drugs. The problem of course is that risk assessments are presented as scientific, and based on probabilities, but how policy makers react to them is highly political and, more importantly, it leaves the policy makers with the judgement of how great a risk is acceptable (see for instance Heimann, 1997: 164 and 168). This led to the banning of products such as the pesticide Alar, which most scientists believed was safe but the public perceived as dangerous, and for Vogel (2001: 4) 'the triumph of "passion" over "sound science" '.

In Britain the first risk assessments were carried out as cost-benefit analyses from the 1950s onwards (Phillips, 2000, Vol. 5: 132). Indeed, this attempt at so-called rational policy making was central in key decisions such as the Roskill Report on London's third airport (Greenaway, Smith and Street, 1992: 18). In the 1970s the Health and Safety Executive developed more sophisticated notions of risk through the notion of reducing risk to: 'As Low as Reasonably Practicable' (ALARP). Subsequently, the use of risk in decision making has spread throughout government departments on issues such as transport, health and, especially, the environment (ILGRA, 1995). Two key factors gave increased impetus to the role of risk. The first was the Conservative government's strategy for deregulation. This was intended to reduce the burdens on industry and so it was necessary to develop a 'scientific' assessment of the risk of particular products. According to ILGRA (1995), the government intended, 'the practice of risk assessment to epitomise the process of policy making in the field of Government regulation'. The second was the commitment in *This Common Inheritance: the second year report* to review the principles for risk assessment in government and to develop 'best practice' (Phillips, 2000, Vol. 5: 134). This commitment led to the establishment of the Interdepartmental Liaison Group on Risk Assessment (ILGRA) in April 1992, which in its first report reviewed risk assessment in government and examined some of the principles underpinning risk in policy making. ILGRA (1995: Chapter 3) discovered 'that the use of risk assessment has not been developed systematically in Government, but has evolved within departments. Yet there is considerable agreement on what a risk assessment involves.'

The Labour government in Britain increasingly sees risk both as something to deal with and as a tool in policy making. In May 1999 there was a conference on risk by key actors within and outside government on the nature, importance and definitions of risk (see 6, 1999). The implications of the debate on risk have worked their way into discussions on improving the policy process. The Strategic Policy Making Team report reflects Beck's view on the growing presence of risk:

> The world for which policy makers have to develop policies is becoming increasingly complex, uncertain and unpredictable. The electorate is better informed, has rising expectations and is making growing demands for services tailored to their individual needs ... the world is increasingly inter-connected and inter-dependent. Issues switch quickly from the domestic to the international arena and an increasing diversity of interests needs to be co-ordinated and harnessed. Governments across the world need to be able to respond quickly to events to provide the support that people need to adapt to change and that businesses need to prosper. (Cabinet Office, 2000: para 2.3)

An important element of the government's White Paper on modernizing government is the need for forward planning in terms of policy making (CM 4310, 2000). The strategic policy review outlines some of the departmental efforts and forward planning. As the White Paper states:

> Government is often criticised for intervening too much to protect people from some risks, while failing to protect them sufficiently from others ... We need consistently to follow good practice in policy making as we assess, manage and communicate risk. (CM 4310, 2000: 16)

Risk is defined as objective and what is important is communication of information. One of the ILGRA reports is concerned with advising departments on how to communicate information of risk (ILGRA, 1998). The principle governing risk was ALARP which provided government with a supposedly scientific basis for making policy but with the clause that risk management should be concerned with what is 'reasonably practicable'.

Interestingly, a further level of risk management has developed within the European Union with the development of significant risk regulation at the EU level. In order to establish a single market, the EU has sought to standardize risk regulation across member states, and to a degree this has been dominated by the more risk-averse regimes of Northern Europe (see Vogel, 2001). Consequently, the EU has developed a comprehensive framework of risk regulation related to health and safety, drugs and food – in particular in relation to genetically modified organisms (Vogel, 2001).

However, recent events such as foot and mouth disease in Britain, avian flu and 11 September 2001 have led to further government thinking about the nature of risk. Daniels *et al.* (2006: 1) suggest that: 'The 9/11 terrorist attacks made it clear to Americans that we are living in a world of geopolitical risk. Hurricane Katrina has shown the world how vulnerable the United States is to natural disaster.' In the United States these events have resulted in a step change in the spread of risk through the governing process. There is a belief that both 9/11 and Katrina were a consequence of poor risk assessment and management and consequently more effort is needed to evaluate risks. As Daniels *et al.* (2006: 3) state: 'Katrina is thus proving to be a story about both recovering from and managing risk.' In addition, the focus on global and natural risk incorporates a more sociological definition of risk into the governmental process. Despite the scientific premises of risk management historically used by government, it seems to have again developed a definition of risk influenced by Beck's risk society. For instance, in Britain, according to a Strategy Unit report published in November 2002 (PIU, 2002):

> Governments have always faced risks and dangers of their own – unforeseen events, programmes going wrong, projects going awry. Such uncertainty is not new. But the nature of risk has changed for two fundamental reasons. First, because of the increasingly rapid pace of development of new science and technology there are new 'manufactured risks'. These require governments and regulators to make judgements about the balance of benefit and risk across a huge range of technologies – from genetically modified food and drugs, to industrial processes or cloning methods. The second new factor is the greater connectedness of the world, through an integrated global economy and communications system and a shared environment.

It may not be a problem that government is now aware of uncertainty and is prepared to build contingency into policy planning. However, it is perhaps more of a concern that risk is being used as a central element in policy making when the definitions used are so often contradictory – a continual shifting from scientific to sociological understandings. As the case study below demonstrates, much risk management is not really about reducing risk to citizens but to government. Governments find it difficult, if not impossible, to manage risk effectively because ultimately risks are the result of uncertainties (such as external development and political arguments) that state actors do not control. Risk is a useful mechanism for government when treated unproblematically because it is an appeal to rational and technocratic policy making. It legitimizes policy choice through the scientific discourse but often the reality is that the concern is governing risk, not using risk for governing. However, the case study demonstrates both the difficulties with positivist and teleological notions of risk, and the contingent nature of risk – in different areas the creation of, response to and management of risk vary greatly.

## Analysing risk in politics

Risk has become a central tool in the process of government, particularly in Britain and the United States. Despite the attention paid to risk, the management of risk has failed because: the notions of risk are contested; risk is intersubjective – intervention creates new risks; and perceptions of risk vary according to political, economic and social positions. Risk is rarely objective. A case study of how the British government dealt with BSE or 'mad cow disease' demonstrates the difficulties for government in using risk assessment because it was impossible to extract the assessment of risk from political relationships. What the case demonstrates is that risk analysis is not an objective assessment of facts but about making a particular interpretation of facts that is highly political.

## Mad cows

The issues surrounding the politics of food and in particular salmonella, BSE and genetically modified organisms (GMOs) initially appear to fit relatively well into the framework outlined by Beck. Modernist solutions to issues of food security produced new risks that are challenged by consumer and environmental interests when the consequences of those solutions become apparent. However, what this case best demonstrates is how a relatively successful system of risk management broke down and this led to clashes between conflicting power/knowledge frameworks.

The power/knowledge framework of British central government has been based on the public service ethos (Richards and Smith, 2000). This ethos, which is a central part of the British tradition, is the view that public servants in Britain are working for the general good and not their own self-interest. Consequently, they can be trusted to make decisions in the public interest and so develop policy with little reference to the public. It is a central element in the British elite conception of democracy which is essentially representative rather than democratic government (Judge, 1999).

The ethos allowed a system of managing risk in food politics that was based on a policy community whereby decisions were made within a closed network that included the Ministry of Agriculture, Fisheries and Food (MAFF) and the National Farmers' Union (NFU). This policy community was able to manage political risks by essentially excluding issues of food quality and food health from the political agenda (Smith, 1990, 1991; Mills, 1992). Whilst issues of food adulteration and food quality had frequently been subject to debate in the 1930s, they almost disappeared from the agenda in the post-war period. Effectively, blame for bad food was passed to consumers; they did not cook it properly.

This process of risk management was extremely effective for nearly

45 years. Problems such as salmonella existed but were effectively side-lined until the eggs debacle of 1988. This issue became salient for a number of reasons (see Smith, 1991) but a central conflict was over different conceptions, perceptions and assessments of risk. MAFF identified a growing problem as early as 1981 but their argument was that it did not present any real risk, rejecting the link between eggs and salmonella. The Department of Health believed that MAFF was ignoring the risk to consumers and after internal conflict released a public warning. Once this was done the media amplified the degree of risk and sales of eggs collapsed. A depoliticized area became highly political and the government was forced to take a number of measures to reassure the public. The risk had existed for many years but was reconstructed in a different form with the crisis.

Similar and much more significant conflicts over the nature and perceptions of risk have occurred in the BSE case. In an attempt to manage risk, despite little explicit discussion of the concept, the government adopted a proportional (regulation should be no more than needed according to the evidence), rather than precautionary (playing safe when in doubt), approach to risk (6, 2000; Phillips, 2000, Vol. 5: 43 and 48). Hence, the absence of information on BSE created a problem as one official admitted:

> [I]t put us in a very difficult position ... nobody was saying to us: 'This disease is likely to be transmissible.' Therefore, we paused a long time before we diagnosed BSE as a zoonosis. On the other hand it did not prevent us doing anything, of course ... One can try to avoid problems arising; but it does mean that one has great difficulty in banning the sale or use of a product. (Phillips, 2000, Vol. 5: 29)

Ministers and officials were not prepared to take action until a link between BSE and CJD was proven and it took eleven years from the identification of the problem to the admission of the link. The government's strategy for much of the period was to manage risk by restating the mantra that 'British Beef is safe' (see Weir and Beetham, 1999). One of the key conclusions of the Phillips Report was that 'excessively reassuring language about the risk from BSE sedated those who needed to act' (Phillips, 2000, Vol. 2: 205). The concern was with underplaying risk in order to avoid panic. In the cases of banning the feeding of meat and bone meal to pigs and poultry and the dissection of cows' eyeballs in schools, action took a long time because risks were underplayed.

The Phillips Report suggests that MAFF was poor at communicating on issues of risk with outsiders and that even in the case of food scientists within the department, their work on risk was seen as 'interesting but academic by their administrative colleagues' (Phillips, 2000, Vol. 5: 34). The assumption was that the risk of transmission to humans was remote and the government failed to adopt a precautionary approach. The BSE inquiry reveals an incremental approach. Even when the 1989 Southwood Report raised the spectre of BSE infecting humans, as late as 1996 it was being treated: 'as if it demonstrated as a matter of scientific certainty, rather than provisional opinion, that any risk to humans from BSE was remote' (Phillips, 2000, Vol. 2: 55). Nevertheless, as the Phillips Report (p. xx) points out 'MAFF officials appreciated from the outset the possibility that BSE might have implications for human health'. But this presumption was not the primary determinant of policy.

The government effectively moved from one form of risk management, exclusion through the policy community, to another, exclusion through the cover of science. The problem was that the government had little evidence. The government's line was that there was *no evidence* of a link between BSE and CJD, when they should have been saying, *they did not have evidence* of a link between BSE and CJD (see Anand, 1998; and indeed this is what Stephen Dorrell later said – see Powell and Leiss, 1997: 12). However, even as the evidence grew that BSE was not the same as scrapie in sheep, 'this was never made clear to the public' (Phillips, 2000, Vol. 2: 37). Indeed, the government initially followed a policy of

> restricting dissemination of information about BSE. The principal reason for this was concern about 'the possible effects on exports and the political implications' should news get out that a possible TSE in cattle had been discovered in Britain. (Phillips, 2000, Vol. 2: 35)

The government's risk management strategy of restricting information and claiming beef was safe was totally undermined on 20 March 1996. The Health Secretary, Stephen Dorrell, following new cases of CJD in young adults, admitted to the House of Commons: 'The most likely explanation at present is that these cases are linked to exposure to BSE before the introduction of the specified bovine offal ban in 1989' (*Parliamentary Debates*, 20 March 1996, cc. 375–7).

The problem from the government's perspective was that it was attempting to make risk assessments in conditions of uncertainty which created space for significant disagreement between elites involved in decision making (Anand, 1998). As the Phillips Inquiry highlighted, there was confusion within MAFF over its role in relation to risk. The Chief Veterinary Officer said the Department of Health: 'was responsible for assessing risk to human health ... He saw MAFF's role as being risk management.' As the report states: 'We have not found it easy to draw a distinction between risk evaluation and risk management' (Phillips, 2000, Vol. 2: 42). There also seemed to be familiar problems of policy chimneys (see Smith, Richards and Marsh, 2000), with MAFF failing to consult fully with the Department of Health (Phillips, 2000, Vol. 2: 45). The problems were threefold: there was disagreement over the science; there were differing perceptions of risk; and the policy community was concerned more with the risks to the beef industry than to the consumer. The ability to identify who is at risk was an important source of power. The initial presumption which was dominant for some time was that it was an animal not human health problem, even though MAFF did not know whether it affected humans (Phillips, 2000, Vol. 2: 45). This created major problems when on its own terms the government was proved to be wrong. The point that Tim Lang makes is that the government completely mismanaged risk. Rather than identifying the problem early and taking action, Lang (1998: 72) argues: 'The source remained in flow, but there was an attempt to reassure consumers by assuring them that the contamination bits were channelled away.' The problem was that the government relied on the scientific assessment of risk rather than consumer perceptions. In Lang's view, the government relied on risk assessment rather than establishing trust. A paradox of the strategy is that risk as a tool for determining policy decisions is flawed because perceptions of risk are different, and so what the government saw as risk management the public saw as obfuscation. The way that the government intervened in managing risk affected the way that the problem was perceived.

This case reveals a central paradox of the increasing use of risk. The statecraft pressures to manage risk in order to preserve governing competence undermined the ability to manage the risk of the problem. The concern was not really the risk of BSE but protecting particular interests. The science was used to legitimize the normal closed behaviour of the agricultural policy community. The consequence of this paradox was that when faced with the subsequent problem of GMOs, there was almost a complete failure to manage the issue. This failure of management arose because it seemed the relationship between the science of risk and the consumers' perception of risk diverged completely. The government's initial position was that GMOs were safe and it supported the testing of GMO crops in order to allow planting in Britain. However, pressure resulted in rather rapid shifts in policy position by the government (see Jordan, 2000: 265). The paradox was that the risk management strategy increased the perception of risk. From the sociological perspective, this problem was a result of industrial food production; but the assumption is that there is a sort of inevitability between modern production and increased risk, whereas the risk actually derived from particular political decisions about agricultural production and decision making. Alternative decision about meat production could have avoided the problem; it was contingent and not structural.

## The analytical implications of risk

The case study illustrates three points. First, risk as a tool for public policy making is inherently flawed because there is little agreement over what constitutes risk (even within government) and this creates conflicts of perceptions. In addition, as John Adams (1995) points out, risk information modifies behaviour thus undermining the predictive capabilities of risk modelling. The conflict of perceptions and behaviour mean that strategies intended to alleviate risks for one group create new risks for another. So attempts to reduce economic risks for farmers increased the perceived risk of consumers. The case of BSE highlights the ambiguities and contested nature of risk. The notion of risk is contested because it contains within it contradictory elements. Risk is both subjective and objective. Whilst elements of risk may in a simple way be objective (the chance of cancer from smoking), how risk affects behaviour is subjective – how the danger of smoking is perceived, whether smoking is culturally acceptable, the costs of smoking versus not smoking or whether individuals will suffer from smoking are always uncertain. Indeed, as we shall see in Chapter 11, in the discussion of obesity governments legitimize the right to intervene in diet because of the associated risks of obesity, even though the facts are disputed. There are scientific assessments of risk (there is little chance of BSE being transmitted) and political/subjective interpretations of the facts (there is a risk of creating a panic when information on BSE is released). Therefore, because risk can never be separated from its subjective elements it remains a problematic policy tool. Mary Douglas and Charles Perrow have long highlighted the political uses of risk but the fact is that government and other decision-makers (like universities) are turning ever more to risk assessment. Failures of risk management are seen as failures of communication (see Powell and Leiss, 1997) and not failures of risk assessment. However, the problem is not the communication, or even the competing interpretations, but the nature of the term which contains within it ambiguities and political calculations.

Second, these political calculations lead to states dealing not with 'the risk', be it BSE or obesity, but with developing risk avoidance strategies as a mechanism for ensuring governing competence. However, these strategies have been unsuccessful in these areas for two reasons. First, the conflict over perceptions has resulted in certain groups perceiving risks as a consequence of risk avoidance strategies. In the food case the government's failure to admit or deal quickly with a problem created a perception of risk in consumers. People have different political interests in risk and therefore assuaging the concerns of one group often creates new perceptions of risk in another group. Because risk is linked to power, arguments about risk will always be political arguments, when the intention of risk assessment is to avoid politics by providing an assessment of the facts.

Third, there is no linear progression in terms of risk. In food, risk has increased not because of modernity but because of a breakdown in the risk management mechanism (the food policy community). Risk is not directly linked to developments in modernity but is linked to political battles. In some ways the perception of risk is more akin to Anthony Downs' 'issue-attention cycles' than any development of a risk society. One hypothesis that may come from this is that interest groups are more attuned to using risk perception as a way of campaigning and this accounts for the rising perceptions of risk.

## Implicit with risk is a notion of power

Risk may not be a form of power in the sense of the other types that we have discussed in this book but it is a mechanism of power because it enables governments to intervene and it ascribes a scientific knowledge to government information. Like surveillance, it also adds a predictive element to the state – allowing state actors to make policy on the basis of their assessments of what may happen in the future. Government's concern with risk is essentially the use of a power/knowledge framework. Risk has mutated into a mechanism of power. There are a number of facets to risk as power. First, governments are using the science of risk assessment to legitimize particular forms of behaviour. Risk assessments are seen as scientific, but because they deal in probabilities and averages they are essentially ambiguous. The chances of pylons causing cancer are small or insignificant and therefore the government does not have to act and it is difficult for non-scientists to object. There is no evidence that GMOs harm humans and therefore the response to GMOs is anti-rational and emotional. On the other hand, if the government wants to legitimize other forms of behaviour it can do so. There is no statistically significant relationship between the use of mobile phones and brain problems but a number of oddities in the data, and therefore parents should take precautions. Risk is an excellent form of knowledge for government because it is scientific and ambiguous at the same time.

Second, the use of risk assessment shifts the site of decision making from politics to science. It is part of a process of depoliticization (see Hay, 2007). Governments through using risk management make a decision, not in the face of political demands, but in relation to the assessment of risk. Which is the bigger risk, a nuclear accident or global warming? If it is the latter then the building of nuclear power stations is justified. However, because risks are contingent, this means the ability to influence political discourse and decisions lies with those who shape risk rather than those who vote or lobby.

Third, risk extends the remit of the state not just to policy but to a diverse range of events such as accidents, obesity, the consequences of alcohol, and environmental changes. State actions then focus not on producing a specific outcome but managing events that *may* happen in the future. In both the United States and Britain government intervened in financial markets in September 2008 because of the risk of not underwriting key financial institutions. Or, in the case of health, risk changes how the state relates to individual behaviour. If I do not reduce what I drink there is a risk of ill-health in the future, and so the government does not just focus on managing my health now but my health in the future (Power, 2007). As Power (2007: 5) points out, this 'reflects increased social expectations about the decidability and management of dangers and opportunities'. In this process interests are collectivized. It is not my risks that are important but the risk to the total population. Therefore, individual feelings of uncertainty can be dismissed as irrational.

Finally, risk emphasizes the role of the state in changing particular forms of behaviour that are seen as high risk. As we will see in the following chapter this involves the state in a moral power that is focussed on modifying behaviour. Again risk legitimizes this form of intervention by measuring current behaviour against future costs.

Risk management, although seen by writers such as Beck and Giddens as reflecting postmodern or postindustrial sensibilities, is in fact an extension of the modernist project. It is a strong belief that through risk analysis and risk management we can calculate the chances of some unknown event occurring. It is an attempt to model and make regular the predictable, and hence supports Cioffi-Revilla's insistence that we can predict the occurrence of war. For Power (2007: 197) 'risk management makes organizations auditable' and so 'project visions of administrative order on nature'. States need not focus on all activities but on assessing risks and then regulating the risky elements of social life. There is within risk management an inherent teleology; a belief that we can predict the future on the basis of the past. This of course does produce new perceptions of risk by creating a new set of future dangers – an obese population that will die younger than the current generation; a bird flu epidemic; climatic global catastrophe. What this search for predictions fails to take account of is the ability of humans to change their behaviour and their understandings of what are dangers.

## Conclusion

Risk analysis and risk management have become important tools in terms of policy making in many states. However, political actors often use risk in conflicting ways. They use it in a sociological sense that we are – because of the changes in later modernity – subject to greater risks than in any preceding era. So politicians like George Bush are able to speak in the language of Beck but at the same time use what are seen as scientific approaches to risk to make decisions. However, risk management is a legitimation process that enables states to intervene in different ways and over different forms of behaviour. Moreover, it allows preventative action and closer management of what is regarded as risky behaviour. This theme is discussed in detail in the next chapter. Risk also changes the way that states relate to situations by presenting problems in terms of probabilities and again individualizing social problems. Risk assessment means that the focus of social intervention is on the probabilities for individuals and not processes of social change.

Risk is an important mechanism of power for two reasons. First, it allows state actors to use knowledge as a mechanism for legitimizing decisions of whether to act. In a sense it presents the decision as scientific and therefore unquestionable. If the government decides to invest in measures for dealing with a flu pandemic, that decision is hard to question if it can be demonstrated that the risk is high. If, on the other hand, there seems to be no risk from mobile phone masts the government can justify allowing them to be erected. What is in fact subjective is presented as objective. Second, risk, like the other new mechanisms of power, changes the locus of power from collective social problems to the individual. How to solve social problems becomes related to the risk factors of the individual and not to the social framework. This point is illustrated in relation to health issues. There is a strong link between health problems and poverty, but by focussing on risk health problems are placed with the risk factors of the individual and not the social situation. Risk reduces the need for the state to take collective action. It also feeds into the new rationality which sees everything as being measurable and subject to rational decisions based on full information.

# Chapter 11

# States and the Moral Order

The aim of this chapter is to demonstrate how the new forms of power outlined above have led to states focussing increasingly on individual behaviour and in doing so developing a new form of moral politics. The relationship between states and morality is complex and varied. For some states there is no distinction between policy and morality; policy is created for reasons of building a good society in accordance with some moral principles; this is the case in both communist and theocratic states. In liberal states, it is often the case that a distinction is made between public and private morality and J.S. Mill's harm principle, that people should be free to act as long as they do not harm others, has to some extent governed legislative behaviour. While liberal states have often intervened in personal, moral decisions to do with drinking, sexuality or marriage, there has been a trend in Western liberal regimes to move away from making explicitly moral decisions for people. Most countries in Europe have legalized abortion, divorce and homosexuality, and some have legalized prostitution and certain drugs. Pragmatically, governments have been wary about taking clear moral positions which may result in them alienating sections of the population, and most Western states have preached a form of value pluralism. Nevertheless, what I want to demonstrate in this chapter is that states have taken on an increasingly moral role (in the sense of developing policies which are normative in terms of the judgements they make about the behaviour of citizens) in recent years, and this is especially true in Britain and the United States. Moreover, the chapter argues that the new forms of power – rationality, surveillance, regulation and risk – are much more focussed on transforming individual behaviour (and indeed focussing on particular individuals) than the more generic, traditional forms of power. Consequently, they allow states both to observe and challenge the behaviour of individuals. Ironically whilst, for example, sexual preferences are now no longer seen as being within the purview of the state, sexual behaviour – and indeed other forms of social behaviour – are increasingly subject to constraints by state actors and policy.

States have long attempted to control sexual behaviour, drinking and social relationships in an attempt to order social lives. Nevertheless, the focus of government action during the period from 1945 has been on collective problems and behaviour, rather than the behaviour of particular individuals. Drinking has not been seen as a problem because it harms the individual but because it causes social disruption (so, for example, in the early twentieth century states controlled drinking but not smoking because the concern was not the health of the individual but the impact that the behaviour had on society or production). The focus of attention in the past has been on groups and classes, more than individuals, and the moral concerns of states have often been rather narrow and limited in impact – states have not traditionally controlled how much people drink or how they bring up their children. However, the new mechanisms of state power have changed the way that states intervene in moral issues. These techniques allow a much more individual focus for state power and, consequently, states have increasingly attempted to modify individual rather than collective behaviour. In areas of anti-social behaviour, parenting, obesity, smoking, teenage pregnancy and welfare dependency we can see the state taking on an increasingly moral position in relation to the behaviour of citizens and shifting away from the liberal premise of negative freedom. For example, in the US, $1 billion of federal funds have been committed for a campaign to promote sexual abstinence amongst teenagers. This chapter begins by looking at how moral politics has developed and then looks in detail at two examples, obesity and anti-social behaviour, to demonstrate the increasingly moral stance of state policy.

## Developing moral politics

Morality is not a new feature of state policy. In the nineteenth century politics was often bound by a strong morality. For instance, the 'purity movement' in the nineteenth century was concerned with regulating sexuality and social behaviour (Hunt, 1998) and temperance movements such as the Pioneers were highly influential in Britain and the United States in terms of policy relating to alcohol. States introduced legislation to regulate sexual behaviour and drinking, and it was during the nineteenth century that police forces became established. Kevin Siena (1998: 555) shows that state and non-state attempts to regulate moral behaviour were a crucial element of the early modern period:

[M]edical authorities employed the frightening image of venereal disease to help create and enforce danger beliefs aimed at policing behavior – behavior that was usually, but not always, sexual.

As today, there was a strong link between health and morality. Sexual activity was increasingly regulated because of the fear of sexually transmitted disease (Siena, 1998). For the developing modern states, the masses were seen as a threat that needed to be controlled, regulated and socialized for living in cities and working in factories. Stanley Cohen, in his seminal text, *Folk Devils and Moral Panics,* highlights how moral panics are an ever-present element of modern society. As he says: 'Working class yobs are the most enduring of suitable enemies. But the roles they played over these decades – football hooligans, muggers, vandals, loiterers, joy riders and mobile phone snatchers – were not represented by distinctive subcultural styles' (Cohen, 2002: viii).

The moral laws introduced in the nineteenth and early twentieth centuries set the framework for most of the twentieth century. However, politics increasingly distanced itself from morality until the 1960s and 1970s, when social and political pressure led to the reforming of the nineteenth-century moral framework with reform of abortion, divorce, laws on homosexuality, and the abolition of capital punishment. The state started to remove itself from governing individual moral behaviour (in different countries in different ways, and with considerable contestation, so that in the United States, for example, issues surrounding abortion and capital punishment have never been resolved). In Britain the Wolfenden Report, which led to the legalization of homosexuality, explicitly accepted Mill's harm principle and supported: 'individual freedom of actions in matters of private morality'. This report set the framework for the state's role in moral matters for the next twenty years.

In the postwar period state involvement tended to be around issues of rights, rather than behaviour, and so the civil rights movements and the women's movement forced legislation which gave equal rights to women and ethnic groups. The 1960s and 1970s (and through to the 1980s) saw states in the developed world adopting a more liberal position, which recognized individual rights and generally abdicated its role of controlling individual behaviour.

The moral abstinence by states, however, was creating a reaction almost as soon as it became established. Rapidly religious and new right groups were attempting to re-establish a politics of personal morality and fighting the liberal position. During the 1980s and 1990s states throughout the world started to develop an increasingly moral position and, as Lawrence Mead (1997) illustrates, an increasing range of policies in the US involved supervizing the behaviour of the poor in return for welfare (see also Smith, 2007). This, of course, was a complex process. Whilst some states were becoming more morally focussed, the newly democratized states in Southern Europe were responding to their new freedom by rapidly liberalizing laws on divorce, abortion and sexuality. Ironically, much of this shift to a new morality is linked to the rise of the new right which, although in principle libertarian in philosophy, pragmatically tied itself to the morality of the traditional right. At the same time its individualist ontology meant that misfortune was laid at the feet of individuals and not structures, and hence it tends to blame poverty on individual failure and not inequality. So whilst state techniques may be important in providing mechanisms for individual intervention, the new right was important in terms of changing the agenda in relation to the purpose of intervention. No longer was the focus on social structure, but increasingly on individual behaviour.

## The new right and individual responsibility

The new right took an explicitly moral position in its critiques of the ills of the United States and Britain, and, more generally, social democracy. The new right essentially rejects structural explanations of inequality and failure, seeing poverty largely as a consequence of individual choices or, in some cases, the lower intelligence of the poor. Resolving social problems could not be based on new social policies but on improving the behaviour of marginal groups. This sense of a moral position is illustrated very much in the debate on the underclass which was developed in the work of Charles Murray. For Murray: as 'a visitor from a plague area come to see whether the disease is spreading' he tells us that the question facing Britain is 'how contagious is this disease?' (1996: 42). Similarly, Ralf Dahrendorf describes the 'underclass' as 'a cancer which eats away at the texture of societies' and its future development as 'critical for the moral hygiene of British society'. The *Sunday Times*, in an editorial to mark its publication of Murray's first British essay, commented that 'the underclass spawns illegitimate children', creating an image of breeding animals. The label 'underclass', with all its negative connotations, now tends to be applied indiscriminately by the media to those in poverty (Lister, 1996: 10).

In the United States, the new right had (and has) close links with the Christian right, and in Britain Margaret Thatcher explicitly linked her project to a restoration of 'Victorian values'. Many of the goals of the new right were linked to moral goals; they wanted to restore the traditional family and the often traditional roles for men and women. In the US the new right has opposed gay rights, fought abortion legislation and demanded the reintroduction of capital punishment. In Britain, Thatcher strongly argued for the rediscovery of traditional values and the development of self-reliance, as an interview with Brian Walden highlights:

> *Walden*: Now obviously Britain is a very different country from the one it was in Victorian times when there was great poverty, great wealth, etc., but you've really outlined an approval of what I would call Victorian values. The sort of values, if you like, that helped to build the country throughout the 19th Century. Now is that right?
>
> *Margaret Thatcher*: Oh exactly. Very much so ... Yes, I want to see one nation, as you go back to Victorian times, but I want everyone to have their own personal property stake. Property, every single one in this country, that's why we go so hard for owner-occupation, this is where we're going to get one nation. I want them to have their own savings which retain their value, so they can pass things onto their children, so you get again a people, everyone strong and independent of Government, as well as a fundamental safety net below which no-one can fall. (Thatcher, 1983)

The work of Charles Murray on the underclass became particularly influential amongst the new right. Murray was in essence arguing that the division between the respectable and unrespectable poor – the deserving and undeserving – was changing, with the undeserving becoming an underclass which was permanently excluding itself from mainstream society. The high moralism of this position is indicated by Murray's argument that the best predictor of the underclass is illegitimacy and that women having children without fathers (husbands) was a major social problem (Murray, 1996: 26). Indeed, for Murray (1996: 27) the particular problem is not the one-parent family but illegitimacy:

> Being without two parents is generally worse for the child than

having two parents, no matter how it happens. But illegitimacy is the purest form of being without two parents – legally, the child is without a father from day one; he is often without one practically as well. Further, illegitimacy bespeaks an attitude on the part of one or both parents that getting married is not an essential part of siring or giving birth to a child; this in itself distinguishes their mindset from that of people who do feel strongly that getting married is essential.

The new right saw the permissiveness of the 1960s leading to family breakdown and the undermining of traditional values which was leading to a permanent underclass which increased the social disruption of society. Moreover, for the new right the welfare state encouraged the underclass by creating dependency. Murray baldly states what he sees as the link: 'long-term welfare dependency is a fact, not a myth, among young women who have children without husbands' (Murray, 1996: 30). This dependency then results in young men choosing 'not to take jobs' (Murray, 1996: 39).

The notion of the underclass picks up a sense that there is an other who does not behave according to the norms of a good society; that illegitimacy, permissiveness and dependency have led to moral degeneration and that we need to restore traditional values in order to resolve social problems. Again for Murray (1996: 42):

As many have commented through the centuries, young males are essentially barbarians for whom marriage – meaning not just the wedding vows, but the act of taking responsibility for a wife and children – is an indispensable civilizing force. Young men who don't work don't make good marriage material. Often they don't get married at all; when they do, they haven't the ability to fill their traditional role. In either case, too many of them remain barbarians.

Individual responsibility is the key to poverty, unemployment and crime and not inequality and social exclusion. For Murray, permissiveness, benefits and a housing act that favours single mothers have resulted in a growth of illegitimacy which has spawned an underclass. His moralising and simple causation may seem extreme, but many of the notions of morality have become part of everyday discourse in politics. Increasingly governments of left and right are attempting to reinforce the family, modify sexual behaviour, limit drinking and eating, and reform the behaviour of individuals. In Britain and the United States, governments have introduced policies which reduced aid to single parent families. In the United States single parent families lost rights to federal aid and were placed on time-limited benefits (as was discussed in Chapter 8). Illustratively, the new legislation was called, Personal Responsibility and Work Opportunity Reconciliation Act (PRWORA), emphasizing notions of responsibility and work. Indeed, for Anna Marie Smith (2007: 8) recent welfare reforms in the US have been specifically aimed at regulating the sexual behaviour of poor, and particularly black, women. Likewise in Britain, under a Labour government, after many years of reducing single parent benefit, the government believes that benefits are guaranteed for too long a period and they are discouraging single parents from work (*BBC News*, 30 January 2007). Indeed one government Minister spoke of depriving people who seemed unwilling to work of social housing. She believed that looking for work should be a condition of access to public housing (*The Guardian*, 5 February 2008).

The new forms of power involve mechanisms for observing and modifying individual behaviour and thus allow states to pursue normative policies directed at particular actions (the new forms of power open up a new field of state action). This is what Foucault, and others, see as biopolitics. As Bryan Turner (1996: 63) points out, for Foucault in modern society:

> [P]ower has a specific focus, namely the body, which is the product of political/power relationships. The body as an object of power is produced in order to be controlled, identified and reproduced. Power over the materiality of the body can be divided into two separated but related issues – 'the disciplines of the body and the regulations of the populations'. (Foucault, 1981: 139)

New forms of power regulate individual behaviour in ways that traditional forms of power such as authority, bureaucracy and force do not. Traditional forms of power are essentially restraints on behaviour and rarely – although this is not always the case – focussed on modifying individual behaviour. States in the nineteenth century were very much concerned with disciplining the newly urbanized workforce and strong codes were imposed in terms of issues such as cleanliness, sexuality and drinking. However, these tended to be class actions rather than a focus on the behaviour of particular individuals. Indeed, Turner highlights how traditionally social theory did not pay attention to 'the body', being concerned with states, classes and social institutions. This focus on the social level to some degree was reflective of how state actors operated. However, new forms of power are, as we have seen, making ontological assumptions about how individuals behave and how measures will affect their behaviour; increasingly it is individuals who are observed. For Foucault, 'life and living being' are now at the centre of politics (Lazzarato, 2002: 99). The moral politics of the late modern state is focussing very much on disciplining the body in terms of regulating social behaviour and regulating populations as a whole through new mechanisms of social control.

Foucault's attention to the body and the nature of the individual is increasingly reflected in both social theory and state power. The focus of states on obesity and individual health more generally, at least in the Anglo-Saxon world, although not exclusively (see Palou, 2007), illustrates the way in which the body has come to the fore in policy making. This focus on the body, however, is part of a more general shift to the idea that humans are reflexive individuals who can be persuaded or incentivized to shift from certain forms of risky behaviour. Despite the *faux* scientism of risk analysis, there is no real attempt to judge which forms of risky behaviour should be discouraged. If these analyses were really about risk and not morality or power, policy makers would be assessing what is more risky: driving a car or smoking a cigarette, climbing a mountain or building a nuclear power station. Instead, the deviant behaviour is a moral, not a scientific, decision. What are presented as being 'good' for us are in fact political and moral decisions about the forms of behaviour that are acceptable.

In short, to make a grand claim – which indeed does oversimplify individual histories and policies – new forms of state power, combined with an increased focus on individualism, have led states to intervene more closely in individual behaviour. As a result, states are developing policies that adopt distinct moral positions, which are then used to attempt to modify individual behaviour. This can be observed in a range of areas such as smoking, drinking, obesity, parenting, anti-social behaviour and teenage pregnancy (some of which are discussed below for illustration). Whilst debates around new forms of governance focus on the declining role of the state, what in fact is happening is that the state is increasing its intervention in society, though focussing on the social rather than the economic. Indeed, it is increasingly the case that in most democratic systems there is little debate over the direction of economic policy and so political divisions focus increasingly on social policy (Smith, 2007; Blakeley, 2004; Delgado and Lopez Nieto, 2008).

The other factor that has been important is the way that in the late modern world health has replaced God as the external fear intended to control social behaviour. Saguy and Riley (2005: 871) point out that a number of commentators have

> argued that the language of medicine merely extends moral judgement in a new guise (Zola, 1972; Illich, 1976), and more recent health surveillance scholarship has demonstrated how concerns about health risk can offer thinly veiled language through which to extend judgments of responsibility, blame and morality (Armstrong, 1995; Crawford, 1980; Lupton, 1995; Nettleton and Bunton, 1995).

Many of the moral policies are focussed around aspects of health and so attempts to control social behaviour are presented in terms of their being bad for our health; so, for example, binge drinking is presented as a health not a social problem. The strength of this moralism has led to examples in Britain where people are being prevented from receiving some treatment if they continue what are regarded as unhealthy activities. A number of health authorities are refusing to provide some treatment for patients who are obese, who smoke or drink (*Western Daily Press,* 3 May 2007). Whilst this is presented as a clinical decision – the treatment will not work if the patient carries on the harmful activity – it is also clearly moral. The extended logic would be not to perform cartilage operations on sports people who refused to give up rugby, or running, nor to treat car drivers in accidents if they continued to drive. However, policy makers are deciding that some risky activities are acceptable but others are not (see Edgar, 2007).

Two important points arise from these developments. First, they can be construed as highly authoritarian. States are often, in these areas, overstepping the harm principle in attempts to discourage or prevent certain activities (Mill, 1974 [1859] and see Mead, 1997: 4). For Mill (1974: 72): 'Each is responsible for his own health'. There seems to be a clear shift into paternalism and increasing acceptance that the state has to intervene for the good of people (Dworkin, 1995). Yet as Loretta Kopelman (2005) argues:

> Interference with the liberty of adults requires a heavy burden of proof to show they are incapacitated, incompetent, or a threat to themselves or others. It requires proving that the probability and magnitude of the possible harm merits the interference and that the means used are effective and the least restrictive means available.

Another feature of the new moralism is that it often contains a class element within the interventions. The issues that have been identified as problems such as obesity, anti-social behaviour, poor parenting and binge drinking are issues that predominantly affect the working class. Much of the moral politics relates to traditional issues of social control within subordinate groups (see for instance Willis, 1977). There is, in other words, a strongly modernist ethos within the moralism; states are increasingly trying to persuade citizens to behave in very similar ways and so are imposing strong conventions of behaviour that fit with a modernist norm. There is an irony to this new form of class politics. Whilst on one side most developed liberal states are attempting to come to terms with multiculturalism and finding different ways of coping with a range of cultural practices within a society, they are becoming less tolerant of particular forms of behaviour amongst traditional 'outsider' groups such as the poor, the working class and, to some degree, the young (the groups which feel most disaffected from politics – see Hay, 2007). This is not to say that states in the West are inclusive in terms of race (this of course varies greatly from state to state; Canada and France operate very differently), but there is no doubt that they are attempting to respond to lifestyles of, say, Muslim groups and how they may be integrated into society; yet there is little reflection on the lifestyles of the poor working class. For example, Rotherham in South Yorkshire has the highest rate of teenage pregnancy in Britain. As we will discuss below, the assumption of policy makers is that this is a bad thing and has to be reduced, but it may be that this is part of the social context of white working class girls in Rotherham who choose to be mothers young (see Wilson and Huntington, 2006). Local state actors are likely to be much more tolerant of young Muslim women who enter arranged marriages and have children in their teenage years than white working class teenage mothers. For one group the state takes a paternalist approach with a strong moralistic position, for the other there is recognition of the need to take account of particular cultural practices. This is illustrated by an examination of teenage pregnancy in another part of South Yorkshire, Doncaster. Here the research suggests that teenage pregnancy is high because of lack of knowledge about contraception and the absence of any discussion of the option of abortion. However the researchers argue:

> Factors related to the informal, cultural framing of sexuality and pregnancy by the community and conventional gender relations are

likely to bring about both initial conception and the subsequent sustaining of the pregnancy. (Tabberer *et al.*, 2000: 20)

The research is underpinned by a progressive sentiment that more information will provide young women with greater knowledge of abortion and hence the option to terminate the pregnancy, and so reduce the number of teenagers with children. However, they are taking a position concerning the cultural framing of reproductive rights in the community that may not be so easily adopted with an ethnic rather than a class group.

For the Right such issues are presented in terms of getting people to 'stand on their own feet' and so not rely on the state. What were moral perspectives on the behaviours of the underclass are presented as turning people into market actors. For the Left it is presented as part of the process of tackling inequality. One left-of-centre politician, 'sanctioned his Cabinet to take a more interventionist approach when it comes to narrowing the life chances between rich and poor' (Revill, 2005). However, the Left is also taking a clear moral position about what is acceptable behaviour and a highly modernist approach in the belief that human beings are improvable.

The irony of these types of intervention is that what started out as an attempt by the new right to break 'welfare dependency' by focussing on individual behaviours, has developed into a wider, and clearly statist attempt to change a range of behaviours (Lawson, 2006; Porter, 2005). A combination of new techniques of power, new ontologies, and a focus on individualism have led to states taking distinctly moral positions which are imposed on people as an extension of social control. The chapter will now examine how these processes have affected policy on obesity and anti-social behaviour.

## Moral panic and obesity

In the 1950s and 1960s governments in Europe, both West and East, had targets for industrial production, economic growth, levels of unemployment and investment. These targets could be very specific and relate to developing particular industries or sectors. Government intervention in this sort of planning has now almost completely disappeared. Governments continue to have targets for inflation and growth but not detailed plans for industrial production. However, the government in Britain does have targets for obesity and child activity. It is a truism in the media that there is an epidemic of obesity. In both the US and Britain an 'obesity epidemic' is stated as a fact (Revill, 2007; Saguy and Almeling, 2005; Courtenay Botterill, 2006).

The issue of obesity is fascinating in terms of state power because it involves the state in particular and personal decisions about what we eat, how much we eat, whether we exercise and our lifestyle. Obesity is particularly interesting because there appears to be an almost universal consensus that obesity is increasing and is now a growing threat to public health (Simmons and Wareham, 2006: 14). It is repeatedly suggested that it is an epidemic with the number of overweight and obese increasing in the US from 45 per cent in 1962 to 66 per cent in 1999–2000. Breslow (2006a: 10) highlighted in 1952 that there is a problem of 'excessive mortality from cardiovascular-renal diseases among American men' and that there seems to be a 'close association between overweight and excessive mortality from several of these chronic diseases'. There are constant references to the growing number of overweight people and that we could be faced with the first generation whose life expectancy declines because of the epidemic of obesity. Abigail Saguy and Rene Almeling (2005: 23) point out that news reports are particularly likely to exaggerate the extent and impact of obesity with over half the articles in their sample using the term epidemic. Yet the scientific evidence for the relationship between weight and health is at best ambiguous. There is little evidence that anything other than extreme obesity has any impact on life expectancy. Even in the extremely obese it may be that obesity is a proxy for other factors, such as poor diet or lack of exercise, which may in fact reduce life expectancy rather than weight (Campos *et al.*, 2006; Saguy and Almeling, 2005; Gard and Wright, 2005; Courtenay Botterill, 2006). There is evidence that those who are fit and overweight do not have increased mortality (although this could be a problem of the BMI which measures weight and not fat; those who are muscular often weigh more than those who are fat) (Breslow, 2006b). If anything, underweight has a stronger association with early death (Campos *et al.*, 2006: 56). Moreover, it seems that the growth in overweight has been exaggerated. Some of the increase is the result of changes in statistical measures so that in terms of the crude Body Mass Index (BMI), which is used as the measure, the point at which overweight is measured has been lowered (Saguy and Almeling, 2005). It is also the case that the sensationalized accounts run together the number of overweight and obese, which are different things. Campos *et al.* (2006: 55) also argue that the weight gain is not generalized and that whilst the heaviest individuals have increased in weight, those in the overweight and lesser obese categories have only increased weight slightly.

Although the discussion of obesity is often phrased in terms of health issues, it undoubtedly has a strong moral element. As Campos *et al.* (2006: 58) argue:

> Targeting obesity has support across the political spectrum. In the US, discussions of the supposed obesity epidemic usually take place within the context of a larger discussion, which assumes that the increasing weight of the population is a sign of increasing moral laxity and that overweight and obesity are playing a significant role in driving up health care costs. This linkage is in responsibility, rather than structural factors that continue to drive health care costs ever upward.

Issues of control of obesity combine all elements of new state power: risk, incentives, and surveillance. In addition, as Saguy and Almeling (2005: 3) highlight, the discussion of obesity is 'highly moralised'. The whole tenor of the debate about obesity is that it is bad to be fat and more particularly that it is a consequence of weakness or sloth (Saguy, 2005). Gard and Wright (2005: 5–6) point out that even amongst scientific papers there is often a shift from a scientific presentation of data to a normative set of conclusions not based on any evidence about the implications. For instance, they quote Bouchard and Blair (1999) saying:

> It will be a daunting task to change the course of nations that have progressively become quite comfortable with an effortless lifestyle in which individual consumption is almost unlimited.

The focus of obesity is very much individual behaviour and indeed individual failure.

Moreover, despite ambiguity in the evidence, governments have decided that obesity is an issue which they have a responsibility to resolve. In Britain there is a cross-government obesity programme which aims at:

- changing population attitudes towards eating and activity
- helping children to be active and eat healthily
- supporting targeted local-level obesity interventions in children
- raising awareness of the importance of healthy weight to children and parents

- working with local partners on delivery and
- developing the knowledge base. (Department of Health, 2007)

The government has identified a problem and sees the solution in terms of changing individual behaviour in relation to food and exercise. Policy adopts a clear normative position and it is not seen as acceptable to allow people to eat what they wish (which indeed contradicts the tenor of food policy for most of the twentieth century, which has been to allow access to cheap food [Blythman, 2004; Walker and Cannon, 1986]). The issue is set up as a moral issue; obesity is considered the consequence of overeating and a sedentary lifestyle – of individual actions – rather than due to a lack of education, poverty, or the structure of the food industry (food companies make considerable money out of highly processed food; sugar and transfats are cheap materials for bulking out food [Blythman, 2004]). There is a notion that specific interventions based both on regulating the body and supervizing the population as a whole are the solution to obesity. The level of surveillance of the population is relatively high in that most developed states have statistics on levels of obesity related to particular categories within the population. In the United States the surveillance is such that in certain states the Body Mass Index scores of pupils are sent home to parents (*New York Times,* 8 January 2007). Governments have also developed specific interventions to change behaviour: one is the creation of a generalized fear of obesity; despite ambiguity in the medical evidence (*Daily Telegraph,* 7 September 2007) that obesity leads to a range of diseases and early death. Other policies, for example in the US, include public education campaigns, exercise campaigns and policies such as those outlined above in terms of providing funds for healthy diets, or what could be seen as the highly authoritarian measure of placing children in care because they are obese (*The Guardian,* 10 September 2007).

The debate about food and obesity is conducted within terms of individual behaviour and little attention is paid to structural factors relating to diet and obesity. Britain has the highest childhood obesity levels in the world and the United States has the highest adult levels. Whilst there is some discussion that these levels of obesity are related to post-industrialism, the policy prescriptions are almost completely individualistic. The focus of attention is on the body and individual behaviour, from the new right view of the poor: it is the individual who is blamed, not the structure of the food industry or the generalized absence of knowledge about food. There is no attempt to tackle the cheap food culture that exists in the United States and Britain, or to examine the structure of the food industry and how it produces and supplies food. It is the behaviour of individuals that has to change. Indeed, there is no attempt to ban or tax cheap, sugary and high-fat food, but to get individuals to resist it despite the advertising and supermarket offers. This is the great irony: individuals face a whole range of highly marketed, cheap, high-calorie foods and the solution to obesity is that individuals should resist what is presented to them; not that there should be any attempt to change what food is on offer. This is almost in a class between two types of power – agenda setting through corporations and direct control of individual behaviour by the state. The state is intervening in ways aimed at the individual and state policies are premised on the idea that those who are overweight have failed. There is little attempt to affect the key companies and advertisers involved in the creation and selling of the food. A more generalized sort of moral behaviour is to be found in the case of anti-social behaviour.

## Anti-social behaviour

Anti-social behaviour is a complex and difficult issue. It could be argued that it does not fit the category of moral politics in the same way as obesity because elements of anti-social behaviour clearly pass the harm principle. However, the point about anti-social behaviour is that it changes the categorization of certain behaviour. Most acts which cause direct harm to people are subject to criminal law (see MacDonald, 2006). Measures related to anti-social behaviour bring what might be seen as social irritations or behaviour that is not deemed as acceptable into the remit of state actors and this has, at least in the case of Britain and some other countries, increased the intervention of the state into social behaviour. Rutter *et al.* (1998: 65) indicate that there is little doubt that crime rates have increased significantly inter-nationally since the 1950s and they focus on how anti-social behaviour amongst the young has become more prevalent. Whilst explanations of increasing crime are obviously many and complex, one of the reasons for growing anti-social behaviour may be a declining tolerance of alter-native forms of behaviour. It is illustrative to read children's novels from the 1940s and 1950s such as *Just William* and *Billy Bunter* to see how activities then regarded as boys being naughty would now be clas-sified as serious anti-social behaviour. Through programmes of anti-social behaviour state actors are making moral decisions about what forms of behaviour are acceptable and to a degree criminalizing what used to be seen as 'high jinks'. This of course reflects a wider process by which societies continually redefine what is acceptable or unacceptable. For example, in the 1950s and 1960s drink-driving was seen as a joke or something to boast about, but today in Britain and the US it is morally reprehensible behaviour that can lead to prison even for celebrities.

The fact that Singapore banned chewing gum has often been cited as an example of the authoritarian nature of the city state (*BBC News*, 15 March 2004). The law is seen as draconian, partly because it oversteps the harm principle. However, under much anti-social regulation, there seems to be a considerable number of what may be seen as draconian measures. In the United States anti-social behaviour policies started with what was called the zero tolerance programme to deal with all forms of crime. George Kelling and James Wilson (1982) develop the thinking behind zero tolerance which held: 'that if not firmly suppressed, disorderly behaviour in public will frighten citizens and attract predatory criminals, thus leading to more serious problems' (Greene, 1999: 172). The premise then is that authorities have to react quickly and that if even minor infractions of the law are treated harshly then serious crime will be diminished.

This policy has developed widely with a zero tolerance policy being used in schools in a number of American states. Any infringement of a school rule can result in severe punishment. However, as a report by the Justice Policy Institute demonstrated, this has in some cases resulted in the criminalization of very minor acts such as the case in Ponchatoula, Louisiana, where:

A 12-year-old who had been diagnosed with a hyperactive disorder warned the kids in the lunch line not to eat all the potatoes, or 'I'm going to get you'. The student, turned in by the lunch monitor, was suspended for two days. He was then referred to police by the principal, and the police charged the boy with making 'terroristic threats'. He was incarcerated for two weeks while awaiting trial. (American Bar Association, 2001)

Zero tolerance is seen as taking a clear moral line. Authorities will not tolerate drugs, underage drinking or misbehaviour. The problem is: what are the limits of the tolerable and who defines it? A writer in the right-wing British paper the *Daily Mail* argues:

Why do I take issue with those who argue that, in refusing to turn a blind eye to 'minor' infringements, the authorities are simply being petty and heavy-handed? Quite simply, because refusing to accept any form of anti-social behaviour is the cornerstone of zero toler-ance – a term that is much talked about, often suggested as a way of curbing our wave of lawlessness, but widely misunderstood. Having witnessed the effects of zero tolerance at first hand, I know that it works – but only if you treat *all* minor infringements with due seri-ousness and don't just pick on easy targets while ignoring the more hardened thugs. (Jones, 2007)

But this sort of position leads to moral decision making – drinking in the street is not tolerated, sometimes there are limits on young people congregating in certain places (as in the case of dispersal orders in Britain where within a defined area people are not allowed to be in groups of more than two) and one example in Britain where a young woman was charged for putting her feet on a train seat. Radley Balko (2003) argues that the extension of zero tolerance of drunkenness has led to 'back-door prohibition' in the United States, and cites a case in Virginia where the police breathalyzed people in a bar and then charged them with 'public intoxication'. According to Judith Greene (1999), it has also resulted in more accusations of police abuse and brutality in New York. Issues of public order take precedence over indi-vidual rights. With dispersal orders individuals who have not commit-ted a crime could be arrested for gathering in a particular area.

Zero tolerance worked within the context of existing law and was based on the idea of equivalence – the view that it is not the crime that is important but the breaking of the law. However, it then tends to draw relative misdemeanors such as drinking into the purview of the state. Anti-social legislation in Britain, and to a degree in other coun-tries such as Spain, goes further. It is based on zero tolerance but not only of 'crime' but of behaviour which is deemed as unacceptable. The aim of anti-social legislation in Britain was to enable the police to deal with minor acts of disorder such as groups of youths threatening people in shopping malls, without resorting to criminal law (where the levels of proof are much higher). Through the ASBO legislation police can impose restrictions on the movements of individuals who have displayed anti-social behaviour through an Anti-Social Behaviour Order (ASBO). Because it is magistrates who issue the order, the police or local authority do not have to prove a crime has been committed but that there has been a consistent pattern of unacceptable behaviour.

However, one of the problems has been defining anti-social behaviour and how the range of activities covered has spread very widely.

The 1998 Crime and Disorder Act defined anti-social behaviour as acts causing 'harassment, alarm or distress'. However, the police had problems in defining anti-social behaviour. These were described in *Policing Antisocial Behaviour* (2000) and in the Executive Summary of the BCS Report (*Antisocial Behaviour and Disorder*, 2001). It found that:

- none of the nine police forces visited had a formal definition of anti-social behaviour;
- the absence of a common definition of antisocial behaviour creates practical difficulties for the police in their efforts to tackle it, because their powers may be unclear and the solution to the problem may lie with other agencies;
- no force restricted itself to one kind of response to antisocial behaviour but used a range of responses depending on the problem.

In their *Tackling Anti-Social Behaviour: What Really Works?* (2002) the National Association for the Care and Rehabilitation of Offenders addressed the problem of definition by listing 17 behaviours which could be defined as anti-social. Some were extremely vague, e.g. noise or 'threats'. These and others would be perceived differently in different communities. Some Crime and Disorder Reduction Partnerships (CDRPs) had as a result adopted local definitions, which the report endorsed. It also mentioned the related problem of measurement of anti-social behaviour and responses to it. The 1998 Act required police forces to develop clear outcome measures. However, there is clearly considerable discretion for police forces to determine the definition of anti-social behaviour.

Despite – or perhaps because of – basic definitional issues, ASB has developed as a long-term policy with a dedicated Home Office unit, the Anti-Social Behaviour Unit, which has recently been supplemented by the development of the 'Respect Agenda' managed at the time of our study by the Office of the Deputy Prime Minister. The ASB policy had a long period of gestation both in the Labour party and the Home Office. New Labour first identified persistent anti-social behaviour as an important and growing problem in a 1995 consultation paper *A Quiet Life: Tough Action on Criminal Neighbours* (Hindmoor, 2004: 324–5). The official position is that ASBOs have been extremely effective because they have allowed communities to deal with issues that are causing considerable distress.

However anti-social behaviour effectively extends the remit of state authorities in controlling behaviour in both public and private spaces. Anti-social policy is about enforcing norms rather than laws and therefore places public authorities in the position of judging what behaviour is acceptable. As Ashworth *et al.* suggest (quoted in MacDonald, 2006: 14):

> Even if the police and local authorities can be trusted to be scrupulous in avoiding discrimination [on grounds of race, religion, sex, sexual orientation or disability] – and we are not sure that they can – this is no obstacle to these orders being used as weapons against other unpopular types, such as ex-offenders, 'loners', 'losers', 'weirdos', prostitutes, travelers, addicts, those subject to rumour and gossip, those regarded by the police or neighbours as having 'got away' with crime, etc.

Moreover, the vague nature of the British legislation means that there is a wide range of activities than can be covered. This ranges from serious criminal activity to the tabloid favourites concerning cases of pigs, parrots and answering front doors without clothes. What is significant is that anti-social behaviour measures allow the state to become involved in particular acts by specific individuals outside criminal law. There is within the legislation and implementation a view that the approach should be flexible, and what is defined in one area as anti-social behaviour is not the same in another. Whilst this allows communities to be involved in defining the anti-social behaviour that affects them it does mean that there is inequality before the law and, of course, confusion amongst the targets about what constitutes anti-social behaviour (see Birmingham City Council, 2006). As Stuart MacDonald (2006: 6–7) points out, there has been 'mission creep':

> By 2002 things such as begging, prostitution and graffiti had been added to the list of behaviours deemed anti-social, reflecting a wider 'sanitising agenda'. Anti-social behaviour was no longer being used simply to connote 'aggressive or selfish individual behaviour affecting neighbours'. Rather, it had been 'adapted ... to describe a diverse mix of environmental and human incivilities that affect neighbourhoods in a more impersonal and generalised way'. At the same time, there is a medicalisation of anti-social behaviour (see Justicea *et al.*, 2006).

Measures to tackle anti-social behaviour are now becoming central aspects of government policy around the world. For example, the United States, Canada, Australia and Spain all have legislation to deal with anti-social behaviour. In Spain the arbitrary nature of the anti-social is illustrated by differences in local application. Anti-social behaviour is dealt with at the regional level and so responds to local concerns. One area to which particular attention has been paid has been the so-called *Botelleons*. Both Barcelona and Andalucía have used anti-social laws to tackle what are essentially street parties where young people meet in the street to drink alcohol (which they see as creating their own social space which is much cheaper than going to bars). This offends several social norms in Spain. Whilst drinking is widely tolerated, drunkenness is not. Moreover, the street is a social space and not seen as one that can be taken over by particular groups. Consequently, the police have taken a very hard line on what in some ways may be seen as the relatively harmless activity of young people getting together, away from parents, and drinking.

The other aspect of anti-social behaviour that is notable is that interventions are coming earlier in the process. In the United States, certain states have introduced a system where the risk factors of anti-social behaviour are identified when a woman is pregnant. At that point, a nurse is attached to the family in order to provide advice on parenting, issues of alcohol and drug abuse and nutrition in order to prevent anti-social behaviour (Ward, 2007). This does, of course, involve identifying children as problem children before they are born. In Britain the government is also using parenting experts to help with children who have behaviour problems and in some cases these parenting classes are compulsory (Ward and Wintour, 2007). There is an evidence-based claim that poor parenting is a significant risk factor in later criminal and anti-social behaviour. Nevertheless, such policies implicate the state deeply in the operation of the family – in this sense politics has become personal. Hence, as we saw in Chapters 9 and 10, surveillance and risk are about identifying what may happen and so taking action to prevent it. The moralism of anti-social behaviour is a development of this policy of anticipation, where those likely to be trouble makers can be identified and subject to early interventions. They do not have to commit crime to come within the purview of the state, just have the potential for criminality.

## Conclusion

States have always taken moral positions and intervened in the lives of citizens in order to modify behaviour and to ensure social order. However, liberal states have tended to respect the harm principle and allow individuals to control their own personal behaviour. The journalist Henry Porter (2006) argues:

> Our bodies used to be ours to do what we would with them. But those liberal days are gone and this development is all part of a much larger movement of intrusiveness, propelled by the evident failure of government in tackling large-scale organized crime, such as people-trafficking. Yet again, for want of any more inspired policy, an intractable problem is resolved in the eyes of the governing class by persecuting the individual and removing his or her freedoms. But this suggestion from the government's sisterhood also demonstrates the migration of individuals' control over their lives to the state and beyond. As more power and decisions are passed to Europe – without our consent – so politicians have to find something to busy themselves with, and what better challenge than 60 million people who fornicate, drink to excess, smoke, eat too much salty and fatty food and harbour all sorts of antisocial and criminal intent?

This chapter has sought to highlight that new forms of state power have enabled a degree and intensity of involvement by the state in social behaviour that is much greater than has ever been the case in the past. The state is increasingly attempting to control sexuality, drinking, eating, and exercise, and to define the norms of acceptable behaviour. As the chapter has demonstrated, this development can be rooted in the new right's individualistic explanation of the causes of poverty and its tendency to see certain forms of behaviour as unacceptable despite its professed libertarianism. The development has been keenly pursued by governments of the centre-left who have seen it both in terms of quality of life issues and as an important mechanism for improving equality of opportunity. However, it is part of a broader conception of state influence which is enabled by new forms of power.

As we saw in Chapter 5, rationalist conceptions of power are based on the notion that individualized incentives can be used to reform behaviour and these have been used particularly in areas of teenage pregnancy and obesity. Mechanisms of surveillance enable state actors to observe in detail transgressions of accepted moral norms, and risk-based policies are based on the assumptions that the risk factors associated with forms of behaviour can be identified (so providing the state with the legitimacy to intervene), and allowing intervention to occur early. These developments are based on the state taking on a regulatory role which is based both on surveillance and risk. The other noteworthy point is that this approach is highly modernist. It assumes both that behaviour can be improved, and that people can be made better, and that the state has the ability, resources and information to make improvements. Moreover, many of these interventions are based on a strong conception of professional knowledge. Whilst the decisions may be seen as moral, they are in fact presented as decisions of scientific knowledge: so teenage pregnancy leads to poverty, obesity leads to death. There is no acknowledgement of the state making moral choices even when the evidence is contested (as in the case of obesity). Finally, despite a general perception of a decline of class politics, and evidence of a decline in class voting, many of these interventions have a strong class element. It is in effect a professional middle class and elite bureaucracy attempting to change the behaviour of groups of the working class (it is not uncommon to see on television relatively rotund middle class doctors providing advice to working class women on healthy eating). This highlights the way in which moral politics relates to the core issue of state power: the problem of order. More particularly, it highlights the complex nature of state power. States have paid much less attention to issues of economic planning and social change and, through new techniques of power, states have focussed instead on individual behaviour, particularly that of groups that are outsiders. The form of state power has changed and with it there has been some change in the gaze of the state.

# Chapter 12

# The Limits of the State: Invisibility, Resistance and Constraint

Much of the debate surrounding the state in the last ten years has been about the growing limits on its power when confronted with the combined forces of neo-liberal public sector reforms and neo-liberal inspired globalization. For much social science literature neo-liberalism is treated as unproblematic and almost as an inexorable force, which both undermines the traditional state, and limits its intervention to welfare policy and the provision of collective goods. Neo-liberalism, however, can only be seen as one element in the processes of change that have occurred within states over the last thirty years; more importantly, neo-liberalism is a fragmented and contested set of ideas that can have varying effects on outcomes. This book has endeavoured to demonstrate that, rather than states losing power, they have developed new forms of power that have been effective in different ways, and to an extent these forms of power are cumulative and so build on existing institutional forms. Moreover, state power is particular, not general; states can have power in one situation and not another. Hence, we cannot see states as having limitless power. For theorists of power like Foucault, power is not about simple domination and, by its very nature, power means resistance (Sharp *et al.*, 2000). We saw in Chapter 7 that even, or maybe especially, in highly authoritarian regimes there are spaces that evade the view of the state. Hence, there are limits on state power. Of course these limits and constraints are many. They can include the electoral system, the media, protest groups, the limits of economic performance, international regulation and organizations, and the power of key economic and social groups like business. This chapter will concentrate on the ways in which state power is limited by focusing on how people are invisible to the state or are able to resist it. The chapter begins by reviewing the debate on the declining role of the state.

## The debate on declining state power

Much of the debate in recent years has been on the declining capabilities and sovereignty of the state. This is seen as a two-fold but connected assault on state power with rising internationalization of fields of policy limiting the state's sovereignty and therefore affecting the state's capabilities to intervene in order to produce public goods. A wide body of literature, ranging from government bodies to fields such as public management (Osborne and Gaebler, 1992), international relations and international political economy, has placed the emphasis on the decline in state power (see Strange, 1996). For much of the 1980s and 1990s organizations like the World Bank saw markets as the mechanism for resolving problems of economic development. Writers from very different perspectives suggested that the era of the state was over. As Van Creveld (1999: 3) argues, 'Somewhere between 1945 and 1975, the type of political construct known as the state and characterized, above all, by the separation between the ruler and the organization peaked and may have gone into decline'. Likewise Scholte (2005: 188) maintains 'The statist mode of governance peaked between the mid-nineteenth to mid-twentieth century'.

The problem with much discussion of power and of the state is that it artificially separates out the state and society and, more problematically, sees the state as operating on subjects whose behaviour it changes. It assumes that a unified state has lost power in a systematic way and it presumes a distinct and bounded state separate from a society that it controls. The reality, of course, is highly complex and, as many authors have emphasized, the distinction between state and society is far from clear (Migdal, 2001; Mitchell, 1999). State power works through operating with and not upon society. We obey the rules of the road not by focusing on state commands but by inculcating within the notion of 'a driver' particular conventions for the road. As Robert Jackman (1993: 41) puts it: 'Compliance thus becomes a habit'. Moreover, it is often the case that what have been described as state powers are enacted by non-state actors. Surveillance does involve the police but it also involves local authorities, private security companies, banks, mobile phone companies and retailers. What the state does is to pull all these sources of information together (in principle). For Joel Migdal (2001: 116):

The state, then, does not generate a single, homogenous response to an issue or problem, or even necessarily a varied but coordinated set of responses. Rather its outcome – the formulations and implementation of its policies – are a series of different actions based on the particular calculus of pressures that each engaged component of the state faces in its particular environment of action.

In other words, how the state exercises power and its impact depends on the particular aspect of the state and the sets of relationships that exist in that area. Global economic relations will have complex effects on the nature of national economic policy (see Hay, 2000). But similarly the state, or aspects of it, will face resistance and failures of capabilities. State failures, or successes, are particular and depend on sets of relations with society. The interaction between state and society creates considerable possibilities for resistance and even effective states have limits on their ability to control behaviour (so in Britain the response to the failure to control obesity is to change the targets). Moreover, as the implementation literature in public policy recognizes, the state's reach depends on the capability of the state to get actors further down the policy chain to act in ways that the government wishes. The crucial point that Michael Lipsky (1980) realized is that often those responsible for policy delivery have considerable autonomy. Power, then, is always contested, resisted and limited and however effective states are there will be areas where they fail. Globalization and neo-liberalism may have changed what states do, but they do not mean the state has been denuded of power. The state is, and always has been limited in what it can do, and to an extent, what it can see.

## Invisibility in the modern state

As we saw in Chapter 5, modern states are based on a desire to name, order and control people (Scott, 1998). With modern states people are drawn into the orbit of the state. States want to control their populations for grounds of security, taxation and to ensure political support. Liberal theory going back to Hobbes and Locke and, in a different tradition, the work of Rousseau is based on the idea of a contract with the state: a presumption that if individuals are within a particular territory, they have some obligation to the state because it bestows certain benefits. Nevertheless, one of the anomalies is that even in authoritarian modern states there are people who avoid the gaze of the state – and in this sense they literally do not exist. Despite new technologies of power, states often do not have some very simple information: how many people are unemployed; how many are immigrants – illegal or otherwise; how many children are not going to school? Often figures for a whole range of government measures – trade, unemployment, the number involved in a demonstration, the number in poverty – are contested because they are difficult to establish and the definition is often political. Indeed, which statistics are chosen for collection and how certain categories are defined, such as unemployed or disabled (Haggerty, 2002), has significant implications for what the state can or cannot do or whom it does not see. As Kevin Haggerty (2002: 91) reminds us:

> The history of the U.S. census nicely demonstrates how political circumstances and priorities can shape statistical practices and institutions. Since its inception in 1790, the U.S. census has been inextricably linked to the political priorities of the day.

Invisibility to the state can come from either side of the state–society relationship. There are groups which states do not have the ability to track and there are those which consciously attempt to hide from the state. There are cases where the state is very keen to track groups or individuals, such as immigrants, but the groups are often keen to evade detection. One of the most obvious examples of these invisibilities and the difficulties that states have in controlling their societies is the existence of the black economy. Central to the modern state is its ability to collect taxes efficiently, which essentially funds all of its activities. Yet every modern society has a large black economy. The notion of the black economy is based on a state's inability to monitor and tax economic activity. Whilst rates – or at least estimated rates – of black economy activity vary, there is little doubt that they are endemic aspects of all societies. The black economy within the EU is equivalent to 16 per cent of gross domestic product (GDP) and in some European countries such as Spain and Greece it is as high as 20 per cent (*International Herald Tribune,* 10 June 1998). In countries such as Nigeria it is estimated to be as high as 75 per cent (Schlosser, 2003).

What is interesting about the black economy is that it is partly economic activity that goes on out of sight of the state. Much economic activity is illegal. For example, it is estimated that the growing of marijuana, illegal labour and pornography now account for 10 per cent of the US economy and it is estimated that marijuana is the largest cash crop in the US (*The Guardian,* 2 May 2003; Schlosser, 2003). What is interesting, however, is the often ambiguous relationship that states have with the black economy. First, it is clear that many societies would have great difficulty surviving without black economies; the legal economy does not have the ability to secure sufficient income. Particularly where there is the absence of a welfare state, quasi-legal activity is the only mechanism for many people to survive (Valante, 2005) (see for example Auyero [2007] who demonstrates that legal authorities could even be complicit in clearly illegal activities such as looting in order to pursue political ends). Second, states are not unaware of the economic benefits of the black economy as a mechanism for reducing labour costs and ensuring competitiveness in certain sectors (Schlosser, 2003). For example, it is argued that in Asia illegal workers are a central part of the economy:

> Japan, South Korea, Singapore, Taiwan, Hong Kong, Macau and Malaysia need (in varying degrees) the migrant workers to help them continue getting a share of the ever growing market domestically and abroad, and to construct the infrastructures for transportation, communication and industries. Another reason is the decreasing number of workers in agricultural and manual work in many receiving countries that made foreign workers the easy substitute. Still another reason is the encouragement by governments in most of these countries, with the exception of Japan. (*Asia Pacific News*, 1996)

However, the use of illegal migrant labour is now a common practice in developed countries. As Gordon Hanson (2007: 10) demonstrates: 'Though the United States does not set the level of illegal immigration explicitly, existing enforcement policies effectively permit substantial numbers of illegal aliens to enter the country'. They now work in a range of areas such as construction, food and retail. The point Hanson makes is that illegal immigrants are more able to respond to the economic needs of the US economy and create a flexible labour market (because legal immigration often lags behind the demand for labour) and consequently they bring significant economic benefits:

> Immigration generates extra income for the U.S. economy, even as it pushes down wages for some workers. By increasing the supply of labor, immigration raises the productivity of resources that are complementary to labor. More workers allow U.S. capital, land, and natural resources to be exploited more efficiently. Increasing the

supply of labor to perishable fruits and vegetables, for instance, means that each acre of land under cultivation generates more output. Similarly, an expansion in the number of manufacturing workers allows the existing industrial base to produce more goods. (Hanson, 2007: 19)

For Hanson the immigration surplus through extra economic production and its suppression of labour costs is 0.2 per cent of US GDP.

Furthermore, often the state is itself engaged in the black economy. For example, in Argentina there are public workers who earn part of their salary as cash in hand (Valante, 2005). In Britain, whilst undoubtedly to the embarrassment of the government, a number of illegal immigrants were caught working as cleaners within the Home Office – the department charged with controlling immigration and catching illegal workers (*Daily Mail*, 19 May 2007). The point is that states often, for obvious reasons, do not have the ability to know how many migrants there are within their borders, particularly when the migration is 'illegal'. Perhaps more importantly states have reasons for not knowing. First, as we have seen, they can become an important element of the economy. Second, immigration is often a politically difficult issue and therefore it is not in the interest of government ministers to highlight the numbers of migrants.

Immigration highlights starkly the complexity of the limits of state power. However globalization is defined, one of the features of the late twentieth and early twenty-first centuries is growing movements of people between countries. Migration has doubled since 1960 and now, according to UN estimates, there are 191 million immigrants worldwide (Grugel and Piper, 2007: 27). Migration is a problem of borders – borders create the problem (because people are only migrants if they cross borders) and states try to use borders as the solution. Despite the changing forms of state power, borders have not disappeared but they have become complex and multivariate.

However hard states try to make borders impermeable, immigrants and goods manage to break through. The United States has expended considerable resources policing the border with Mexico but in early 2006 it discovered a tunnel leading from Mexico directly into a warehouse in the United States. This was the 21st tunnel to be discovered since 2001. Donato *et al.* (1992) illustrate how the Immigration Reform and Control Act (1986) attempted to increase control over illegal immigration into the US from Mexico by making it illegal for employers to employ illegal immigrants and by increasing the resources of the Immigration and Nationalities Service to enforce the border. However, as they point out: 'Apprehended or not, every migrant who attempted to enter the United States eventually got in' (1992: 51). Sherrie Kossoudji (1992) finds that the Act has had a perverse effect with illegal migrants returning to the US more often and for longer periods. So despite all the billions of dollars spent on border control, the impact is negative. The point is that the controls did not work despite the border becoming more of a physical reality. States cannot control immigration even though they continually attempt to create measures for that end.

Immigrants exist within a paradoxical situation. Often, because of immigration controls, they are regarded as illegal workers. However, many economies and particular employers depend on them. States take explicit measures to deal with 'illegal immigrants' but are aware of their economic importance. States consequently produce contradictory policy responses. In October 2007 the US Security Chief Michael Churtoff said his department would expel all illegal immigrants. However, 80 per cent of Mexicans arrested are released because there is nowhere to hold them, and US policy towards Cuban immigrants is not to expel them (Breitbart.com, 18 October 2007). Indeed, different parts of the US do not have a consistent policy toward migrants. States may desire to expel illegal immigrants but in countries such as the United States where the numbers are in the millions and they are imbricated in all aspects of economic life, it is impossible to achieve (Jacoby, 2007). As Jeff Jacoby (2007) highlights:

> But no one this side of the fever swamps really believes that 12 million people – the population of Pennsylvania – can be rounded up and expelled ...To deport ... that number would require the iron fist of a Stalin. No sane American would tolerate it.

Likewise, in Britain, whilst 314,000 asylum claims were rejected between 1997 and 2004, only 75,000 people were removed from the country (National Statistics Office, 12 December 2007). In Spain there is recognition of the difficulty of controlling illegal immigrants with periodic processes of legalizing illegal immigrants through an amnesty. One of the fascinating aspects of illegal immigration is that whilst states take considerable measures to prevent it, they often lack the capabilities to find and return immigrants once they are within a border.

States create an immigration problem by enforcing borders and in reinforcing the borders they create new problems. There is an economic drive for a flexible labour market and so global capitalism sucks in low-skilled, cheap workers whom nation states see as illegal. Consequently, illegal immigrants do not receive the protections that exist for other workers; the state does not see them as anything other than a problem and so the law does not apply to them. There are attempts to develop rights for migrant workers (Grugel and Piper, 2007), but the application and enforcement of rights requires some degree of recognition. This recognition identifies illegal workers and so subjects them to the possibility of expulsion.

Illegal immigrants are one group of 'missing people' who, to use Corbridge *et al.*'s (2005) term, are not seen by the state. However, they are only one out of a range of groups and individuals that fall outside the state's purview. In Chapter 5 we highlighted James Scott's argument that a key element of the creation of the modern state is the naming and registering of individuals. However, Jean Grugel and Nicola Piper (2007: 135) illustrate that many modern states in the developing world are still relatively imperfect when it comes to the process of registration. For example, in Bolivia 50 per cent of children under one and 12 per cent of children between one and nine do not have birth certificates and therefore do not exist in the eyes of the state. Consequently, they do not have access to welfare services. As Grugel and Piper illustrate, even in Argentina, which is a relatively developed state, 'poor children are still often unregistered' even though registration has existed for over 100 years (Grugel and Piper, 2007: 135).

Missing children are not confined to what may be seen as developing countries. In Britain when the torso of a murdered child was found in the Thames it highlighted a hidden world of children moving in and out of Britain without the knowledge of local or national authorities. A BBC report highlighted that in order to identify the body the police had asked education authorities how many black boys between four and seven had left school and it emerged that 300 had disappeared. The police officer involved suggested that they were children 'lost into the system'. It seems that many were trafficked, or at least moved out of Britain, and there were no records of their movement. However, a headteacher suggested that the children had just moved to another school but again, despite the growth of surveillance, they are not tracked (*BBC News*, 13 May 2005). The point is that the state does not control the movement of these children and nor is it able to trace them. Moreover, the fact that trafficking of children into countries such as Britain (even if in relatively small numbers) occurs means that there are a number of children who are not subject to the normal protection of the law or access to the normal system of welfare (*BBC News*, 17 May 2005). The problem is exacerbated by the existence of private fostering where children can come into the country to be looked after by relatives and therefore exist outside a process controlled by social services.

Of course, the problem of missing children does not apply just to children who are trafficked. There are also children within the bounds of nation states who disappear. In the United States, of the 876,213 people who go missing every year, 85 to 90 per cent are children. Of these about 90 per cent are found but still 10,000 children a year are lost, and of course this is just the children who are reported missing. There are obviously some – like the boy found in the Thames – who are never reported and may never be missed in an official sense. This weakness of even strong and highly developed states is one that is rarely discussed: the fact that states with all their bureaucracy, regulation and, as we have seen in Chapter 11, increasingly interventionist approach to moral behaviour, have an inability to control what may be the weakest and most vulnerable people within society. There is little acknowledgement that many statistics are estimates and by the very nature of certain activities they miss parts of the population. Like the black economy, states are poor at dealing with systematic illegality that does not directly harm the interests of what might be called established society. When a child like Madeleine McCann (a four year old British girl who disappeared in Portugal) goes missing the disappearance receives considerable attention from the media and various public bodies; but when some children disappear (particularly from amongst groups on the edge of society) no one notices. In Britain the mass murderer Fred West had been murdering young women for many years, but in seven cases the women were not reported missing and as the police did not find any bodies, nothing sparked a murder inquiry for many years (*The Independent*, 3 January 1995).

Consequently, those who are missing from the purview of the state include both people who evade the state – as in the case of the black economy – and those whom the state cannot or does not want to see, such as illegal immigrants. In either case there are considerable numbers of people within a whole range of state systems who do not come within the state's radar. This of course limits the ability of the state to intervene. If the state cannot see a particular group, they cannot be controlled and states cannot develop policies to deal with them. Sometimes this is convenient and sometimes it limits state power. However, whilst the missing may be passive, there are many groups that actively resist the state.

## Resistance

Whilst this book has sought to demonstrate the new and various ways in which the modern state exercises power, there is little doubt that state actors fail to exert the degree of control they wish. New forms of power are attempts to control more directly the power of individuals. However, as Foucault and Hobbes were aware, within power there is resistance (Burgess, 1994). Indeed, for Foucault there cannot be power without resistance (Hartmann, 2003). For Foucault resistance comes through opening up new fields of action and new possibilities that threaten the existing processes of normalization (Pickett, 1996). But more importantly, resistance is part of self-realization and therefore it is the act of rejecting the normalization process which categorizes people in certain ways or imposes certain forms of behaviour. States attempt to impose forms of behaviour but people are able to resist them often in little ways by realizing parts of themselves. These forms of resistance can be found in the office worker who sneaks off for a ciga-rette in work time, the factory workers who work at a set speed, the student who sends texts in lectures, each realizing within a framework of power relations their own desires and spaces of self-expression. At a more consciously political level social movements are often involved in struggles and resistance that open up spaces for new interests or forms of behaviour, and this raises the issue of previously ignored social inter-ests (Routledge, 1999).

Scott (1990: 13) suggests that, 'Social science is ... focussed resolutely on the official or formal relations between the powerful and weak' but he argues that much resistance is hidden and behind the scenes. The weak resist in ways that do not reveal their opposition to the powerful. Moreover, Scott (1990) highlights the argument discussed in Chapter 7, concerning how in highly authoritarian regimes there are spaces outside the reach of the state where people are able to act in 'relatively' unrestricted ways. For Scott, in authoritarian relationships there are hidden transcripts of power – what he calls infrapolitics – where the oppressed can develop their strategies of resis-tance:

> Infrapolitics is, to be sure, real politics. In many respects it is conducted in more earnest, for higher stakes, and against greater odds than political life in liberal democracies. Real ground is lost and gained. Armies are undone and revolutions facilitated by the desertions of infrapolitics ... Resistant subcultures of dignity and

vengeful dreams are created and nurtured. Counter hegemonic discourse is elaborated. Thus infrapolitics is ... always pressing, testing, probing the boundaries of the permissible. (Scott, 1990: 200)

Resistance to the state can be overt through strikes, demonstrations, riots or terrorism. Whilst there are numerous examples of this type of resistance, its impact – despite its overt force – can often be limited. Terrorism, for instance, has complex and various impacts with the state. Often the aim of terrorism is to produce greater state repression in order to produce new supporters and to legitimize the struggle of the terrorist groups. Likewise, states often say that they will not negotiate with terrorists but are often forced into negotiations in order to resolve the problem. Margaret Thatcher, for example, rejected the idea that governments should make concessions to terrorists. She stated that her policy was determined by the needs of improved security and that the defeat of terrorism was through depriving terrorists of domestic and international support (Thatcher, 1993: 384). However, this was effectively a rhetorical position. For whilst the government's extant position was one of no negotiation with terrorists, the Conservative government opened up channels for communication with the IRA in the late 1980s. These openings developed into secret talks with the IRA in the early 1990s which were to become the basis of the negotiations which finally led to a ceasefire in 1994 and the Good Friday Agreement in 1998 (*The Observer*, 28 November 1993). Interestingly, a similar process has occurred in Iraq in terms of the relationship between the US and the insurgents. Despite the strong claims by George Bush that he would never concede to the terrorists involved in opposing the elected Iraqi government and US troops, the US has started discussions with Sunni rebels (*Time*, 20 February 2005) and it is a local agreement with insurgents that allowed the British troops to withdraw from Basra in Southern Iraq (*The Independent*, 4 September 2007).

Simon Tormey (2006), amongst others, has focussed on how new forms of politics are concerned with resisting traditional state forms. Many new political movements are concerned both with creating political organizations outside the state and with not expressing grievances through traditional mechanisms of representation. In challenging how politics is organized these new political movements are resisting existing forms of power. Daniel Drache (2008: 7) claims:

Publics have become highly critical of institutionalized authority in general. ... While traditional clubs and organizations, from mass political parties to the Elks and the Masons, have experienced falling memberships, more people are active in public than ever before, signing petitions, holding boycotts, and joining online communities.

Most forms of representation support essentially elitist forms of political organization where voters choose leaders to take decisions on their behalf. A number of movements consciously resist the state and traditional forms of political organization as a mechanism for mobilization. Tormey (2006) cites the example of the Zapatistas in the Chiapas region of Mexico whose aim is not to represent the rural power but to give them voice and ensure that their multiple voices are heard. Neil Harvey (1998: 199) points out that the Zapatista uprising was not a traditional revolutionary protest but an attempt to engage with the oppressed groups in order to allow their interests to be revealed. They were not the vanguard.

These forms of resistance are not limited to rebellions but inform a number of different political movements where people try to organize outside the state in order to resist it. One of the best known is the 'reclaim the street' movement which attempts to take control of the streets away from the traditional authorities. Perhaps the largest is the anti-globalization movement which essentially sees states and capitalism as the causes of all the world's problems from poverty to environmental degradation (Lloyd, 2001). There is a rejection of modernist notions of the state as a mechanism for progress and conflict resolution. Consequently, the movement is focussed on resistance to the state and existing forms of institutional politics. For John Lloyd (2001: 55) these global movements have reached a 'high water mark' and have forced both corporations and governments to make concessions around issues of the environment, child labour, drugs and aid. For example, the Make Poverty History movement seems in principle to have forced governments to change their position considerably on Third World debt.

Many theories of the state emphasize the resistance not of excluded groups but of powerful groups such as business. Charles Lindblom (1977) highlights the dependent relationship that the state has with business, and elitists like C.W. Mills (1956) and Marxists like Ralph Miliband (1969) emphasize the way that business elites dominated the processes of governing. Consequently, there are many examples where governments are constrained by the requirements of satisfying the

interests of business. This is a large issue, but it is worthwhile recording the areas such as climate change, discussed below, taxation, welfare
spending, and many others where the resources of business constrain
government from acting. This can often be directly in terms of threats
of disinvestment or through shaping the agenda in terms of what is
acceptable behaviour. Whatever the nature of globalization there are
tremendous economic pressures on states to maintain economic activity, and therefore in an international market where sub-prime lending
in the US can affect economies throughout the world, states are highly
limited in their options as long as they are unwilling to challenge the
interests of key economic actors. As the banking crisis of 2008 demonstrated, when faced with severe economic problems states have little
option but to intervene and take over where banks have failed to
manage risk. There are two interesting points that arise from these
events: first, states in the US and Europe had to act because of their
dependence on avoiding economic crisis; and second, despite the
processes of globalization and state reform that have occurred, states
clearly could intervene in decisive and – at least in the short-term –
effective ways. This example illustrates the complex nature of state
power. States are on one side overwhelmed by economic events and
constrained by the need to secure their banking systems, but on the
other they have access to resources and capabilities that enable
economic intervention on a large scale. Despite the clear resources of
business and the way it limits state options, it is important to recognize
that states and businesses are often in complex processes of negotiation
where the interests of business are not essentially or uniformly para-
mount (see Strong, 2009). States have their own resources and other
constituencies, and through processes of regulation they are often
attempting to limit and control the actions of business.

## Implementation and subversion

Public policy literature has frequently observed the difficulty that state
actors have in implementing their plans. One of the key problems for
state actors is compliance – something that the forms of power outlined
in previous chapters were intended to redress; but states are in a continual process of trying to get people to submit to state proposals. For
example, Kathryn Stoner-Weiss (2006) highlights the continual failure
of the Russian state to get regional authorities to comply with its policies. Max Weber famously defined the ideal type of delivery in his

description of bureaucracy. In principle, the modern state would be able to ensure that decisions made at the centre were delivered on the ground, through a process of hierarchical organization with clear lines of control and subordination. However, leaving aside the question of whether hierarchy in this form ever really existed, it is increasingly the case that the hierarchical model of delivery has been challenged through the development of new modes of governance and marketization. A considerable literature analyzes the ways in which hierarchical bureaucratic forms often fail to deliver intended policy outcomes (for example, Pressman and Wildavsky, 1984; Lipsky, 1980, O'Toole, 1986; Marsh and Rhodes, 1992b, Hill and Hupe, 2003; Hill, 2003). These authors postulate that, rather than government directly controlling the delivery of public goods, more effective mechanisms include 'hands-off' approaches operated either through market incentives or through diversifying the delivery process so that agencies on the ground work together and have some autonomy to decide how best to deliver public goods.

A problem identified by Lipsky (1980) was that, whatever the intentions of politicians and senior bureaucrats, it is 'street level bureaucrats' who hold responsibility for the delivery of government policies and services on the ground. Lipsky (1980: 13) points out that: 'unlike lower level workers in most organizations, street level bureaucrats have considerable discretion in determining the nature, amount, and quality of benefits and sanctions provided by their agencies'. More recently Norma Riccucci (2005: 115) highlighted that one of the problems for policy delivery is that: 'professional norms, work customs and occupational culture' are better at explaining the actions of street level bureaucrats than management. Yet this is only part of the problem. Heather Hill observes that policy may not be based on shared meanings between different actors and that meanings can be vague and unclear (Hill, 2003). The dangers and difficulties of implementation gaps, failures and unintended consequences are readily apparent and highlight the question of how politicians and senior officials can attempt to ensure that their intended goals are effectively delivered. The implementation literature illustrates the absence of direct control that exists in the hands of the state. States can use force, but as we have seen this is not a very effective mechanism for achieving state goals. Authority and legitimacy depend on a mutual recognition of rights to rule, and the newer mechanisms of rationality, surveillance and incentives are indirect and open to subversion. Consequently when dealing with complex social problems such as anti-social behaviour, the difficulty for states to solve the problem in

ways that they wish is very great. There is a fundamental belief with
state actors that not only can they control very large organizations –
government bureaucracies – but that they can also control societies.
Yet all state actions depend on millions of actions by individuals who
are not directly controlled, and people make decisions within the
framework of their organization concerning how they should implement decisions. It is relatively easy for people to tick the boxes that are
needed to convince their superiors that they are doing their job, but
what they actually do is almost impossible to control because there are
so many actions involved. As David Knights and Darren McCabe
(2000: 434) highlight:

> Gurus, consultants and practising managers will never give up on
> their search for the 'perfect' technology of controlling labour. One
> saving grace is the consideration that the concept of subjectivity
> encourages us to believe that, even in the most oppressive regimes,
> there will be spaces and opportunities for escape and perhaps even a
> bit of misbehaviour.

The discussion of anti-social behaviour in Chapter 11 highlights how
states are trying to iron out misbehaviour; the problem is that not only
do they have to control those who act anti-socially, but also all those
from civil servants to local authorities, to social workers, judges, and
police officers who have to implement the policy. The process of implementation subverts the outcome and limits the control of the state. For
example, despite the fact that police officers face targets on dealing
with anti-social behaviour, once on the beat they will act as they see fit
(Geddes *et al.*, 2007: 22):

> Possibly because I'm in quite a unique position in that I've got
> twenty-five years and I've only five years left, but I don't feel like I've
> got any pressure on me whatsoever to achieve any particular target.
> To be honest I'm not particularly interested, and that's my own
> personal opinion as well. I'm not working towards a figure, and I
> totally refuse to work to a figure. I'm not going to hit a particular
> figure to try and meet just a target. I will go out and police my area
> as I see fit and as I deem necessary, and I will justify that decision if
> I need to.

One thing is clear, that however many targets a government introduces
or programmes it develops, anti-social behaviour will not go away.

What may disappear is the attention that state actors, and the media, pay to it.

## External limits – the case of climate change

States are clearly limited in what they can do despite the range or resources and mechanisms available. The globalization literature has emphasized the growing difficulty that the state has in an international context. As we have seen with issues such as migration states have considerable difficulty in controlling issues which cross frontiers and are dependent on more than one nation state to resolve. New international problems such as avian flu, the AIDS pandemic, and global warming starkly highlight the limits on states' power.

The example of climate change illustrates the problems for states. First, it is a classic collective action problem. Addressing climate change depends on every state cutting carbon emissions but reductions in individual outputs make little difference. As in the chicken game, there is a strong incentive for defection; to wait for the other to act and to receive the benefits of their action. However, as everyone waits the problem becomes worse. Second, whilst agreement is international, implementation is local (Cooper, 1998) and so it is easy for states to sign up to an international agreement but then to pay little attention to implementation. So whatever the goals of one state in terms of global warming, they are in fact dependent on the actions of other countries if the policy is to have an impact.

Climate change creates further problems for states because it is not arrayed along a single dimension but is a consequence of a number of policy areas such as housing, transport, energy, economic policy and even areas such as health and education policy (Strong, 2009). Moreover, it is multi-level in that it involves sets of decisions at local, national, regional and supranational level. Decisions about climate change policy within EU states involve decisions that combine setting targets and Kyoto, at the EU level and nationally. This has led to a situation in Europe in which EU and national targets are stronger than the international targets (Strong, 2009). However, whilst the British and German governments may wish to reduce carbon emissions, the leading producers of carbon – the United States and China – reject targets and consequently, despite clear policy goals, the EU is in effect unable to reverse carbon outputs. Some individual nation states such as Iceland and Denmark have made strong commitments to becoming carbon neutral but whilst they may be able to achieve that goal, it will have no impact on outcomes. Whilst the Bali Conference appeared to create a framework for an international agreement on climate change, it is not clear that an agreement will be reached that will significantly reduce carbon production (Monbiot, 2007). The point is that whatever the desire of states to reduce carbon in order to tackle global warming, it is beyond their capabilities:

> Between 2000 and 2005, emissions grew four times faster than in the preceding 10 years, according to researchers at the Global Carbon Project, a consortium of international researchers. Global growth rates were 0.8% from 1990 to 1999. From 2000 to 2005, they reached 3.2%. (Brahic, 2006)

As Catherine Brahic (2006) illustrates, even to stabilize carbon emissions would take considerable effort, and considering the inability of the international community to control the outputs of the US and China, this is not a likely outcome. The British government, for example, has reached its Kyoto target (Strong, 2009) but this will have little or no impact on global warming because worldwide emissions continue to increase.

The case of climate change demonstrates how, despite the new forms of power illustrated throughout this book, states face continual limits on their capacities. Confronted by a problem that affects all nation states, but requires both national and international action, the mechanisms for implementing policy do not exist. States are increasingly using incentives to try to get individuals to change behaviour in terms of carbon production, but these policies make little or no difference within an international context that they cannot affect.

Climate change also illustrates the different types of constraints on states. Firstly, the problem is international and so it cannot be tackled easily at the domestic level. Secondly, the actual mechanisms for reducing carbon emissions are complex and diffuse. Do states use coercion, incentives, the development of new technologies or persuasion? Thirdly, states are faced by complex and contradictory interests. Often these conflicts are internal. For example, in the case of global warning governments have a commitment to reducing carbon emissions but want to ensure continued economic activity (and, for example, the expansion of airports) and do not want to alienate the electorate. It would be relatively easy to reduce carbon emissions from cars by doubling or trebling the price of fuel but governments will not consider the economic and electoral consequences of such action. Consequently, the limits on state power are not solely about a lack of capabilities but often a lack of clarity in what they are trying to achieve. Carbon emissions could be drastically reduced if government were to focus on that goal, but states are continually constrained by other goals and interests. The complex array of interests facing states can have the effect of dissipating governments' endeavours. Moreover, as most state instruments are not direct, state goals involve including numerous institutions and interests in the delivery process, and with a policy such as global warming the vast range of actors needed to achieve the goals means that compromises in goals can occur in literally millions of individual decisions. One person may decide to insulate their house, whilst another may choose to buy a bigger car.

## Conclusion

Much of the hyperbolic literature on the decline of states confuses the failures of states with the disappearance of states. States clearly have considerable limits on their power; these are both internal and external. They have difficulty observing all that goes on within their territory and in implementing their goals. States are not abstract organizations but they depend on the behaviour of millions of people to achieve their goals. The problem for states is that these people are reflexive beings who can consciously subvert the intentions of state actors and make it difficult to extend state policy to what occurs on the ground. Both those who deliver and receive state policies have the ability to change the intended outcomes of politicians and civil servants. Moreover, there are also groups, organizations and individuals who consciously and actively resist the state. Consequently, state actors then have to change policy, compromise or use force, which may then create further sets of problems. Migdal (2001: 12) neatly summarizes the complexity of state power:

> States must contend with opposing groupings, some of which are quietly and indirectly subversive ... others of which are openly confrontational. These multiple groupings of opposition have created coalitions to strengthen their stance, and these have cut right into the very structures of states themselves. The resulting coalitional struggles have taken their toll: state policy implementation and the outcomes in society have ended up quite different from the state's original blueprint.

Whilst it is clear that states often fail and in particular are unable to achieve their goals, this does not mean that they do not affect people's lives or shape outcomes. States continually affect the lives of citizens but there are numerous limits on the state. Even in failing to achieve the intended outcomes, state actors are continually organizing policy and shaping a whole series of actions and outcomes, even if in unintended ways. This illustrates the points made in Chapter 4 that state actors are continuously involved in a series of dependent relationships and therefore there is no such thing as an independent tool of state power. States exercise power in multiple ways but that power is limited by their inability to direct and control the myriad mechanisms necessary for outcomes to be implemented.

# Chapter 13

# Conclusion

The focus of this book has not been on theories of power or of the state but on the mechanisms of state power; the ways in which states attempt to achieve goals. The book has argued that the way states exercise power has changed, and that while we have not seen a decline in state power, we have seen that states always vary in their effectiveness. Consequently, in order to overcome failures or weaknesses states have attempted to develop new ways of achieving social and political outcomes. This concluding chapter will review the key findings of the book and discuss what this means for our understanding of the state in the twenty-first century.

## Modernism and exceptionalism

The postwar states in the developed world were exceptional institutional conglomerations. They appeared to have complete control of their borders and territory, and of most of their citizens. For the first time in history, the end of the Second World War created a situation whereby states seemed to exercise both internal and external sovereignty. Within the context of this new vision of the impermeable border, states developed complex welfare programmes and often quite detailed mechanisms of economic intervention and planning. In the years of optimism that followed the Second World War, when developed states were the closest they ever came to the Weberian ideal, politicians believed that they could change the world. As John F. Kennedy said in his inaugural speech in 1960:

> To those people in the huts and villages of half the globe struggling to break the bonds of mass misery, we pledge our best efforts to help them help themselves, for whatever period is required – not because the communists may be doing it, not because we seek their votes, but because it is right. If a free society cannot help the many who are poor, it cannot save the few who are rich.

Indeed, the whole speech is a statement of the modernist wishes of the most powerful state in the world. The US had a vision of its ability to shape both its internal and external destiny; improving the circumstances not only of its own citizens but of all those who followed the progressive path. The US dream was intended for both a domestic and international audience.

However, this exceptional moment was precisely that – exceptional and spatially and temporally limited. It applied to very few states – a select few in Western Europe, the US and perhaps Australia and New Zealand and, in a different form, the Soviet Union, where in the Khrushchev era there was a belief that the country was on the cusp of a new era. Khrushchev's hubris was perhaps greater than Kennedy's, believing that the Soviet Union would soon overtake the US, which could then decide whether it wanted to adopt communism and catch up, or remain capitalist and stay where it was:

> Well then we will say America has been in existence for 150 years and this is the level she has reached. We have existed not quite 42 years and in another seven years we will be on the same level as America. When we catch you up, in passing you by, we will wave to you. Then if you wish we can stop and say: Please follow us. Plainly speaking, if you want capitalism you can live that way. That is your own affair and doesn't concern us. We can still feel sorry for you but since you don't understand us – live as you do understand.

However, in Eastern Europe states lacked sovereignty through being part of the Soviet orbit. In Western Europe, sovereignty was equally compromised through the Marshall Plan and the Cold War, which forced states under the US umbrella. Southern Europe (with the exception of Italy) was still tied to wartime dictatorships and much of the rest of the world was grappling with the remnants of empire and oppressed by long-term underdevelopment.

In Western Europe even this postwar optimism was short lived. Economic growth and social change were perhaps less a consequence of state planning than an artefact of expanding US markets and expenditure, primary commodity producers with little market power, and the development of new means of production in the wake of the destruction of the Second World War. Whilst welfare states and new types of social policies were effective at removing the worst excesses of poverty (although this may have been a consequence of economic boom rather than social intervention), they had trouble tackling deep-seated inequalities. Not long after the establishment of welfare systems, states were confronted with the problems of cost and were increasingly criticized for their bureaucracy, inefficiency and openness to fraud.

Powerful, unified and sovereign modernist states were always exceptional and even the most modernist of states were replete with failures to control (as we saw in Chapter 7 with the discussion of the limits on authoritarian regimes). The idea of the state as an all-powerful actor was mythical and, therefore, the idea of the state hollowing out or retreating is misplaced because states never had the degree of control that such analyses suggest. Hollowing out is a concept applied to a state that did not exist; states have always had a degree of hollowness. Globalization may have affected what the state can do but it is one of a number of real world phenomena that have limited how states impact on societies (see Chapter 12). States are always partial in their reach. They rely on a range of actors and institutions to deliver goals and therefore their impact is continually mediated. Moreover, they often attempt to tackle problems that are insurmountable and, whilst they can perhaps focus considerable resources on particular problems, they cannot do everything or 'see' all that is within their remit.

## Theories and their limitations

Hence, what this book has attempted to demonstrate is that our understanding of the state has been limited by understandings of power and the state that have oversimplified the nature of the way the state operates. In other words, as Joel Migdal points out, theorists have been more focussed on the idea of the state's power, rather than the empirical reality of what states do. Theories of power have, as we have seen, focussed on the theoretical nature of power and what it means rather than how it is exercised. The book has highlighted how state actors are not interested in philosophical consistency and so the nature of state power in reality is multi-dimensional and relational. States never have total power, but the exceptional period of postwar modernism has generated an erroneous understanding of the state that has persisted. States can be very direct, as with the use of coercion, but also more subtle, for example, through the processes of legitimation. Yet whatever form of power they use, they never completely control outcomes because of their dependence on other actors. Moreover, government policies are contradictory and confused. Governments are presented with often intractable problems and offer solutions that have little possibility of tackling the issues they face. For example, how do policy makers reduce crime – put more people in prison, improve the minimum wage, retrain police officers or spend more on public relations? The modern state is based on a presumption of rational solutions to problems but this is a misplaced faith because state powers are limited and social problems have an intractable complexity.

At the same time, theories of the state offer little help in dealing with these problems. Essentialist theories of the state tend to be a misnomer. They are not concerned with what the state does but in whose interest the state operates and as a consequence they pay little attention to what the state does. The paradox of state theory is that it generally accepts the myth of the modern state with the idea that the policies it adopts are delivered. It assumes, in effect, that the state works; or, at best, pays little attention to how states work, the mechanisms that they have available and how policies can be inconsistent, indeterminate and often arbitrary.

What we have seen with the development of the modern state is the creation of a range of connected techniques based on the triad of bureaucracy, coercion and legitimacy. The point is that these three mechanisms are interconnected and central to the idea of the modern state. Pre-modern states were essentially based on force and, as Mann (1986) amongst others illustrates, this severely limited the abilities of states. Modern states successfully extended their reach through the development of bureaucracy which allowed the state to develop new capabilities. These capabilities permitted a new range of social interventions, ranging from welfare states to the Nazi Holocaust. Bureaucracy is effective because it can organize information and delivery systems, but these only work because bureaucracy is backed up on one side by legitimacy and on the other by force. Bureaucracy is rule-governed power and hence people obey it to the extent that it is legitimate. However, bureaucracy also involves coercion. In some senses this is subtle in that state bureaucracy is often based on a requirement to act, and at other times less subtle in that failure to obey the requirements of the state can be met with direct force – such as imprisonment.

The underlying presumption of this triad was that the state was rational and that it could through rational policy making and collective actions make social improvements. These social improvements ranged from economic development through to eliminating poverty to the creation of a new society. However, the mechanisms and the solutions were collective, and with these powers we saw the creation of the large and directive modernist states of the postwar period in both their liberal and communist forms.

## States after the crises

Both conservative and radical critics of modernism see the modern state as containing the seeds of its own destruction. The more states intervene, the more problems they create and, as they attempt to resolve problems, the more action they take which creates further problems. The economic crises of the 1970s and growing disillusionment with state socialism in its democratic and communist forms led to a range of critiques of the state. The 1970s and 1980s saw widespread legitimation crises for states in the East and West and the apparent failure of the modernist project (Habermas, 1976). Within the new right, particularly in the United States and Britain, a coherent critique of the state developed which saw states more as the cause of, rather than solution to, economic and social problems. The neo-liberal project was based on rolling back the state through the setting free of markets, privatization and the introduction of a managerial ethos into government. Neo-liberalism aimed at taking the state out of resolving collective action problems, believing that these were best dealt with by the market.

At the same time the external context of states appeared to be changing. Neo-liberalism went hand-in-hand with processes of globalization which seemed to shrink the possibilities of nation states to control their borders and their economies. As we have seen, the more extreme globalization theorists saw the national state as becoming irrelevant, whilst the more circumspect recognized that the state was operating in a very different environment. The combination of neo-liberal policy presumption and global economic developments seemed to remove the state from economic policy and push many states to attempt to limit and reform their welfare commitments. The assumption was that states lost power. For many the state was becoming postmodern. It was fragmenting and losing its narrative of progress. The days of the large postwar state seemed over.

Yet the presumption of this book is that the issue of states losing power is not the relevant point. States have always been partial and constrained. Their successes have been contingent on a series of circumstances. There is a range of empirical evidence to suggest that states throughout the world continue to be large and high spending organizations and, at least in Western Europe, they continue to maintain large welfare states (with considerable opposition to any attempts at dramatic restructuring of welfare provision). Economic intervention continues but often in less systematic ways than the postwar programmes based on planning and nationalization. State intervention has been much more concerned with supply and micro-economic interventions than the macro interventions of the Keynesian era (nevertheless states have continued to use public spending and borrowing as mechanisms for influencing the economy). The book has argued that what we have seen with states is a development, or at least, enhancement of new forms of power; we have seen the development of the *past*-modern state. A state with a framework of modernism, but developing new mechanisms of power and new patterns of intervention.

Whilst the modern state was built on the bureaucratic triad, the *past*modern state has built a new set of mechanisms on the modernist foundations. In other words, these mechanisms supplement rather than replace the traditional forms of state power. States cannot escape from the Hobbesian problem of order. For the state to survive, state actors have to ensure order within their territory. Consequently, whatever the impact of globalization and neo-liberalism, states will try to control their populations. The banking crisis of 2008 starkly illustrates the imperative for (or will of) states to intervene when the economic order is threatened. What we have seen in recent years has been the development of new and powerful mechanisms of control by states. These mechanisms have focussed on surveillance, risk, rationality and regulation. As with the traditional triad, these conceptions are strongly interlinked.

Surveillance has always been a core element of the modern state. Modern states exist on the basis of being able to observe their populations. However, the development of digital technologies has resulted in a step change in the ways in which data are collected and stored. It permits the focus on individual data, the storing of considerable amounts of data and the ability to connect this data together. As a result we are watched in ways that are qualitatively and quantitatively different, and this has changed the relationship between the state and citizens. Surveillance has become a mechanism of maintaining order by watching what people do (it is not a *post hoc* reconstruction) and increasingly predicting how people will behave. Consequently, surveillance data can be linked to risk analysis to model how individuals could behave in the future and thus what incentives and regulations should be put in place to prevent deviant activities. States are not focussing only on collective behaviours – as they did in the past – but on individual behaviour. Increasingly, social problems are not seen as having structural causes but as being the consequence of individual behaviour and choices. It is interesting to note the way in which individualistic ontologies have permeated collectivist ideologies such as social democracy and traditional conservatism. This has led states to try to change the behaviour of individuals. The focus on rational choice has led to a belief that the focus of state intervention is on the individual.

As a result, in addition to the bureaucratic triad of the modern state we now have the addition of a set of mechanisms which emphasize individual intervention. These have led states away from focusing solely on macro interventions through economic planning and welfare programmes to individual interventions that focus on the moral behaviour of actors, such as drinking, parenting, eating or anti-social behaviour. For example, in the area of unemployment the focus has shifted from labour market policies to foster economic growth and skills training to one where the focus is on the individual choices of the unemployed and how they can be changed to fit into the existing labour market. The failure to get employment can be linked to the moral failure of the individual rather than social failure. This is not to make a normative judgement about what is best for states but to illustrate how states have developed a new set of tools which allow for different forms of intervention and policies. It could be argued that state actors are addressing the reality of the constraints that they face and are developing techniques that work within a new political framework and global political economy.

Nevertheless, the argument of this book is not that old forms of intervention have disappeared – clearly most developed states still have large-scale welfare policies – but that new forms of intervention have emerged. Nevertheless, these new techniques and new contexts do not change the partiality of states, nor the observation that these new techniques have not created new all-powerful states. This point highlights how arguments about the declining role of the state do not pay sufficient attention to the ways in which states operate and how their success in terms of social intervention is always variable. States can be highly effective organizations when they pay sufficient attention to a problem. However, the resources of states are always limited and their impacts will always be limited. States can never be one hundred per cent effective.

The events of 11 September 2001 and the 2008 banking crisis starkly illustrate the strength/weakness paradox of states in the twenty-first century. Both 2001 and the banking crisis have elicited strong responses from particular states, with considerable public resources going into both the 'war on terror' and underwriting banks. Both events have also seen the use of new forms of state power such as surveillance and regulation. Both demonstrate that in the global era states can be decisive actors that command resources unavailable even to the financial masters of the universe. Nevertheless, in both cases the impact of states has been very limited. The US and its allies have far from defeated al-Qa'eda and Islamic fundamentalism, and the massive economic interventions have not stabilized banks or stock markets or, seemingly, prevented recessions. States can take actions and use a vast array of mechanisms but their impact will always be limited and constrained. This is not new, but how states intervene and what they do has changed.

As we discussed in Chapter 12, there are considerable areas where the state faces constraints, or perhaps more importantly, groups and individuals exist away from the gaze of the state. To a degree the rich and powerful can often avoid the gaze of the state but there are groups of the less powerful such as illegal immigrants, those working in the black economy and those who go 'missing' who confound the state by their ability to avoid surveillance. Moreover, politics continues. Groups develop to resist the state. Increasingly, there are networks of social activists around a range of issues that are prepared to challenge state policies. States cannot afford to ignore political protest because legitimacy remains a core resource for the state, and governments in both Britain and the US have continued to face problems of legitimacy because of their involvement in a war in Iraq that is not seen as legitimate, either in the Middle East or within their own polities.

The explanation of the development of these new forms of power is complex and manifold. It is partly a consequence of the crisis of the state in the 1970s and 1980s. The modern state with its traditional mechanisms was seen to have failed and as a result state actors looked for new ways to influence outcomes. At the same time the new right moved away from the idea of collective solutions to social problems and by adopting the ontological assumptions of rational choice developed social policies based on the idea of individual rather than social failure. There has also been a technological drive to change. The development of digitized forms of data and surveillance – and more complex forms of performance management – has allowed states access to much more detailed information about society and hence enabled much more detailed intervention. Whilst technology may have allowed states to focus downward, changes at the level of the international economy seem to have led states to believe that their room for economic manoeuvre is limited. Consequently, the gaze of states has been much more on aspects of individual behaviour – which state actors think they can control – rather than economic policy – which they believe they cannot control. The combination of new techniques and new ideas about what states should do has led to the growing individuation of state power.

## Conclusion

The state in the twenty-first century is not a single type of state. All states are, as ever, different. They use a range of mechanisms and varying scales of intervention. The object of this book has been to demonstrate that states have developed new mechanisms of power for intervening in society. These mechanisms have not replaced the traditional modes of intervention but are built on top of them. Consequently, state actors have a new range of resources available to them that allow new forms of social and political control. These new mechanisms focus state power differently and add a new point of intervention in enabling states to concentrate much more on the activities of individuals. Social control is now orientated much more to the future than it has been traditionally.

In terms of traditional theories of power and the state, there are a number of lessons that we can draw from this book. First, power is much more about mechanisms than understanding the philosophical basis of power. This means that power as an empirical object is not a single thing but is multidimensional, partial and inconsistent. State actors are not theorists and so they can be inconsistent in how they conceive of power and how they exercise it. Consequently, it is not uncommon to see states operating policies that are incompatible in terms of the assumptions they make about human behaviour. Theories of power help us to frame what we are looking for – what we mean by power – but they say little about how it works empirically. Notions of power are a heuristic, not a closed conceptual framework. Second, theories of the state continue this reductionism by focussing more on for whom the state rules rather than how it actually rules. States, however, are mixed in their motivations and partial in their impacts. In order to understand the nature of states we need to understand how they exercise power and what impact that exercise of power has. States may rule in the interest of particular groups (although that must be an empirical question) but we need to understand what mechanisms they have to make that rule effective. It is the issue of effectiveness that is crucial to understanding modern states. They have a range of mechanisms and they face ever-changing circumstances. People are reflexive and resistant and, therefore, states will always have problems implementing their policies. Their ability to do so to some extent depends on the ability of state actors to adapt to changing circumstances – to patch up the multiple ways in which people can defy, ignore and bypass government policies.

So, in analysing state power in the twenty-first century, what we see are states that are developing new ways of intervention and with that, different forms and types of policy. States continue as central organizations in the developed world because of the resources they control and the mechanisms that they have available to them, but their power continues to be partial, always affected by the particular context in which decisions are made and implemented.

# Bibliography

Aalberts T.E. (2004) 'The Future of Sovereignty in Multilevel Governance Europe – A Constructivist Reading', *Journal of Common Market Studies*, 42 (1), 23–46.

Abelson, R.P. (1996) 'The Secret Existence of Expressive Behavior', in Friedman, J. (ed), *The Rational Choice Controversy: Economic Models of Politics Reconsidered* (New Haven: Yale University Press).

Adams, J. (1995) *Risk* (London: UCL Press).

Alford, R.R. and Friedland, R. (1985) *Powers of Theory: Capitalism, the State and Democracy* (Cambridge: Cambridge University Press).

Allison, G. T. and Zelikow, P. (1999) *Essence of Decision: Explaining the Cuban Missile Crisis*, second edition (Harlow: Longman).

Althusser L. (1971) *Lenin and Philosophy* (London: Verso).

American Bar Association (2001) *Zero Tolerance Policy*, http://www.abanet.org/crimjust/juvjus/zerotolreport.html

Amidon, S. (2000) 'Herbert Marcuse's One-dimensional Man', *New Statesman*, 27 November.

Amoore, L. (2007) 'Vigilant Visualities: The Watchful Politics of the War on Terror', *Security Dialogue* 38 (2), 215–32.

Anand, P. (1998) 'Chronic Uncertainty and BSE Communications: Lessons from (and Limits of) Decision Theory', in Ratzan, S.C. (ed), *The Mad Cow Crisis: Health and the Public Good* (New York: New York University Press).

Ansell, C. (2004) 'Restructuring Authority and Territoriality', in Ansell, C. and Di Palma, G. (eds), *Restructuring Territoriality: Europe and the United States Compared* (Cambridge: Cambridge University Press).

Applebaum, A. (2003) *Gulag: A History* (Harmondsworth: Penguin).

Aretxaga, B. (2000) 'A Fictional Reality: Paramilitary Death Squads and the Construction of State Terror in Spain', in Sluka, J. (ed), *Death Squad: The Anthropology of State Terror* (Philadelphia: University of Pennsylvania Press).

Armstrong, D. (1995) 'The Rise of Surveillance Medicine', *Sociology of Health and Illness*, 17: 393–404.

Asia Pacific News (1996) 'Migrant Workers and Human Rights', 4, June.

Atkinson, R. and Blandy, S. (2005) 'Introduction: International Perspectives on the New Enclavism and the Rise of Gated Communities', *Housing Studies*, 20: 175–86.

Auyero, J. (2007) *Routine Politics and Violence in Argentina: the Gray Zone of State Power* (Cambridge: Cambridge University Press).

Axelrod R. (2008) 'Political Science and Beyond: Presidential Address to the American Political Science Association', *Perspectives on Politics*, 6(1): 3–9.

Bachrach, P. and Baratz, M.S. (1962) 'The Two Faces of Power', *American Political Science Review,* 56 (4): 947–52.

Baldwin, P. (2003) 'The Return of the Coercive State: Behavioral Control in Multicultural Society', in Paul, T.V., Ikenberry, G.J. and Hall, J.A. (eds), *The Nation State Under Challenge: Autonomy and Capacity in a Changing World* (Princeton, NJ: Princeton University Press).

Bale, T. (2007) 'Are Bans on Political Parties Bound to Turn Out Badly? A Comparative Investigation of Three Intolerant Democracies: Turkey, Spain and Belgium', *Comparative European Politics,* 5 (2): 141–57.

Balko, R. (2003) 'Back Door to Prohibition: The New War on Social Drinking', *Policy Analysis,* 501, December, 1–25.

Bamford, B. (2005) 'The Role and Effectiveness of Intelligence in Northern Ireland', *Intelligence and National Security*, 20(4): 581–607.

Barry, B. (1989) *Democracy, Power and Justice: Essays in Political Theory* (Oxford: Clarendon Press).

Barry, B. (1991) *Democracy and Power: Essays in Political Theory I* (Oxford: Oxford University Press).

Barry, B. (2002) 'Capitalists Rule OK? Some Puzzles About Power', *Politics, Philosophy and Economics,* 1 (2): 155–84.

Barzel, Y. (2002) *A Theory of the State: Economic Rights, Legal Rights and the Scope of the State* (Cambridge: Cambridge University Press).

Bauer, R., De Sola Pool, I and Dexter, L. (1972) *American Business and Public Policy: The Politics of Foreign Trade,* second edition (Chicago, Il: Aldine).

Bauman, Z. (1989) *Modernity and the Holocaust* (Cambridge: Polity).

BBC (1999) *Horizon* 'The Midas Formula', BBC 2, 2 December.

BBC (2003) 'Rifkind brands poll tax "a mistake" ' http://news.bbc.co.uk/1/hi/scotland/3251300.stm

BBC (2005) 'The Power of Nightmares: The Shadows In The Cave', BBC 1, 20 January.

BBC (2007) 'A&E success "not sustainable"', BBC News Online, 17 January http://news.bbc.co.uk/1/hi/health/6267897.stm.

Beck, U. (1992) *Risk Society: Towards a New Modernity* (London: Sage).

Beck, U. (1994) 'The Reinvention of Politics: Towards a Theory of Reflexive Modernization' in U. Beck, A. Giddens and S. Lash,

*Reflexive Modernization: Politics, Tradition and Aesthetics in the Modern Social Order* (Cambridge: Polity).

Beck, U. (2000) 'Risk Society Revisited: Theory, Politics and Research Programmes' in B. Adam, U. Beck and J.V. Loon (eds.) *The Risk Society and Beyond: Critical Issues for Social Theory* (London: Sage).

Beck, U. (2005) *Power in the Global Age: A New Global Political Economy* (Cambridge: Polity).

Beetham, D. (1991) *The Legitimation of Power* (Basingstoke and New York: Palgrave Macmillan).

Beevor, A. (2006) *The Battle for Spain: The Spanish Civil War 1936–1939* (London: Weidenfeld & Nicolson).

Bellamy, C. and Raab, C. (2005) 'Multi-agency working in British social policy: Risk, information sharing and privacy', *Information Polity*, 10 (1–2): 51–63.

Bennett, P.G. (1995) 'Modelling Decisions in International Relations: Game Theory and Beyond', *Mershon International Studies Review*, 39 (1): 19–52.

Bernhard, M. (1993) 'Civil Society and Democratic Transition in East Central Europe', *Political Science Quarterly*, 108( 2): 307–26.

Bevir, M. and Rhodes, R. (2006) *Governance Stories* (London: Routledge).

Birch, A. (1984) 'Overload, Ungovernability and Deligitimation: The Theories and the British Case', *British Journal of Political Science,* 14: 135–60.

Birmingham City Council (2006) *Anti-Social Behaviour: Overview and Scrutiny Committee Report* (Birmingham: Birmingham City Council).

Blakeley, G. (2004) ' "It's Politics, Stupid!: The Spanish General Election of 2004', *Parliamentary Affairs*, 59 (2): 331–49.

Blyth, M. (2008) 'ELEN Degenerates – or – Four (Plus Two) Reasons to Take Ideas Very Seriously Indeed', in Beland, D. and Cox R. (eds), *Ideas and Politics in Social Science Research*.

Blythman, J. (2004) *Shopped: The Shocking Power of British Supermarkets* (London: Fourth Estate Ltd).

Bouchard, C. and Blair, S.N. (1999) 'Introductory Comments for the Consensus on Physical Activity and Obesity', *Medicine and Science in Sports and Exercise*, 31(11) Supplement 1: S498.

Bourdieu, P. (1989) 'Social Space and Symbolic Power', *Sociological Theory*, 17 (1): 14–25.

Bourdieu, P. (1999) 'Rethinking the state: Genesis and Structure of the Bureaucratic Field', in G. Steinmetz (ed.), *State/Culture: State Formation After the Cultural Turn* (Ithaca, NY: Cornell University Press).

Boyne, G. and Law, J. (2005) 'Setting Public Service Outcome Targets:

Lessons from Local Public Service Agreements', *Public Money and Management*, 25( 4): 253–60.

Braham, M. and Holler, M.J. (2005) 'The Impossibility of a Preference-Based Power Index', *Journal of Theoretical Politics*, 17 (1): 137–57.

Brahic, C. (2006) 'Carbon Emissions Rising Faster than Ever', *New Scientist*, 10 November.

Brenner, N. (2004) *New State Spaces: Urban Governance and the Rescaling of Statehood* (Oxford: Oxford University Press).

Breslow, L (2006a) 'Public Health Aspects of Weight Control', *International Journal of Epidemiology*, 35: 10–12.

Breslow, L. (2006b) 'Commentary: On 'Public Health Aspects of Weight Control', *International Journal of Epidemiology*, 35: 12–14.

Brower, D.R. (1987) 'Stalinism and the View from Below', *Russian Review*, 46 (4): 379–81.

Brujin, H. de (2006) 'One Fight, One Team: the 9/11 Commission Report on Intelligence, Fragmentation and Information', *Public Administration*, 84( 2): 247–67 .

Buller, J. (2000) *National Statecraft and European Integration* (London: Pinter).

Buller, J. and Flinders, M. (2005) 'The Domestic Origins of Depolitization in the Area of British Economic Policy', *British Journal of Politics and International Relations*, 7( 4): 526–43.

Bullock, A. (1991) *Hitler and Stalin: Parallel Lives* (London: HarperCollins).

Bulpitt, J. (1986) 'The Discipline of the New Democracy: Mrs Thatcher's Domestic Statecraft', *Political Studies,* 34: 19–39.

Burgess G. (1994) 'On Hobbesian Resistance Theory', *Political Studies,* 42 (1): 62–83.

Burgess, S., Propper, C. and Wilson, D. (2005) *Will More Choice Improve Outcomes in Education and Health Care? The Evidence from Economic Research* (Bristol: Centre for Market and Public Organisation).

Burke, E. (1999) *Reflections on the Revolution in France* (Oxford: Oxford University Press).

Burnham, P. (2007) 'The Politicisation of Monetary Policy in Postwar Britain', *British Politics*, 2( 3): 395–419.

Bush, G. W., (2005) President Commemorates Veterans Day, Discusses War on Terror, Tobyhanna, PA, November 11.

Butler, D., Adonis, A. and Travers, T. (1994) *Failure in British Government: The Politics of the Poll Tax* (Oxford: Oxford University Press).

Cabinet Office (2000) *Professional Policy Making for the Twenty First Century* (London: Cabinet Office).

Camerer, C. *et al.* (1997) 'Labor supply of New York City Cabdrivers: One Day at a Time', *Quarterly Journal of Economics*, 112: 407–41.

Campos, P., Saguy, A., Ernsberger, P. Oliver, E. and Gaesser, G. (2006) 'The Epidemiology of Overweight and Obesity: Public Health Crisis or Moral Panic?', *International Journal of Epidemiology*, 35: 55–60.

Carey, G. and Gottesman, I. (1996) 'Genetics and Antisocial Behaviour; Substance versus Soundbites', *Politics Life Sciences*, 15 (1): 88–90.

Carrol, J. (2003) 'Power and Resistance in the Later Foucault', presented at the 3rd Annual Meeting of the Foucault Circle Cleveland, OH, 28 February–2 March.

Carter, N. (1989) 'Performance Indicators: Back Seat Driving or Hands Off Control', *Policy & Politics*, 17 ( 2): 131–8.

Castells, M. (1996) *The Rise of the Network Society: The Information Age: Economy, Society and Culture: Volume I* (Oxford: Blackwell).

Chandler, D. (1999) *Voices from S-21: Terror and History in Pol Pot's Secret Prison* (Berkeley: University of California Press).

Chote, R. and Emerson, C. (2005) *Public Spending*, IFS, election briefing.

Cioffi-Revilla, C. (1998) *Politics and Uncertainty: Theory, Models and Applications* (Cambridge: Cambridge University Press).

Clarke, K. (2006) 'Childhood, parenting and early intervention: a critical examination of the Sure Start National Programme', *Critical Social Policy*, 26 (4): 699–721.

CM 4310 (2000) *Modernising Government* (London: Stationery Office).

CMPS (2000) Joint Policy Seminar *Risk, Policy Development and Service Delivery*, Admiralty House, 28 March.

Cohen, S. (1988) *The Making of United States International Economic Policy* (New York: Praeger).

Cohen, S. (2002) *Folk Devils and Moral Panics; the Creation of the Mods and Rockers* (London: Routledge).

Cohen, S. (2003) *The Resiliance of the State: Democracy and the Challenges of Globalisation* (London: Hurst).

Cole, A. and Jones, G. (2005) 'Reshaping the State: Administrative Reform and New Public Management in France', *Governance*, 18 (4): 567–88.

Committee on Legal Affairs and Human Rights (2006) *Alleged secret detentions and unlawful inter-state transfers involving Council of Europe member states* (Council of Europe).

Conquest R. (1987) 'Revisioning Stalin's Russia', *Russian Review*, 46 (4): 386–90.

Cooper, R. (1998) 'Toward a Real Global Warming Treaty', *Foreign Affairs*, March/April.

Corbridge, S. Williams, G, Srivastava, M. and Vernon, R. (2005) *Seeing the State: Governance and Governmentality in India* (Cambridge: Cambridge University Press).

Costello, C. and Henry, J. (2003) *Across America: Preventing Teen Pregnancy in California, Georgia and Michigan* (Washington DC: National Campaign to Reduce Teen Pregnancy).

Courtenay Botterill, L. (2006) 'Leaps of Faith in the Obesity Debate: a Cautionary Note for Policy Makers', *The Political Quarterly*, 77 (4): 493–500.

Cox, R. (2005) 'An Essay on Method', in Amoore, L (ed.), *The Global Resistance Reader* (London: Routledge).

Crawford, R. (1980) 'Healthism and the Medicalization of Everyday Life', *International Journal of Health Services*, 10: 365–88.

Crenson, M.A. (1971) *The Un-Politics of Air Pollution: A Study of Non-Decisionmaking in the Cities* (Baltimore: Johns Hopkins University Press).

Dahl, R.A. (1957) 'The Concept of Power', *Behavioural Science*, 2: 201–15.

Dahl, R.A. (1961) *Who Governs?* (New Haven: Yale University Press).

Dahl, R.A. (1963) *Pluralist Democracy in the United States: Conflict and Consent* (Chicago: Rand and McNally).

Danaher, G., Schirato, T. and Webb, J. (2000) *Understanding Foucault* (London: Allen and Unwin).

Dandeker, C. (1990) *Surveillance, Power and Modernity: Bureaucracy and Discipline from 1700 to the Present Day* (Cambridge: Polity).

Daniels, R., Kettl, D. and Kunreuther, H. (2006) 'Introduction' in Daniels, R., Kettl, D. and Kunreuther, H. (eds), *On Risks and Disaster: Lessons from Hurricane Katrina* (Philadelphia: University of Pennsylvania).

Dannreuther, C. and Lekhi, R. (2000) 'Globalization and the Political Economy of Risk', *Review of International Political Economy*, 7 (4): 574–94.

Danziger, S., Heflin, C., Corcoran, M., Oltmans, E. and Wang, H. (2002) 'Does It Pay to Move from Welfare to Work?', *Journal of Policy Analysis and Management* 21(4): 671–92.

Davenport, C. (2005) 'Understanding Covert Repressive Action', *Journal of Conflict Resolution*, 49: 120–40.

Davies, R.W. and Wheatcroft, S.G. (2004) *The Years of Hunger: Soviet Agriculture, 1931–1933* (London: Palgrave).

Dean, M.M. (1999) *Governmentality: Power and Rule in Modern Society* (London: Sage).

Delgado, I. and Lopez Nieto, L. (2008) 'Spain', *European Journal of Political Research*, 47 (7–8): 1140–2.

Dell, E. (1996) *The Chancellors* (London: HarperCollins).

Department of Communites and Local Government (2006) *Anti-social Behaviour Intensive Family Support Projects*( London: DCLG).

Department of Education and Skills (2006) *Teenage Pregnancy: Accelerating the Strategy to 2010* (London: Stationery Office).

Department of Health (2007) 'The Government's Obesity Programme', http://www.dh.gov.uk/en/Policyandguidance/Health andsocialcaretopics/Obesity/DH_4133951

Digeser, P. (1992) 'The Fourth Face of Power', *The Journal of Politics*, 54, (4): 977–1007.

Donato, K.M., Durand, J. and Massey, D.S. (1992) 'Stemming The Tide? Assessing the Deterrent Effects of the Immigration Reform and Control Act', *Demography*, 29( 2): 139–57.

Douglas, M. (1985) *Risk Acceptability According to the Social Sciences* (London: Routledge),

Douglas, M. (1992) *Risk and Blame* (London: Routledge).

Douglas, M. (1994) *Dominant Rationality and Risk Perception*, PERC Occasional Paper, Number 4, University of Sheffield.

Douglas, M. and Wildavsky, A. (1983) *Risk and Culture* (Berkeley: University of California Press).

Dover, R. (2007) 'For Queen and Company: The Role of Intelligence in the UK's Arms Trade' *Political Studies* 55( 4): 683–708.

Dowd, K. (1998) *Beyond Value at Risk: The New Science of Risk Management* (Chichester: Wiley).

Dowding, K. (1991) *Rational Choice and Political Power* (London: Edward Elgar).

Dowding, K. (1996) *Power* (Milton Keynes: Open University Press).

Dowding, K. (2002) 'Resources, Power and Systematic Luck: A Response to Barry, Lukes and Haglund', http://personal.lse.ac.uk/DOWDING/Files/Dowding_BarryReply_09_02.pdf

Dowding, K., Dunleavy P., King, D. and Margetts, H. (1995) 'Rational Choice and Community Power Structures', *Political Studies*, 43: 265–77.

Downes, D. and Rock, P. (1971) 'Social Reaction to Deviance and Its Effects on Crime and Criminal Careers', *British Journal of Sociology*, 22 (4): 351–64.

Downs, A. (1957) *An Economic Theory of Democracy* (New York: Harper and Row).

Downs, A. (1967) *Inside Bureaucracy* (Boston: Little, Brown).

Drache, D. (2008) *Defiant Publics: the Unprecedented Reach of the Global Citizen* (Cambridge: Polity).

Dryberg, T.B. (1997) *The Circular Structure of Power: Politics, Identity, Community* (London: Verso).

Dunleavy, P. (1991) *Democracy, Bureaucracy and Public Choice* (Hemel Hempstead: Harvester Wheatsheaf).

Dunleavy, P. (1994) 'The Globalization of Public Services Production: Can Government be "Best in the World" ', *Public Policy and Administration,* 9 (2): 36–64.

Dunleavy, P. and O'Leary, B. (1985) *Theories of the State* (London: Macmillan).

Dworkin, G. (1995) 'Paternalism', in Audi, R. (ed.) *Cambridge Dictionary of Philosophy* (New York: Cambridge University Press).

Edgar, D. (2007) 'These medical moralizers might as well try banning sex', *The Guardian*, 7 June.

Elliot, A. (2002) 'Beck's Sociology of Risk: A Critical Assessment', *Sociology*, 36; 293–315.

Elliot, R. (2006) 'An Early Experiment in National Identity Cards: The Battle Over Registration in the First World War', *Twentieth Century British History*, 17 (2): 145–76.

Engster, D. (2001) *Divine Sovereignty: The Origins of Modern State Power* (DeKalb, IL: Northern Illinois University Press).

Escolar, M. (2003) 'Exploration, Cartography and the Modernization of State Power' in Brenner, N., Jessop, B., Jones, M. and Macleod, G. (eds), *State/Space: A Reader* (Oxford: Blackwell).

Evans, P.B. (1997) 'The Eclipse of the State? Reflections on Stateness in an Era of Globalization', *World Politics*, 50 (1): 62–87.

Evans, P.B., Rueschemeyer, D. and Skocpol, T. (1985) *Bringing the State Back In* (Cambridge: Cambridge University Press).

Farmer, P. (2005) *Pathologies of Power: Health, Human Rights and the New War on the Poor* (Berkeley: University of California Press).

Félez, E.A. (2005) 'The future of private data in private companies', *Jusletter*, 3, October.

Ferrera, M. And Rhodes, M. (2000) 'Building a Sustainable Welfare State', *West European Politics*, 23: 257–82.

Fischer, F. (2003) *Reframing Public Policy* (Oxford: Oxford University Press).

Fitzpatrick, S. (1982) *The Russian Revolution* (Oxford: Oxford University Press).

Fitzpatrick, S. (1986) 'New Perspectives on Stalinism', *Russian Review*, 45: 357–414.

Fleischacker, S. (2005) *On Adam Smith's Wealth of Nations: A Philosophical Companion* (Princeton: Princeton University Press).

Flinders, M. V. (2008) *Delegated Governance and the British State: Walking without Order* (Oxford: Oxford University Press).

Flyvbjerg, B. (1998) *Rationality and Power* (Chicago: Chicago University Press).

Foucault, M. (1979) *Discipline and Punish* (Harmondsworth: Penguin).

Foucault, M. (1981) *The History of Sexuality: Volume 1* (Harmondsworth: Penguin).

Foucault, M. (2002a) *Power: Essential Works of Foucault 1954–1984, Volume 3* (Harmondsworth: Penguin).

Foucault, M. (2002b) 'The Eye of Power' in Levin, T., Frohne, U. and Weibel, P. (eds), *CTRL [SPACE]: Rhetorics of Surveillance from Bentham to Big Brother* (Cambridge, MA: The MIT Press).

Frank, T. (2004) *What's the Matter with Kansas?: How Conservatives Won the Heart of America* (New York: Henry Holt).

Franklin, J. (1998) 'Introduction', in Franklin, J. (ed.), *The Politics of the Risk Society* (Cambridge: Polity).

Frederick, S., Loewenstein, G. and O'Donoghue, T. (2002) 'Time Discounting and Time Preferences: A Critical Review', *Journal of Economic Literature*, 40: 351–401.

Frentzel-Zagorska, J. (1990) 'Civil Society in Poland and Hungary', *Soviet Studies,* 42 (4): 759–77.

Frey, B. (1993) 'From Economic Imperialism to Social Science Inspiration', *Public Choice,* 77: 95–105.

Fried, R. (1991) *Nightmare in Red: the McCarthy Period in Perspective* (Oxford: Oxford University Press).

Friedman, J. (1996) 'Introduction: Economic Approaches to Politics' in Friedman, J. (ed.), *The Rational Choice Controversy* (New Haven: Yale University Press).

Friedman, R.B. (1990) 'On the Concept of Authority in Political Philosophy', in Raz, J. (ed.), *Authority* (New York: New York University Press).

Fukuyama, F. (2005) *State Building: Governance and World Order in the Twenty First Century* (London: Profile).

Funder, A. (2003) *Stasiland* (London: Granta).

Fussey, P. (2008) 'Beyond Liberty, Beyond Security: The Politics of Public Surveillance', *British Politics,* 3: 120–35.

Gallie, W.B. (1956) 'Art as an Essentially Contested Concept', *The Philosphical Quarterly,* 6 (23): 97–114.

Gamble, A. and Kelly, G. (2000) 'The British Labour Party and Monetary Union', *West European Politics,* 23: 1–25.

Gard, M. and Wright, J. (2005) *The Obesity Epidemic: Science, Morality and Ideology* (London: Routledge).

Garfinkel, S. (2000) *Database Nation: The Death of Privacy in the 21st Century* (Sebastopol, CA: O'Reilly).

Garrett, G. and Tsebelis, G. (1999) 'Why resist the temptation to apply power indices to the European Union?', *Journal of Theoretical Politics,* 11 (3): 291–308.

Gaventa, J. (1980) *Power and Powerlessness: Quiescence and Rebellion in the Appalachian Valley* (Oxford: Oxford University Press).

Geddes, A., Richards, D., Smith, M.J. and Mathers, H. (2007) 'Analysing Delivery Chains in the Home Office: Cases of Anti-Social Behaviour and the Street Crime Initiative' (University of Sheffield).

Geronimus, A. (1997) 'Teenage Childbearing and Personal Responsibility: An Alternative View', *Political Science Quarterly,* 112(3): 405–30.

Gibson, J.L. (1988) 'Political Tolerance and Political Repression During the McCarthy Scare', *American Political Science Review,* 82 (2): 511–29.

Giddens, A. (1984) *The Constitution of Society* (Cambridge: Polity).

Giddens, A. (1985) *The Nation State and Violence* (Cambridge: Polity).

Giddens, A. (1991) *The Consequences of Modernity* (Cambridge: Polity).

Giddens, A. (1995) 'Affluence, poverty and the idea of a post-scarcity society', UNRISD Discussion Paper.

Giddens, A. (1998) 'Risk Society: the Context of British Politics' in Franklin, J. (ed.), *The Politics of Risk Society* (Cambridge: Polity Press).

Gill, P. (2006) 'Not Just Joining the Dots But Crossing the Borders and Bridging the Voids: Constructing Security Networks after 11 September 2001', *Policing and Society,* 16(1): 27–49.

Giroux, H.A. (2004) 'War on Terror: the Militarising of Public Spaces and Culture in the United States', *Third Text,* 18 (4): 211–21.

Gladwell, M. (2004) 'Big and Bad', *New Yorker,* 12 January.

Goffman, E. (1990) *The Presentation of Self in Everyday Life* (Harmondsworth: Penguin).

González Rossetti, A. and Mogollón, O. (2002) 'La Reforma de Salud y su Componete Político: un Análisis de Factibilidad', *Gaceta Sanitaria,* 16 (1): 39–47.

Gopal, P. (2006) 'The Story Peddled by Imperial Apologists is a Poisonous Fairytale', *The Guardian,* 28 June

Goverde, H., Cerny, P., Haugaard, M. and Lentner, H. (2000) 'General Introduction', in Goverde, H., Cerny, P., Haugaard, M. and Lentner, H. (eds), *Power in Contemporary Politics: Theories: Practices: Globalisations* (London: Sage).

Graham, S. and Wood, D. (2003) 'Digitizing surveillance: Categorization, space, inequality', *Critical Social Policy,* 23(2): 227–48.

Gramsci, A. (1971) *Selection from Prison Notebooks* (London: Lawrence and Wishart).

Gray, J. (2003) *Al Qaeda and What it Means to be Modern* (London: Faber and Faber).

Greenaway, J., Smith, S. and Street, J. (1992) *Deciding Factors in British Politics* (London: Routledge).

Greene, J. (1999) 'Zero Tolerance: A Case Study of Police Policies and Practices in New York City', *Crime & Delinquency,* 45 (2): 171–87.

Gregory, P.R. (1990) *Restructuring the Soviet Economic Bureaucracy* (Cambridge: Cambridge University Press).

Grey, S. (2006) *Ghost Plane* (London: Hurst & Co.).

Griffin, P. (2007) 'Sexing the Economy in a Neo-Liberal World Order: Neo-Liberal Discourse and the (Re)Production of Heteronormative Heterosexuality', *British Journal of Political Science*, 9(2): 220–38.

Grugel, J. (2001) *Democratization* (London: Palgrave).

Grugel, J. and Piper, N. (2007) *Critical Perspective on Global Governance: Rights and Regulations in Governing Regimes* (London: Routledge).

Grugel, J. and Riggirozzi, M.P. (2007) 'The Return of the State in Argentina', *International Affairs*, 83 (1) 87–107.

Habermas, J. (1976) *Legitimation Crisis* (London: Heinemann).

Hacking, I. (2004) 'Between Michel Foucault and Erving Goffman: Between Discourse in the Abstract and Face-to-Face Interaction', *Economy and Society*, 33 (3): 277–303.

Hagen, E.H. and Hammerstein, P. (2006) 'Game Theory and Human Evolution: A Critique of Some Recent Interpretations of Experimental Games', *Theoretical Population Biology*, 69 (3): 339–48.

Haggerty, K. (2002) 'The Politics of Statistics: Variations on a Theme', *Canadian Journal of Sociology*, 27 (1): 89–105.

Hailsham, Lord (1947) *The Case for Conservatism* (London: Penguin).

Hall, J. (1994) *Coercion and Consent: Studies on the Modern State* (Cambridge: Polity).

Hall, P. and Soskice, D. (2001) *Varieties of Capitalism* (Oxford: Oxford University Press).

Hanson, G. H. (2007) 'The Economic Logic of Illegal Immigration', Council on Economic Relations, Council Special Report, 26 April.

Harris, P. (2006) 'I like Driving my Car', *Observer*, 18 May.

Harris, S. (2006) 'TIA Lives On', *National Journal*, 23 February.

Harris, S. (2007) *The Governance of Education* (London: Continuum).

Harrop, J. (1998) 'The European Union and National Macroeconomic Policy: an Empirical Overview', in Forder, J. and Menon, A. (eds), *The European Union and National Macroeconomic Policy* (Cambridge: Polity).

Hart, O. and Holmstrom, B. (1987) 'The Theory of Contracts' in Bewley, T. (ed.) *Advances in Economic Theory* (Cambridge: Cambridge University Press).

Hartmann, J. (2003) 'Power and Resistance in the Later Foucault', Paper presented at the 3rd Annual Meeting of the Foucault Circle at John Carroll University, Cleveland, OH, 28 February to 2 March.

Harvey, D. (1990) *The Conditions of Postmodernity* (Oxford: Blackwell).

Harvey, D. (2005) *A Brief History of Neoliberalism* (Oxford: Oxford University Press).

Harvey, N. (1998) *The Chiapas Rebellion: The Struggle for Land and Democracy* (Durham, NC: Duke University Press).

Haugaard, M. (2000) 'Power, Ideology and Legitimacy', in Goverde, H., Lentner, H., Cerny, P. and Haugaard, M. (eds), *Power in Contemporary Politics* (London: Sage).

Hausman D. and Le Grand, J. (1999) 'Incentives and Health Policy: Primary and Secondary Care in the British National Health Service', *Social Science and Medicine*, 49 (10): 1299–307.

Hay, C. (1997) 'Divided by a Common Language: Political Theory and the Concept of Power', *Politics*, 17: 45–52.

Hay, C. (2000) 'Contemporary Capitalism, Globalisation, Regionalisation and the Persistence of National Variation', *Review of International Studies*, 26 (4): 509–32.

Hay, C. (2002) *Political Analysis: a Critical Introduction* (London: Palgrave).

Hay, C. (2004a) 'Theory, Stylized Heuristic or Self-Fulfilling Prophecy? The Status of Rational Choice Theory in Public Administration', *Public Administration,* 82 (1): 39–62.

Hay, C. (2004b) 'The Normalizing Role of Rationalist Assumptions in the Institutional Embedding of Neoliberalism', *Economy and Society*, 33(4): 500–27.

Hay, C. (2006a) 'What's Globalisation Got to Do with It? Economic Interdependence and the Future of the Welfare State', *Government and Opposition*, 14 (1): 1–22.

Hay, C. (2006b) '(What's Marxist about) Marxist State Theory', in Hay, C., Lister, M. and Marsh, D. (eds), *The State: Theories and Issues* (London: Palgrave).

Hay, C. (2007) *Why We Hate Politics* (Cambridge: Polity).

Hayek, F. (1944) *The Road to Serfdom* (London: Routledge & Kegan Paul).

Hayward, C. (2000) *Defacing Power* (Cambridge: Cambridge University Press).

Heimann, C.F.L. (1997) *Acceptable Risks: Politics, Policies and Risky Technologies* (Michigan: University of Michigan Press).

Held, D. (1989) *Models of Democracy* (Cambridge: Polity).

Held, D. (1996) *Models of Democracy,* revised second edition (Cambridge: Polity).

Helm, C. and Morelli, M. (1979) 'Stanley Milgram and the Obedience Experiment: Authority, Legitimacy and Human Action', *Political Theory*, 7: 321–45.

Hemerijck, A. and Vail, M. (2006) 'The Forgotten Center: State Activism and Corporatist Adjustment in Holland and Germany', in Levy J. (ed.), *The State after Statism* (Cambridge, MA: Harvard University Press).

Henley, J. (2004) 'A Horrifying Hypothesis', *The Guardian*, 30 July.

Hennessy, P. (2000) *Government and Risk* (London: Public Management Foundation).

Hetherington, M.J. (1998) 'The Political Relevance of Political Trust', *The American Political Science Review*, 92: 791–808.

Hewitt, C.J. (1974) 'Elites and the Distribution of Power in British Society', in Giddens, A. and Stanworth, P. (eds), *Elites and Power in British Society* (Cambridge: Cambridge University Press).

Higgs, E. (2001) 'The Rise of the Information State: the Development of Central State Surveillance of the Citizen in England, 1500–2000', *Journal of Historical Sociology*, 14 (2): 175–93.

Hill, H. C. (2003) 'Understanding Implementation: Understanding Street Level Bureaucrats' Resources for Reform', *Journal of Public Administration Research and Theory*, 13 (3): 265–82.

Hill, M. and Hupe, P. (2002) *Implementing Public Policy* (London: Sage).

Hill, M. and Hupe, P. (2003) 'The Multi-Layer Problem in Implementation Research', *Public Management Review*, 5 (4): 471–490.

Hindess, B. (2006) 'Bringing States Back In', *Political Studies Review*, 4 (2): 115–23.

Hindmoor, A. (2004) *New Labour at the Centre* (Oxford: Oxford University Press).

Hindmoor, A. (2006) 'Public Choice', in Hay, C., Lister, M and Marsh, D. (eds), *The State: Theories and Issues* (London: Palgrave).

Hirst, P. (1994) *Associative Democracy(* Cambridge: Polity).

Hirst, P. (2005) *Space and Power: Politics, War and Architecture*, (Cambridge: Polity).

Holland, D. (2009) The Problem of 'Interdisciplinarity: A Critical Realist Investigation', unpublished thesis, University of Sheffield.

Hood, C.C. (1995) 'Contemporary Public Management: A New Global Paradigm', *Public Policy and Administration*, 10: 104–17.

Hood, C.C. (2001) 'The Risk Game and the Blame Game', *Government and Opposition*, 37: 15–37.

Hood, C.C. (2003) 'The Tax State in the Information Age', in Paul, T.V., Ikenberry, G.J. and Hall, J.A. (eds), *The Nation State in Question* (Princeton: Princeton University Press).

Hood, C.C. and Margetts, H.Z. (2007) *The Tools of Government in the Digital Age* (London: Palgrave).

Hood, C., Rothstein, H. and Baldwin, R. (2001) *The Government of Risk: Understanding Risk Regulation Regimes* (Oxford: Oxford University Press).

Horn, M. (1995) *The Political Economy of Public Administration* (Cambridge: Cambridge University Press).

Hoxby, C. (2002) 'How School Choice Affects the Achievement of Public School Students', in Hill, P. (ed.), *Choice with Equity* (Stanford, CA: Hoover Press).

Hugh, J. (2008) 'New Labour, Motivation and Welfare Reform', University of Sheffield, Department of Politics, mimeo.

Hunt, A. (1998) 'The Great Masturbation Panic and the Discourses of Moral Regulation in Nineteenth- and Early Twentieth-Century Britain', *Journal of the History of Sexuality*, 8 (4): 575–615.

Ikenberry, G.J. (2003) 'What States Can Do Now', in T.V. Paul, G. John Ikenberry and J.A. Hall (eds), *The Nation State in Question* (Princeton: Princeton University Press).

ILGRA (1995) *Use of Risk Assessment within Government Departments* (London: ILGRA).

ILGRA (1998) *Risk Communication: A Guide to Regulatory Practice* (London: HMSO).

Illich, I. (1976) *Medical Nemesis: The Expropriation of Health* (New York: Panthean).

Inda, J.X. (2006) *Targeting Immigrants: Government, Technology and Ethics* (Oxford: Blackwell Publishing).

Information Commissioner (2006) *A Report on the Surveillance Society*. http://www.ico.gov.uk/upload/documents/library/data_protection/practical_application/surveillance_society_full_report_2006.pdf

Innes, M. (2003) *Understanding Social Control* (Milton Keynes: Open University Press).

Jackman, R.W. (1993) *Power Without Force* (Michigan: Michigan University Press).

Jacob, B. and Levitt, S. (2003) 'Rotten Apples: An Investigation of the Prevelance and Predictors of Teacher Cheating', *The Quarterly Journal of Economics*, 118(3): 843–77.

Jacoby, J. (2007) 'Illegal Immigrants are Here to Stay', *Boston Globe*, 14 March.

Jaeger. P, Bertot, J. and McClure, C. (2003) 'The Impact of the USA Patriot Act on Collection and Analysis of Personal Information under the Foreign Intelligence Surveillance Act' *Government Information Quarterly*, 20: 295–314.

Jasanoff, S. (1999) 'The Songlines of Risk', *Environmental Values*, 8: 135–52.

Jayasuriya, K. (2001) 'Globalization and the Changing Architecture of the State: the Regulatory State and the Politics of Negative Co-ordination', *Journal of European Public Policy*, 8 (1): 101–23.

Jenkins, R. (2008) 'Goffman: a Major Theorist of Power', *Journal of Power*, 1 (2): 157–68.

Jessop, B. (1982) *The Capitalist State* (Oxford: Martin Robertson).

Jessop, B. (1990) *State Theory: Putting Capitalist States* (Cambridge: Polity).

Jessop, B. (2002) *The Future of the Capitalist State* (Cambridge: Polity).

Jessop, B. (2004) 'Multi-level Governance and Multi-level Metagovernance: Changes in the European Union as Integral Moments in the Transformation and Reorientation of Contemporary Statehood', in Bache, I and Flinders, M. (eds), *Multi-level Governance* (Oxford: Oxford University Press).

Jessop, B. (2008) *State Power* (Cambridge: Polity).

John, P. (1998) *Analysing Public Policy* (London: Pinter).

Jones, D. (2007) 'Zero tolerance must mean exactly that ... even if she's a sweet maths student', *Daily Mail*, 5 September.

Jordan, A. (2000) 'Environmental Policy' in P. Dunleavy, A. Gamble, I. Holliday and G. Peele (eds), *Developments in British Politics 6*, (London: Macmillan).

Jordan, A.G. (1990) 'Sub-Governments, Policy Communities and Networks: Refilling Old Bottles', *Journal of Theoretical Politics*, 2 (3): 319–38.

Judge, D. (1993) *The Parliamentary State* (London: Sage).

Judge, D. (1999) *Representation* (London: Routledge).

Justicea, F. *et al.* (2006) 'Towards a New Explicative Model of Antisocial Behaviour', *Electronic Journal of Research in Educational Psychology*, 9 (4): 131–50.

Kahneman, D. and Tversky A. (1984) 'Choices, Values and Frames', *American Psychologist*, 39 (4): 341–50.

Kahneman, D. and Tversky, A. (1990) 'Prospect Theory: an Analysis of Decision Under Risk', in Moser, P. (ed.), *Rationality in Action: Contemporary Approaches* (Cambridge: Cambridge University Press).

Kelling, G. and Wilson, J. (1982) 'Broken Windows', *Atlantic Monthly*, March.

Kelman, H. and Hamilton, V.L. (1989) *Crimes of Obedience* (New Haven: Yale University Press).

Kennedy-Pipe, C. and Mumford, A. (2007) 'Torture, Rights, Rules and Wars: Ireland to Iraq', *International Relations*, 21: 119–26.

Keohane, R. (2002) *Power and Governance in a Partially Globalized World* (London: Routledge.

Kerr, O. (2003) 'Internet Surveillance Law After the US PATRIOT Act', *Public Law Research Paper*, No. 42, The George Washington University Law School.

Kershaw, I. (1998) *Hitler: 1889–1936 Hubris* (London: Allen Lane).

King, A. (1975) 'Overload: Problems of Governing in the 1970s', *Political Studies*, 23 (2–3): 284–96.

King, R. (2007) *The Regulatory State in an Age of Governance* (London: Palgrave).

Knights, D. and McCabe, D. (2000) ' "Ain't Misbehaving"? Opportunities for Resistance Under New Forms of "Quality" Management', *Sociology*, 34 (3): 421–36.

Kopelman, L. (2005) 'On Distinguishing Justifiable from Unjustifiable Paternalism', http://www.ama-assn.org/ama/pub/category/11857.html

Kossoudji, S. (1992) 'Playing Cat and Mouse at the US-Mexican Border', *Demography*, 29 (2): 159–80.

Kunreuther, H. and Slovic, P. (1996) 'Science, Values, Risk', *Annals of the American Academy of Political and Social Science*, 545 (1): 116–25.

Lane, J-E. and Maeland, R. (2006) 'International Organisation as Coordination in N-Person Games', *Political Studies* 54 (1): 185–215.

Lang, T. (1998) 'BSE and CJD: Recent Developments', in S.C. Ratzan (ed.), *The Mad Cow Crisis* (London: UCL Press).

Langford, I. (2002) 'An Existential Approach to Risk Perception', *Risk Analysis*, 22: 101–20.

Lave, L.B. (1962) 'An Empirical Approach to the Prisoner's Dilemma Game', *Quarterly Journal of Economic*, 76, (3) 424–36.

Lawson, D. (2006) 'Smokers, Tattoos and Barmy NHS Priorities', *The Independent*, 24 October.

Lazzarato, M. (2002) 'From Biopower to Biopolitics', *Pli*, 13: 99–113.

Le Grand, J. (2003) *Motivation, Agency and Public Policy: Of Knights and Knaves, Pawns and Queens* (Oxford: Oxford University Press).

Lee, C.-J., Scheufele, D.A. and Lewenstein, B.V. (2005) 'Public Attitudes toward Emerging Technologies: Examining the Interactive Effects of Cognitions and Affect on Public Attitudes toward Nanotechnology', *Science Communication*, 27 (2): 240–267.

Levi-Faur, D. (2005) 'The Global Diffusion of Regulatory Capitalism', *The Annals of the American Academy of Political and Social Science*, 598: 12–32.

Levitt, S. and Jacob, B. (2003) 'Rotten Apples: An Investigation of the Prevalence and Predictors of Teacher Cheating', *Quarterly Journal of Economics*, 118 (3): 843–77.

Levy, J. (2006) 'The State also Rises: the Roots of Contemporary State Activism', in Levy J. (ed.) *The State after Statism* (Cambridge, MA: Harvard University Press).

Levy, J., Miura, M. and Park, G. (2006) 'Exiting *Etatisme*? New Directions in State Policy in France and Japan', in Levy, J. (ed.) *The State after Statism* (Cambridge, MA: Harvard University Press).

Lewin, M. (1985) *The Making of the Soviet System* (New York: Panthean).

Lewin, M. (1991) 'Russia/USSR in Historical Motion: An Essay in Interpretation', *Russian Review*, 50, 3: 349–66.

Lindblom, C.E. (1977) *Politics and Markets* (New York: Basic Books).

Lindblom, C.E. (1982) 'Another State of Mind', *American Political Science Review*, 76: 9–21.

Lipsky, M. (1980) *Street-level Bureaucracy: Dilemmas of the Individual in Public Services* (New York: Russell Sage Foundation).

Lipton, D., Sachs, J., Fischer, S., and Kornai, J. (1990) 'Creating a Market Economy in Eastern Europe: The Case of Poland', *Brookings Papers on Economic Activity*, 1990: 1, Macroeconomics, 75–147.

Lister, R. (1996) 'Introduction : In Search of the Underclass', in Lister R. (ed.) *Charles Murray and the Underclass: the Developing Debate* (IEA: London).

Lloyd, J. (2001) *The Protest Ethic: How the Anti-Globalisation Movement Challenges Social Democracy* (London: Demos).

Locke, J. (2002 [1752]) *Two Treatises on Government* (Harmondsworth: Penguin).

Lodge, M. (2002) 'Varieties of Europeanisation and the National Regulatory State', *Public Policy and Administration*, 17 (2): 43–67.

Lukes, S. (1974) *Power: A Radical View* (London: Macmillan).

Lukes, S. (2005) *Power: A Radical View*, 2nd edn (Basingstoke and New York: Palgrave Macmillan).

Lukes, S. and Haglund, L. (2005) 'Power and Luck', *European Journal of Sociology*, 46: 45–66.

Lupton, D. (1995) *The Imperatives of Health* (London: Sage).

Lyon, D. (2003) *Surveillance After September 11* (Cambridge: Polity).

McDermott, R. (1998) *Risk-Taking in International Politics* (University of Michigan Press).

McFarland, A.S. (2004) *Neopluralism: The Evolution of Political Process Theory* (Kansas: University Press of Kansas).

McGreal, C. (2006) 'Shameful legacy', *The Guardian*, 13 October.

McLean, I. (2001) *Rational Choice and British Politics: An Analysis of Rhetoric and Manipulation from Peel to Blair* (Oxford: Oxford University Press).

McLennan, G. (1989) *Marxism, Pluralism and Beyond* (Cambridge: Polity).

MacDonald, S. K. (2006) 'A Suicidal Woman, Roaming Pigs and a Noisy Trampolinist: Refining the ASBO's Definition of Anti-Social Behaviour', *Modern Law Review*, 69.

Macdonald, T. (2008) 'What's So Special about States? Liberal Legitimacy in a Globalising World', *Political Studies*, 56 (3): 544–65.

MacIntyre, A. (1962) 'A Mistake about Causality in Social Science', in P. Laslett and W.G. Runciman (eds), *Philosophy, Politics and Society* (Second Series) (Oxford: Basil Blackwell: 48–70).

Macpherson, C.B. (1962) *The Political Theory of Possessive Individualism: Hobbes to Locke* (Oxford: Clarendon Press).

Mandel, M. (2005) 'A Nobel Letdown in Economics', *Business Week*

*Online*, http://www.businessweek.com/bwdaily/dnflash/oct2005/nf20051011_3028_db084.htm

Manley, J.F. (1983) 'Neo-Pluralism: A Class Analysis of Pluralism I and Pluralism II', *American Political Science Review*, 77: 368–83.

Mann, M. (1970) 'The Social Cohesion of Liberal Democracy', *American Sociological Review*, 35: 423–39.

Mann, M. (1973) *Consciousness and Action among the Western Working Class* (London: Macmillan).

Mann, M. (1984) 'The Autonomous Power of the State: its Nature, Causes and Consequences', *Archives Européennes de Sociologie*, 25: 185–213.

Mann, M. (1986) *The Sources of Social Power, Volume One: A History of Power from the Beginning to AD 1760* (Cambridge: Cambridge University Press).

Mann, M. (1993) *The Sources of Social Power, Volume Two: The Rise of Classes and Nation States* (Cambridge: Cambridge University Press).

Mann, M. (1997) 'Has Globalization Ended the Rise and Rise of the Nation State?', *Review of International Political Economy*, 4 (3): 472–96.

Mann, M. (2006) 'The Sources of Social Power Revisited: a Response to Criticism', in Hall, J. and Schroeder, R. (eds), *An Anatomy of Power: the Social Theory of Michael Mann* (Cambridge: Cambridge University Press).

Marcuse, H. (1964) *One-Dimensional Man: Studies in the Ideology of Advanced Industrial Society* (London: Sphere Books).

Marcuse, H. (1965) 'Socialism in the Developed Countries', *International Socialist Journal*, 2 (April): 139–52.

Margolis, H. (1996) *Dealing with Risk: Why the Public and the Experts Disagree on Environmental Issues* (Chicago: University of Chicago Press).

Marsh, D. (2002) 'Pluralism and the Study of British Politics: It is Always the Happy Hour for Men with Money, Knowledge and Power', in C. Hay (ed.) *British Politics Today* (Cambridge: Polity).

Marsh, D. and Chambers, J. (1981) *Abortion Politics* (London: Junction Books).

Marsh, D. and Hay C. (1998) *Demystifying Globalisation* (London: Palgrave).

Marsh, D. and Read M. (1988) *Private Members' Bills* (Cambridge: Cambridge University Press).

Marsh, D. and Rhodes, R.A.W. (1992a) *Policy Networks in British Government* (Oxford: Oxford University Press).

Marsh, D. and Rhodes, R.A.W. (1992b) *Implementing Thatcherism* (Milton Keynes: Open University Press).

Marsh, D., Richards, D. and Smith, M.J. (2001) *Changing Patterns of Governance in the UK*, London: Palgrave.

Marsh, D., Richards, D. and Smith, M.J. (2003) 'Unequal Plurality: Towards an Asymmetric Power Model of British Politics', *Government and Opposition*, 38 (3): 306–22.

Marshall, B.K. (1999) 'Globalisation, Environmental Degradation and Ulrich Beck's Risk Society', *Environmental Values*, 8: 253–75.

Marshall, T.H. (1950) *Social Class and Citizenship* (Oxford: Oxford University Press).

Matthews, M. (1993) *The Passport Society: Controlling Movement in Russia and the USSR* (Boulder, CO: Westview).

Mead, L. (1997) 'The Rise of Paternalism', in Mead, L. (ed.), *The New Paternalism: Supervisory Approaches to Poverty* (Washington, D.C.: Brookings Institute Press).

Merelman, R.M. (2003) *Pluralism at Yale: The Culture of Political Science in America* (Wisconsin: University of Wisconsin Press).

Migdal, J.S. (2001) *State in Society: Studying How States and Societies Transform and Constitute One Another* (Cambridge: Cambridge University Press).

Milgram S. (1974) *Obedience to Authority: An Experimental View* (New York: Harper and Row).

Miliband, R. (1969) *The State in Capitalist Society* (London: Quartet).

Mill, J.S. (1974) [1859] *On Liberty* (Harmondsworth: Penguin).

Miller, P. and Rose, N. (2008) *Governing the Present* (Cambridge: Polity).

Mills, C.W. (1956) *The Power Elite* (Oxford: Oxford University Press).

Mills, C.W. (1970) *The Sociological Imagination* (Harmondsworth: Penguin).

Mills, M. (1992) 'Networks and Policy on Diet and Heart Disease', in D. Marsh and R.A.W. Rhodes (eds), *Policy Networks in British Government* (Oxford: Oxford University Press).

Mitchell, K. (2001) 'Transnationalism, Neo-Liberalism, and the Rise of the Shadow State', *Economy and Society*, 30 (2): 165–89.

Mitchell, T. (1991) 'The Limits of the State: Beyond Statist Approaches and their Critics', *The American Political Science Review*, 85 (1): 77–96.

Mitchell, T. (1999) 'Society, Economy and the State Effect', in Steinmetz, G. (ed.) *State/Culture: State Formation after the Cultural Turn* (Ithaca, NY: Cornell University Press).

Moe, T. (2005) 'Power and Political Institutions', *Perspectives on Politics*, 3: 215–33.

Monbiot, G. (2007) 'We've been suckered again by the US', *The Guardian*, 17 December.

Moran, M. (2003) *The British Regulatory State: High Modernism and Hyper-Innovation* (Oxford: Oxford University Press).

Morriss, P. (2002) *Power: A Philosophical Analysis* (Manchester: Manchester University Press).

Morriss, P. (2006) 'Steven Lukes on the Concept of Power', *Political Studies Review*, 4 (2): 124–35.

Murray, C. (1996) 'The Emerging British Underclass', in Lister R. (ed.) *Charles Murray and the Underclass: the Developing Debate* (IEA: London).

Napel, S. and Widgrén, M.T. (2005) 'Power Measurement as Sensitivity Analysis: A Unified Approach', *Journal of Theoretical Politics*, 16 (4): 517–38.

National Research Council (1983) *Risk Assessment in the Federal Government: Managing the Process* (Washington, DC: National Academy Press).

Needham, C. (2007) *The Reform of Public Services under New Labour: Narratives of Consumerism* (Bristol: Polity Press).

Nettleton, S. and Bunton, R. (1995) 'Sociological Critiques of Health Promotion' in Bunton, R., Nettleton, S. and Burrows, R. (eds), *The Sociology of Health Promotion* (London: Routledge).

New Economic Foundation (2005) *Behavioural Economics: Seven Principles for Policy Makers* (London: NEF).

Newton, K. (2001) 'Trust, Social Capital, Civil Society, and Democracy', *International Political Science Review / Revue internationale de science politique*, 22 (2): 201–14.

Newton, K. (2006) 'Political Support: Social Capital, Civil Society and Political and Economic Performance', *Political Studies*, 54 (4): 846–64.

Niskanen, W.A. (1973) *Bureaucracy: Servant or Master* (London: Institute of Economic Affairs).

Nordlinger, E. (1981) *On the Autonomy of the Democratic State* (Cambridge, MA: Harvard University Press).

Norris, C. McCahill, M. and Wood, D. (2004) 'The Growth of CCTV: A Global Perspective on the International Diffusion of Video Surveillance in Publicly Accessible Space', *Surveillance and Society*, 2 (2–3): 110–35.

North, D.C., Wallis, J.J. and Weingast, B.R. (2005) 'The Natural State: the Political-Economy of Non-Development', http://www.international.ucla.edu/cms/files/PERG.North.pdf.

Nove, A. (1987) 'Stalinism: Revisionism Reconsidered', *Russian Review*, 46 (4): 412–17.

O'Toole, L.J. (1986) ' Policy Recommendations for Multi-Actor Implementation: An Assessment of the Field', *Journal of Public Policy*, 6: 181–210.

Oakeshott, M. (1962) *Rationalism in Politics* (London: Methuen).

Offe, C. (1984) *Contradictions of the Welfare State* (London: Hutchinson).

Offe, C. (1996) *Modernity and the State* (Cambridge: Polity).

Ohmae, K. (1996) *The End of the Nation State: the Rise of Regional Economies* (London: HarperCollins).

Olson, M. (1965) *The Logic of Collective Action* (Cambridge, MA: Harvard University Press).

Olson, M. (2000) *Power and Prosperity* (New York: Basic Books).

Osborne, D. and Gaebler, T. (1992) *Reinventing Government: How the Entrepreneurial Spirit is Transforming the Public Sector* (London: Plume).

Overy, R. (2004) *The Dictators: Hitler's Germany and Stalin's Russia* (London: Allen Lane).

Paes-Machado, E. and Noronha, C.V. (2002) 'Policing the Brazilian Poor: Resistance to and Acceptance of Police Brutality in Urban Popular Classes', *International Criminal Justice Review*, 12 (1): 53–76.

Paine, M. (2004) 'Old Ideas + New Technology + New Technology = Crash Savings', http://www.mynrma.com.au/files/1/new_technology_paine.pdf

Palou, A. (2007) 'El sector alimentario europeo contra la obesidad: ¿medidas persuasivas o imperativas?', *Revista Española de Obesidad*, 5 (4): 189–90.

Paté-Cornell, E (2002) 'Risk and Uncertainty Analysis in Government Safety Decisions', *Risk Analysis*, 22: 633–46.

Pei, M. (2003) 'Rotten from Within: Decentralized Predation and the Incapacited State' in T.V. Paul, G. John Ikenberry and J.A. Hall (eds), *The Nation-State in Question* (Princeton: Princeton University Press).

Per, P. and Christianson, T. (2006) (eds), *Control and Autonomy in Modern Governments* (London: Edward Elgar).

Pereira, A.W. (2005) *Political (In)Justice: Authoritarianism and the Rule of Law in Brazil, Chile, and Argentina* (Pittsburgh: Pittsburgh University Press).

Performance and Innovation Unit (PIU) (2002) *Adding it Up: Improving Analysis and Modeling in Central Government* (London: Cabinet Office).

Perrow, C. (1999) *Normal Accidents: Living with High-risk Technologies* (Princeton: Princeton University Press).

Phillips, Lord (2000) *The Inquiry into BSE and Variant CJD in the United Kingdom* (London: Stationery Office).

Pickett, B. (1996) 'Foucault and the Politics of Resistance' *Polity*, 28 (4): 445–66.

Pierre, J. and Peters, B.G. (2000) *Governance, Politics and the State* (London: Palgrave).

Pierson, C. (1998) *The Modern State* (London: Routledge).

Pierson, P. (1995) *Dismantling the Welfare State: Reagan, Thatcher and the Politics of Retrenchment* (Cambridge: Cambridge University Press).

Pion-Berlin, D. and Lopez, G. (1991) 'Of Victims and Executioners: Argentine State Terror, 1975–1979', *International Studies Quarterly*, 35: 63–86.

Poggi, G. (2000) *Forms of Power* (Cambridge: Polity).

Poggi, G. (2006) *Weber: a Short Introduction* (Cambridge: Polity).

Pollack, M. (2001) 'International Relations Theory and European Integration', *Journal of Common Market Studies*, 39(2): 221–44.

Polsby, N.W. (1963) *Community Power and Political Theory* (New Haven: Yale University Press).

Porter, H. (2006) 'Surveillance is really getting under my skin', *The Observer*, 19 November.

Porter, R. (2000) *Enlightenment: Britain and the Creation of the Modern World* (London: Allen Lane).

Poster, M. (1990) *The Mode of Information* (Cambridge: Polity).

Poulantzas, N. (1978) *State, Power, Socialism* (London: Verso).

Powell, D. and Leiss, W. (1997) *Mad Cows and Mother's Milk: The Perils of Poor Risk Communication* (Montreal and Kingston: McGill-Queen's University Press).

Power, M. (2007) *Organized Uncertainty: Designing a World of Risk Management* (Oxford: Oxford University Press).

Pressman, J.L. and Wildavsky, A. (1984) *Implementation: How Great Expectations in Washington are Dashed in Oakland; Or, Why It's Amazing that Federal Programs Work at All* (Berkeley: University of California Press).

Public Administration Select Committee (2004/5) *Choice, Voice and Public Services* (London: Stationery Office).

Rakove, J. N. (2001) *The Unfinished Election of 2000: Leading Scholars Examine America's Strangest Election* (New York: Basic Books).

Reichman, H. (1988) 'Reconsidering "Stalinism"', *Theory and Society*, 17 (1): 57–89.

Reuben, E. and Van Winden, F. (2005) 'Negative Reciprocity and the Interaction of Emotions and Fairness Norms', CREED working paper, University of Amsterdam.

Revill, J. (2005) 'Pregnant women to get cash for good diet', *The Observer*, 9 September.

Rhodes, R.A.W. (1994) 'The Hollowing Out of the State: The Changing Nature of Public Service in Britain', *Political Quarterly*, 65: 138–151.

Rhodes, R.A.W. (1997) *Understanding Governance* (Milton Keynes: Open University Press).

Riccucci, N.M. (2005) *How Management Matters: Street-level*

*Bureaucrats and Welfare Reform (Public Management and Change)* (Georgetown: Georgetown University Press).

Richards, D. and Smith, M.J. (2000) 'Gatekeepers of the Common Good – Power and the Public Service Ethos', *West European Politics*, 23 (3): 45–66.

Richards, D. and Smith, M.J. (2002) *Governance and Public Policy in the UK* (Oxford: Oxford University Press).

Riker, W. (1986) *The Art of Political Manipulation* (New Haven: Yale University Press).

Riley, P (1973) 'Will and Legitimacy in the Philosophy of Hobbes: Is he a Consent Theorist?' *Political Studies* 21 (4): 500–22.

Ron, J. (1997) 'Varying Methods of State Violence', *International Organisation*, 51 (2): 275–300.

Rose, N. (1992) 'Governing the Enterprising Self' in Heelas, P. and Morris, P. (eds), *The Values of the Enterprise Culture: the moral debate* (London: Routledge).

Rosen, N. (2007) 'Ten Ways to Thwart Big Brother', *The Observer*, 28 October.

Routledge, P . (1999) 'Critical Geopolitics and Terrains of Resistance', *Political Geography* 15, (6/7): 509–31.

Rudolph, L.I. and Jacobsen, J.K. (2006) 'Conclusion: Sovereignty Unbound: Experiencing the State after 9/11' in Rudolph L. and Jacobson J. (eds), *Experiencing the State* (New Dehli: Oxford University Press).

Ruggie, J.G. (1993) 'Territoriality and Beyond: Problematizing Modernity in International Relations', *International Organization*, 47, 1: 139–74.

Rummel R.J. (1994) *Death by Government* (New Jersey: Transaction Press).

Rutter, M., Giller, H. and Hagell, A. (1998) *Antisocial Behaviour by Young People* (Cambridge: Cambridge University Press).

Sabine, G.H. (1974) *A History of Political Theory* (London: Dryden Press).

Saguy, A.C. (2005) 'French Women Don't Get Fat? French News Reporting on Obesity', *Health at Every Size*, 91 (4): 219–32.

Saguy, A.C. and Almeling, R. (2005) 'Fat Devils and Moral Panics: News Reporting on Obesity Science', American Sociological Conference, Philadelphia.

Saguy, A.C. and Riley, K.W. (2005) 'Weighing Both Sides: Morality, Mortality and Framing Contests over Obesity', *Journal of Health Politics, Policy and Law*, 30 (5): 869–923.

Salter, B. and Jones, M. (2002) 'Regulating Human Genetics: The Changing Politics of Biotechnology Governance in the European Union', *Health, Risk & Society*, 4 (3): 325–340.

Sanders, D. (1990) *Losing an Empire: Finding a Role* (London: Macmillan).

Sanders, D. (1996) 'Economic Performance, Management Competence and the Outcome of the Next General Election', *Political Studies*, 44: 203–31.

Sartre, J.-P. (1966) *Being and Nothingness* (New York: Washington Square).

Saurugger, S. (2007) 'Democratic "Misfit"? Conceptions of Civil Society Participation in France and the European Union', *Political Studies*, 55 (2): 384–404.

Saward, M (1990) 'Cooption and Power: Who Gets What From Formal Incorporation', *Political Studies* 38 (4): 588–602.

Schaede, U. (1995) 'The "Old Boy" Network and Government-Business Relationships in Japan', *Journal of Japanese Studies*, 21 (2): 293–317.

Schmidt, V. (2002) *The Futures of European Capitalism* (Oxford: Oxford University Press).

Schlosser, E. (2003) *Reefer Madness: Sex, Drugs and Cheap Labor in the American Black Market* (New York: Houghton Mifflin).

Scholte, J. (2005) *Globalization: A Critical Introduction* (London: Palgrave Macmillan).

Schroeder, R. (2006) 'Introduction: The IEMP Model and its Critics', in Hall, J.A. and Schroeder, R. (eds), *An Anatomy of Power: The Social Theory of Michael Mann* (Cambridge: Cambridge University Press).

Schultz, B. and Schultz, R. (1989) *It Did Happen Here: Recollections of Political Repression in America* (Berkeley: University of California Press).

Scott, A. (2000) 'Risk Society or Angst Society? Two Views of Risk, Consciousness and Community', in B. Adam, U. Beck and J.V. Loon (eds), *The Risk Society and Beyond* (London: Sage).

Scott, J.C. (1990) *Domination and the Arts of Resistance: Hidden Transcripts* (New Haven: Yale University Press).

Scott, J.C. (1998) *Seeing Like a State: How Certain Schemes to Improve the Human Condition have Failed* (New Haven: Yale University Press).

Scott, J.C. (2006) 'High Modernist Social Engineering: The Case of the Tennessee Valley Authority', in Rudolph L and Jacobson J. (eds), *Experiencing the State* (New Delhi: Oxford University Press).

Sen, A.K. (1977) 'Rational Fools: A Critique of the Behavioural Foundations of Economic Theory', *Philosophy and Public Affairs*, 6: 317–44.

Sen, A.K. (1999) *Development as Freedom* (Oxford: Oxford University Press).

Shapiro, I. (2005) *The Flight from Reality in Human Science* (Princeton: Princeton University Press).

Shapiro, I. (2006) 'On the Second Edition of Lukes' Third Face', *Political Studies Review*, 4: 146–55.

Sharp, J.P., Routledge, P., Philo, C. and Paddison, R. (eds), (2000) *Entanglements of Power: Geographies of Domination/Resistance* (London: Routledge).

Shavell, S. (1979) 'Risk Sharing and Incentives in the Principal and Agent Relationship', *Bell Journal of Economics*, 10 (1): 55–73.

Shaw, M. (2003) 'The State of Globalization: Towards a Theory of State Transformation', in Brenner, N., Jessop, B., Jones, M. and Macleod, G. (eds), *State/Space: A Reader* (Oxford: Blackwell).

Shore, C. and Wright, S. (1999) 'Audit Culture and Anthropology: Neo-Liberalism in British Higher Education', *Journal of the Royal Anthropological Institute*, 5: 557–75.

Siddiqui, T.A.(2006) 'The Dynamics of Bureaucratic Rule in Pakistan: A Personal View', in Rudolph L. I. and Jacobsen J. (eds), *Experiencing the State* (New Delhi: Oxford University Press).

Siena, K. P. (1998) 'Pollution, Promiscuity, and the Pox: English Venereology and the Early Modern Medical Discourse on Social and Sexual Danger', *Journal of the History of Sexuality*, 8 (4): 553–74.

Simmons, R.K. and Wareham, N.J. (2006) 'Commentary: obesity is not a newly recognized public health problem – a commentary of Breslow's 1952 paper on "public health aspects of weight control"', *International Journal of Epidemiology*, 35 (1): 14–16.

6, Perri (1999) 'Understanding, Presenting and Managing Risk in Public Policy', *Ditchley conference report no D99/0[xx]*

6, Perri (2000) 'The Morality of Managing Risk', *Journal of Risk Research*, 3 (1): 135–165.

6, Perri, Leat, D., Seltzer, K. and Stoker, G. (2002) *Towards Holistic Governance* (London: Palgrave).

Skocpol, T. (1979) *States and Social Revolutions* (Cambridge: Cambridge University Press).

Skocpol, T. (1985) 'Bringing the State Back In: Strategies of Analysis in Current Research', in Evans, P.B., Rueschemeyer, D. and Skocpol, T. (eds), *Bringing the State Back In* (Cambridge: Cambridge University Press).

Slovic, P., Flynn, J.H., and Layman, M. (1991) 'Perceived Risk, Trust, and the Politics of Nuclear Waste', *Science*, 254: 1603–7.

Sluka, J. (2000) ' "For God and Ulster": The Culture of Terror and Loyalist Death Squads in Northern Ireland', in Sluka, J. (ed.), *Death Squad: The Anthropology of State Terror* (Philadelphia: University of Pennsylvania Press).

Smith, A.M. (2007) *Welfare Reform and Sexual Regulation* (Cambridge: Cambridge University Press).

Smith, D. (1987) *The Rise and Fall of Monetarism: the Theory and Politics of an Economic Experiment* (Harmondsworth: Penguin).

Smith, M. (2000) *Rethinking State Theory* (London: Routledge).

Smith, M.J. (1990) *The Politics of Agricultural Support in Britain* (Aldershot: Dartmouth).

Smith, M.J. (1991) 'From Policy Community to Issue Network: Salmonella in Eggs and the New Politics of Food', *Public Administration*, 69: 235–55.

Smith, M.J. (1993) *Pressure, Power and Policy* (Hemel Hempstead: Harvester Wheatsheaf).

Smith, M.J. (1999) *The Core Executive in Britain* (London: Macmillan).

Smith, M.J. (2005) 'It's Not the Economy, Stupid! The Disappearance of the Economy from the 2005 Campaign', in Geddes, A. and Tonge, J. (eds) *Britain Decides: The UK General Election of 2005* (London: Palgrave).

Smith, M.J. (2006) 'Pluralism', in Hay, C., Lister, M. and Marsh, D. (eds), *The State: Theories and Issues* (Basingstoke and New York: Palgrave Macmillan).

Smith, M.J., Richards, D. and Marsh, D. (2000) 'The Changing Role of Central Government Departments', in R.A.W. Rhodes (ed.), *Transforming British Government* (London: Macmillan).

Sorenson, G. (2004) *The Transformation of the State: Beyond the Myth of State Retreat* (London: Palgrave).

Stanley, J. and Steinhardt, B. (2003) *Bigger Monster, Weaker Chains: the Growth of an American Surveillance Society* (New York: American Civil Liberties Union).

Stevens, J. (2003) *Stevens Inquiry 3: Overview and Recommendations* (London: Stationery Office).

Stevens, M. (2003) *Privacy: Total Information Awareness Programs and Related Information Access, Collection, and Protection Laws*, Report for Congress, 21 March.

Stoner-Weiss, K. (2006) *Resisting the State: Reform and Retrenchment in Post-Soviet Russia* (Cambridge: Cambridge University Press).

Stones, R. (1988) 'The Myth of Betrayal: Structure and Agency in the Labour Government's Policy of Non-Devaluation 1964–70', University of Essex: unpublished thesis.

Stones, R. (1992) 'Labour and International Finance', in D. Marsh and R.A.W. Rhodes (eds), *Policy Networks in British Government* (Oxford: Oxford University Press).

Stones, R. (1996) *Sociological Reasoning: Towards A Past-Modern Sociology* (London: Macmillan).

Stones, R. (2005) *Structuration Theory* (London: Palgrave).

Strange, S. (1971) *Sterling and British Policy* (Oxford: Oxford University Press).

Strange, S. (1996) *The Retreat of the State: The Diffusion of Power in the World Economy* (Cambridge: Cambridge University Press).

Strange, S. (1998) *Mad Money* (Manchester: Manchester University Press).

Strategic Policy Making Team (1999) *Professional Policy Making for the Twenty First Century* (London: Cabinet Office).

Strategy Unit PIU (2002) *Risk and Uncertainty* (London: Cabinet Office).

Strong, L. (2009) *The Role of Business in Climate Change Policy*, unpublished thesis, University of Sheffield.

Sum, N.-L. (2003) 'Rethinking Globalisation; Re-articulating the Spatial Scale and Temporal Horizons of Trans-Border Spaces', in Brenner, N., Jessop, B., Jones, M. and Macleod, G. (eds), *State/Space: A Reader* (Oxford: Blackwell).

Tabberer, S., Hall, C. Prendergast, S. and Webster, A. (2000) *Teenage Pregnancy and Choice: Abortion or Motherhood* (York: Joseph Rowntree Foundation).

Taylor, A. (2005) 'Stanley Baldwin, Heresthetics and the Realignment of British Politics', *British Journal of Political Science*, 35, 429–63.

Taylor, P.J. (1994) 'The State as Container: Territoriality in the Modern World-System', *Progress in Human Geography*, 18 (3): 151–62.

Taylor, P.J. (2003) 'The State as Container: Territoriality in the Modern World-System', in Brenner, N. Jessop, B., Jones, M. and MacLeod, G. (eds), *State/Space: A Reader* (Oxford: Blackwell).

Taylor-Gooby, P. (2000) 'Risk and Welfare', in P. Taylor-Gooby (ed.), *Risk, Trust and Welfare* (London: Macmillan).

Thatcher, M. (1983) 'Interview London Weekend World', 16 January. http://www.margaretthatcher.org/speeches/displaydocument.asp?docid=105087

Thatcher, M. (1993) *The Downing Street Years* (London: Harper-Collins).

Thatcher, M. and Stone Sweet, A. (2002) 'Theory and Practice of Delegation to Non-Majoritarian Institutions', *West European Politics*, 25 (1), 1–22.

Thompson, H. (2006) 'The Modern State and its Adversaries', *Government and Opposition*, 14 (1): 23–42.

Thompson, M. and Rayner, S. (1998) 'Risk and Governance Part I: The Discourse of Climate Change', *Government and Opposition*, 33 (2): 139–66.

Titmuss, R. (1970) *The Gift Relationship* (London: Allen & Unwin).

Tormey, S. (2006) ' "Not in my Name" Deleuze, Zapatismo and the Critique of Representation', *Parliamentary Affairs*, 59 (1): 138–54.

Toynbee, P. (2003) *Hard Work* (London: Fourth Estate).

Trotksy, L. (1938) 'Their Morals and Ours', *The New International*, 6 (6): 163–173.

Tsebelis, G. (1990) 'Penalty has no Impact on Crime: A Game-Theoretic Analysis', *Rationality and Society*, 2 (3): 255–86.

Turner, B. (1996) *The Body and Society: Explorations in Social Theory* (London: Sage).

Tversky, A. and Kahneman, D. (1981) 'The Framing of Decisions and the Psychology of Choice', *Science*, 211 (4481): 453–8.

Tyler, T.R. (1990) 'The Social Psychology of Authority: Why do People Obey an Order to Harm Others?', *Law and Society Review*, 24 (4): 1089–102.

Urban, M. (1992) *Big Boys' Rules: The Secret Struggle Against the IRA* (London: Faber and Faber).

Valante, M. (2005) 'Labour-Argentina: The "Black" and "Grey" Economy', *Latin American News Review*, 7 October, http://lanr. blogspot.com/2005/10/labour-argentina-black-and-grey.html.

Van Creveld, M. (1999) *The Rise and Fall of the State* (Oxford: Oxford University Press).

Van den Broek, D. (2003), 'Privacy and Work Intensification within Call Centres', *Worksite*, http://www.econ.usyd.edu.au/wos/work-site/surveillance.html

Ventosa, I.P. (2002) 'Incentivos económicos para avanzar hacia la reducción y el reciclaje de residuos urbanos', *Revista Interdisciplinar de gestión ambiental*, 48: 22–32.

Vogel, D. (2001) *The Politics of Risk Regulation in Europe*, LSE: Centre for Analysis of Risk and Regulation Discussion Paper.

Von Winterfeldt, D. (2006) 'Using Risk and Decision Analysis to Protect New Orleans', in Daniels, R. Kettl, D. and Kunreuther, H. (eds), *On Risks and Disaster: Lessons from Hurricane Katrina* (Philadelphia: University of Pennsylvania).

Walker, C. and Cannon, G. (1986) *Food Scandal: What's Wrong with Britain's Diet and How to Put it Right* (London: Edbury Press).

Ward, H. (1987) 'Structural Power: A Contradiction in Terms?', *Political Studies*, 35 (4): 593–610.

Ward, H. (2002) 'Rational Choice' in Marsh, D. and Stoker, G. (eds), *Theory and Methods in Political Science* (London: Palgrave).

Ward, L. (2007) 'Unborn babies targeted in crackdown on criminality', *The Guardian*, 16 May.

Ward, L and Wintour, P. (2007) 'State supernannies to help struggling parents', *The Guardian*, 22 November.

Waring, A. and Glendon, A.I. (1998) *Managing Risk: Critical Issues for Survival and Success into the 21st Century* (London: Thomson Business Press).

Wasserman, D.T. and Wachbroit, R. (2001) *Genetics and Criminal Behavior* (Cambridge: Cambridge University Press).

Watson, M. and Hay, C. (2003) 'The Discourse of Globalisation and the Logic of No Alternative: Rendering the Contingent Necessary in the Political Economy of New Labour', *Policy & Politics*, 31 (3): 289–305.

Weber, M. (1978) *Economy and Society: An Outline of Interpretive Sociology* (Berkeley, CA: University of California Press).

Weir, S. and Beetham, D. (1999) *Political Power and Democratic Control in Britain* (London: Routledge).

Weiss, L. (1998) *The Myth of the Powerless State* (Ithaca, NY: Cornell University Press).

Weiss, L. (1999) 'Managed Openness: Beyond Neoliberal Globalism', *New Left Review*, I, 238–57.

Weiss, L. (2003) *States in the Global Economy* (Cambridge: Cambridge University Press).

WERG (2006) *Sussex Incentives Recycling Project* (Brighton: University of Sussex).

Werner, W.G. and De Wilde, J.H. (2001) 'The Endurance of Sovereignty', *European Journal of International Relations*, 7 (3): 283–313.

Weyland, K. (1998) 'The Political Fate of Market Reform in Latin America, Africa, and Eastern Europe', *International Studies Quarterly*, 42(4): 645–73.

Weyland, K. (2000) 'Neopopulism and Market Reform in Argentina, Brazil, Peru and Venezuela', *Paper to the 22nd International Congress of the Latin American Studies Association*, Miami, 16–18 March.

Whitaker, R. (1999) *The End of Privacy: How Total Surveillance is Becoming a Reality* (New York: The New Press).

White, A. (2009) 'The Regulation of Privatised Security', unpublished thesis, University of Sheffield.

Whittaker, G.M. (2000) 'Asymmetric Wargaming: Toward A Game Theoretic Perspective', Bedford, MA: The MITRE Corporation.

Willis, P. (1977), *Learning to Labour. How working class kids get working class jobs* (Farnborough, Hants: Saxon House).

Willmott, P. and Young, M. (1960) *Family and Class in a London Suburb* (London: Routledge and Kegan Paul).

Wilson, H. and Huntington, A. (2006) 'Deviant (M)others: The Construction of Teenage Motherhood in Contemporary Discourse', *Journal of Social Policy*, 35 (1): 59–76.

Wilson, J. (1980) *The Politics of Regulation* (New York: Basic Books).

Woodworth, P. (2001) *Dirty War, Clean Hands: ETA, GAL and Spanish Democracy* (Cork: Cork University Press).

Wrong, D. (1988) *Power, Its Form, Bases and Uses* (Oxford: Basil Blackwell).

ZD Net (2007) 'Britain and Ireland Call for EU Data Sharing', http://news.zdnet.co.uk/security/0,1000000189,39288092,00.htm, 21 March.

Zey, M. (1998) *Rational Choice and Organizational Theory: A Critique* (London: Sage).

Zola, I. (1972) 'Medicine as an Institution of Social Control', *Sociological Review,* 20: 487–504.

# Index

Printed and bound by CPI Group (UK) Ltd, Croydon, CR0 4YY